MARK MY WORDS

• • •

Tales of Brandon Webb, O.J. Mayo, and
Other Sports Legends of Northeastern Kentucky

MARK MY WORDS

• • •

Tales of Brandon Webb, O.J. Mayo, and
Other Sports Legends of Northeastern Kentucky

by
MARK MAYNARD

ISBN: 1-931672-55-5

Book Design by

Suzanna & Anthony Stephens
www.designs-on-you.net

Published by

Jesse Stuart Foundation
1645 Winchester Avenue • P.O. Box 669
Ashland, Kentucky 41105-0669
(606) 326-1667
JSFBOOKS.com

TABLE OF CONTENTS

• • •

This book is dedicated to my late father Clarence Maynard, who instilled in me a love of God, family, and sports.

• • •

INTRODUCTION

· · ·

The last thirty-four years has been one wild ride. As a sports writer, sports editor, and managing editor of *The Independent*, a daily newspaper in Ashland, Kentucky, I have had the absolute privilege of covering sports of all kinds in northeastern Kentucky. There have been heart-warming stories, heart-breaking stories, funny stories, and unbelievable ones. All the way, with pen and pad in hand, I have watched as Little Leaguers became Major Leaguers, as state championships were won and lost, as a seventh-grader took the area by storm, as friends who were sports legends have come and gone. As far as coverage, I have run the gamut. I was there when Duke's Christian Laettner broke Kentucky's hearts everywhere with that dagger of a shot in 1992 in Philadelphia. I was there when Ashland and Russell won state football championships. I covered the football team that everyone called "JAWS" and have learned and written about area teams of the past—many of them long before my time—and how they made history with amazing performances that are still talked about today.

What you will find inside the pages of this book are a collection of my sports columns and stories that were in the pages of *The Independent* from 1977 to 2009. They carry some opinion and much history of one of the greatest sports places in Kentucky. Just ask anybody who has lived here. I hope you enjoy reading them as much as I enjoyed writing them.

—*Mark Maynard*

A GREAT DAY AT SHEA
October 2008

• • •

The wrecking ball will make Shea Stadium a mere memory during the offseason.

It may be the ugly stepsister to Yankee Stadium, but there were plenty of important happenings at the forty-four-year-old stadium.

It's where the Beatles played a thirty-minute concert in 1965. It was the home of the Amazin' Mets of 1969, the place where Bud Harrelson and Pete Rose mixed it up in the 1973 playoffs and the site where the ground ball rolled under Bill Buckner's glove in 1986. It was the home for the Jets of Broadway Joe Namath.

Yes, Shea had her memories.

For me, the memories of Shea involve an adventuresome road trip in my mini-van and the start of a major league career that could only be described as, well, "amazing" for one of Ashland's favorite sons.

It was April 27, 2003 and Brandon Webb was scheduled to make the first start of his career. It would be against the Mets, and one of his sports heroes growing up—Tom Glavine. His real hero, his father, would be in the stands watching. Phil Webb was one of the five who made the drive from Ashland to New York City with only a Map Quest word map as our guide.

Brandon Webb puts on his glove to go pitch in Cincinnati's Great American Ball Park in August 2003. KEVIN GOLDY/THE INDEPENDENT

The others on the trip with me were Brandon's grandfather Bob Carr, my pastor Floyd Paris and his son Philip.

We departed Ashland with this ominous message from the Weather Channel: The forecast for New York on Saturday was 100 percent chance of rain. Not 70 percent. Not 80 percent. Not even 90 percent. It was 100 percent. It was going to rain.

Undaunted by that forecast—Hey, how many times are these guys wrong?—we loaded up the mini-van from the church parking lot on a Friday night and away we went. Like most trips of anticipation, we were all pretty excited.

Brandon's father was excited and nervous, although not as nervous as he would be when his son took the mound later in the weekend. I'd say a lump the size of a baseball was in both of their throats.

None of us had been to Shea Stadium, so the adventure actually even went beyond Brandon's appearance.

Shea was not Yankee Stadium but, for me anyway, it always was a magical place. The story of the '69 Mets was always one of my favorites. As an eleven-year-old boy, I remember following that World Series and really falling in love with baseball's magic. Of course, the days of the Big Red Machine would follow and I was hooked forever.

Namath's guarantee in Super Bowl III also was one of those great sports moments for me, too. And Shea is where Namath did his thing to get to that Super Bowl.

Brandon was scheduled to pitch on Saturday—the day of the 100 percent rain forecast—and we decided to split the long trip into two days. We drove about eight hours—mostly in rain—before stopping for the night.

We got up the next morning refreshed and ready to complete the drive to New York. And, true to the forecast, it rained some more.

Somehow, even with the Map Quest as our only mapping tool, we made it to the parking lot at Shea Stadium. That was Miracle No. 1 of the weekend.

Brandon left everyone tickets, but I had also secured media credentials to cover "The Big Event." That gave me a little more access than the rest of the gang as we waited out the rain delay, hoping we hadn't made this twelve-hour trip—in the rain—for nothing.

While checking out the media accommodations, I actually—and almost literally—bumped into Tom Seaver. The Hall of Fame pitcher is now a Mets' television announcer. I nervously introduced myself, stumbling over words while telling him how I'd followed his career and how my mom and dad had front-row seats for his no-hitter against the Cardinals when he pitched for the Reds.

Seaver was nice about it, almost seeming interested in what I was saying. I gave him some background on Brandon. He appreciated it, stuffed it in a pocket, and went on.

I found my seat in the Mets' press box and then headed back to the concourse to find out the fate of the Saturday afternoon game. It was still raining and the field was covered. There was hardly anyone sitting in those bright orange seats, one of Shea's trademarks.

Eventually, the game was called but a doubleheader was scheduled for Sunday—a day with a forecast for sunny skies—and Webb was the scheduled starter for Game 1.

We'd come this far, so we weren't turning back now. But our Map Quest mapping only took us to Shea, and we didn't have a "real" map between us. Now the adventure really begins.

We left Shea Stadium with another passenger—Brandon Webb had joined us in the mini-van. So here I was, driving in New York City, to the hotel where the Diamondbacks were staying. It was near Grand Central Station—are you kidding me? Driving in that town, as you can imagine, was a rather nerve-wrecking experience. There were yellow cabs everywhere and, apparently, they do own the road.

My only previous experience in The Big Apple was in 1996 when Kentucky was in the Final Four in New Jersey. But I flew into the city, stayed in the media hotel downtown and took shuttles to and from the arena. That was nothing. This was something.

Somehow—maybe Miracle No. 2—we arrived at the hotel and the Diamondbacks helped arrange for a couple of rooms. That night, we talked with Brandon and went to dinner with him. He was so excited yet amazingly calm.

My guess is that neither Brandon nor Phil slept well that night. And neither did I, my nerves shattered by the whole driving-in-New York experience.

I told everyone before we went to our rooms that night we needed to leave early on Sunday because I had no idea where I was going. This was the days before the GPS, and this Map Quest turn-by-turn map from Ashland to Shea Stadium wasn't doing me a whole lot of good now.

So we left early, it seems like around 9:30, for the journey back to Shea Stadium. It turned out the trip wasn't going to take three hours as I had anticipated. The streets of New York are pretty quiet on Sunday morning. I mean, it was like a ghost town. I felt like I was driving in downtown Ashland (except for when I went the wrong way on a one-way street).

We were back at Shea Stadium's parking lot in no time, probably less than thirty minutes from when we left the hotel. We pulled onto the parking lot and there was NOBODY there. I mean, nobody. It was too early for ticket-takers, maintenance, anybody—except these five guys from Ashland.

We walked around the grand old stadium a couple of times and took in the surrounding sites, like the home of the U.S. Open tennis championships. Eventually, the workers began showing up. We were able to make our way into the stadium and begin what would be a memorable afternoon.

I was able to talk the Mets' public relations personnel into letting Phil into the clubhouse to talk to his son before the game—that may have been Miracle No. 3. I imagine it was calming for both of them.

Instead of going to the press box, I chose to watch the game with my group. I gave Phil my portable radio with earplugs so he could listen to the Mets' broadcast as the game unfolded—plus block out everyone else. The story, I figured, was right there for me anyway: A father from Ashland watching his son, who grew up playing on our fields, pitch in the big leagues. What could be better?

How about this: Webb pitched seven shutout innings, struck out ten and walked one in a 6 - 1 victory. He even laid down two sacrifice bunts. A crowd of 36,491 showed up for that Sunday twin bill and everyone was buzzing about the kid from Kentucky.

After the game, the D-backs actually "sent" Webb back to the minors to make room on the roster for Randy Johnson. All that meant was that he couldn't be seen on the Arizona bench for the second game. It didn't matter. Webb was in the clubhouse, meeting the New York media and starting a career that most could only dream about. His father got to tell him, in person, how proud he was of him.

Five years later, Webb is the winningest pitcher in the major leagues and a top contender for his second National League Cy Young Award.

For the five of us who decided to make the amazing journey from Ashland to New York, we drove home happy, satisfied that we made memories that would last a lifetime.

My nerves have since calmed.

Mayo's Time Has Arrived
June 2008

• • •

Even after watching him play for the first time, you knew there was something different.

He had "it," even as a sixth-grader.

We'd heard the talk and the hype before, but this time, it was different.

He had it and he knew it, even as a sixth-grader.

Already, his posse was growing. That's what happens to the "It" players. And it was happening to O.J. Mayo even before he enrolled at Rose Hill Christian School to repeat the sixth grade.

He was there to stay away from the wrong element, to be in a Christian environment. That's what the family said anyway. Truth be told, that was only part of it. He was there to hone his basketball skills, to play on the varsity level for two years—something he wasn't going to be able to do in Ohio or West Virginia—before considering other options.

Mayo was at Rose Hill for three years, leading the Royals to unprecedented levels, while turning basketball in the 16th Region into the hottest ticket around. His Legend grew with every dribble, every shot. They would line up after games for his autograph and came to watch this phenom by the thousands. Even ESPN came to witness "Mayo-mania."

Mayo brought fire with him and Rose Hill developed a rivalry with Ashland that bordered on hatred. There were sellout crowds and people wearing Rose Hill gear who may not have known the school even had a basketball team before Mayo came to town. Ashland's fans often carried signs—some clever and some cruel—with them to every game. They questioned Mayo's age, where he lived, how he arrived at school every day.

Those great Rose Hill-Ashland battles were some of the most intense I've witnessed in thirty years of covering games for this newspaper. But while adults bickered over Rose Hill's sudden (too sudden?) rise—and the rights and wrongs about the situation—the players on both teams carried a healthy respect for each other. They just wanted to play the game. Nothing else really mattered to them. They competed like crazy and it turned into some of the greatest games this region may ever see.

Mayo was ready to play, ready to lead, and ready to star when he was a seventh-grader. Other schools hurried their young players along too, maybe in hopes of finding the "Next O.J." They brought them up from the middle schools to join the varsity. Some parents decided to have their child repeat a grade, even when academics dictated it wasn't necessary, in hopes of gaining an athletic edge. Mayo's emergence changed the way people thought.

But O.J. Mayo was a player with a talent that this region is likely to never see again. Everybody knew then that Mayo would be playing in the NBA some day. It wasn't a dream, it was a matter of time.

Mayo's days at Rose Hill seem more like a blur now. It's been five years since he abruptly decided to leave after leading the school to its only 16th Region title in 2003, taking his game to a bigger market in the Cincinnati area. For two years, he had Rose Hill among the state's elite. Then, just like that, he was gone even after Mayo and his father assured reporters only two weeks earlier at the State Tournament that he was coming back to Rose Hill. Many soon followed him out the open door, leaving Rose Hill to wonder if it was all worth it.

Some would say Mayo used Rose Hill. But in reality—and for better or worse—it was more like they used each other.

Mayo's high school career post-Rose Hill is well-chronicled: two Ohio state titles at North College Hill when he was a sophomore and a junior and one West Virginia state title his senior year at Huntington High.

Then it was on to USC, where he kept making national headlines like he'd done since he was a sixth-grader—some good, some bad but always interesting. Nobody ever got to know O.J. that well. He was always polite, even charming with the media. But the only thing we all really knew was basketball made him tick. His talent was enormous and his work ethic unmatched. He never allowed anyone to get too close, perhaps fearing they would reveal a weakness. The mystery was part of the appeal. Not even the national media has been able to crack that shell.

All of his life has been geared for this moment, when NBA commissioner David Stern will call his name Thursday night in the NBA Draft.

It doesn't matter who takes him or when they take him—although he's likely to be one of the top three players selected—Mayo will have done what he was destined to do since he was a young lad. He will be a top NBA draft choice and begin the career that has been mapped out for him his entire life.

What he does from here is anybody's best guess. There are still

19

issues of impropriety aimed at him by one from his former inner circle. The college posse had different characters than in his high school days, but the motive was still the same. Ride O.J.'s coattails to the pot of gold at the end of the rainbow.

But this much is for sure: We'll all be watching, just like we did when he walked into the 16th Region seven years ago and turned it on its head. After all, basketball phenoms don't come along very often.

Rose Hill's O.J. Mayo slams down a dunk during the Touchstone Energy All "A" Classic semifinals in 2003. JOHN FLAVELL/THE INDEPENDENT

MEMORIES ABOUND AT CP-1
August 2008

• • •

Even though the event wasn't scheduled to begin until 1:30 in the afternoon, they started showing about 10:30 in the morning.

The stories started a couple of minutes later, almost before car doors were completely shut.

By noon, it was a steady parade making their way down to Ernie Chattin Field in Central Park.

If you build it, they will come.

They sure did.

If you missed Saturday afternoon's CP-1 Reunion in Central Park, you missed a lot.

More than 120 gathered at the main baseball diamond—fondly and formerly known as CP-1—to talk about the old days. It was like a who's who of Ashland area sports stars from the 1950s and 1960s.

Don Gullett, the McKell High School phenom who played on four consecutive World Series champions, was there. So was Ashland great and Rupp Runt Larry Conley. They were probably the two biggest names, but hardly the only ones area fans would recognize.

Russell great Mickey Sydenstricker was there. So were Holy Family stars like Jim Stephenson, J.D. Browne, and Fred Simpson. Booker T. Washington was well represented with the likes of Reese Banks, Bobby Simpson, and Wilson Barrow. And there were many Tomcats on hand, too numerous to mention here.

Just call it Tomcat Legend Day in the park.

Ashland super-fan David Payne called "it the greatest collection of Tomcat athletes ever assembled in one place." I couldn't argue.

They came because of their bond to Central Park and to each other. The park was their playground. Parents didn't worry about what the kids were doing. They were at the park. It was safe. It was "Everybody's Backyard."

The summer meant baseball from daylight to dark. There was no place like it.

"This was basically our second home," Conley said.

They looked over the transformation that has taken place at CP-1, where a $125,000 donation has started a project that will make the field a showplace, and they smiled a smile broad enough to reach from first base to third base. Their summer home was getting a makeover.

"When you see people from four corners of the United States come back for something like this, it says a lot about the feelings those people had for Central Park," said Browne, who traveled from Naples, Florida, himself.

The sentiments were unanimous: It was good to be home.

For many of the former athletes who came, it really was home. They spent their free time on the Central Park playground.

"I was talking to Dean Church about what a great time to have grown up in Ashland," Browne said. "You don't appreciate things like that until you get a little older. Maybe it's a little luck to be born at the right time in the right community."

Don Gullett, Bobby Simpson, and Larry Conley pose for a photo during th CP-1 Reunion in August 2008. MARK MAYNARD

Banks and Simpson were the first two blacks to play baseball on integrated youth league teams in Ashland. But when they crossed the lines, they said they were family. There were no racial barriers, at least not on the field.

"This is like being home," Simpson said, as he sat under a tent in center field. "They were like our family, in essence. I never felt downgraded by teammates. Some of the parents were obstacles. They didn't like us."

All day long, stories were traded and told, games were replayed and moments remembered. It was something else.

The competition was always fierce in the park and it only fueled

Ashland to greater heights during the 1950s and '60s. Everybody knew everybody.

"At the time we were playing baseball here, we took it for granted," Stephenson said. "It's what it was all about, at least in the sports world in Ashland. This field was our center ring. It brings back a lot of memories."

It was a day for remembering and being thankful for the time of their lives.

"Big Chief" Rides Again
March 2008

• • •

What makes a legend?

Memorable stories.

Successful career.

Great nickname.

Check, check, and check.

Say hello to Orb "Big Chief" Bowling, a 6-foot-10 giant of a man who trudged up and down hollows and up and down the basketball court for Sandy Hook High School some fifty years ago.

While a half-century has passed since the "Big Chief" played for Sandy Hook, he's still one of that town's most memorable characters—maybe as much for the stories told about him as his actual basketball abilities.

And even though he now lives in a suburb of Memphis, Tennessee, "Big Chief" is still a fan of basketball in Sandy Hook, especially the brand being played by Elliott County High School these days. He follows the team through the hometown newspaper he receives in the mail every week, from the school's newsletter and with phone calls back home. Like so many others who played at Sandy Hook High School and then Elliott County High School, last year's 16th Region championship—the first in school history—was a triumph for anyone who ever wore a Lions' uniform.

Sandy Hook High School was changed to Elliott County High School in 1973. But the change was in name only. There was no consolidation as was going on in so many other surrounding counties.

Sandy Hook and Elliott County are one and the same.

But there has been only one "Big Chief," the biggest player to ever play basketball in that town and in 1958 the biggest player on a Kentucky high school roster.

Fifty years from now, it could be this current group of Elliott County players that are likely to be revered with such legendary status in Sandy Hook. But, more than likely, the "Big Chief" will still be talked about too.

"He's still a legend," said Elliott County superintendent John Williams. "We have his picture hanging in the gym."

"Big Chief" is memorable in Sandy Hook, memorable in Knoxville and a rags-to-riches tale like you wouldn't believe. Basketball took him places like you wouldn't believe either. After a college career at Tennessee, he was drafted by the New York Knicks in the 11th round. He went to camp with the Knicks but soon found out he wasn't NBA material. Instead, he had a better idea. "Chief" signed to play for the Washington Generals—the patsy team for the Harlem Globetrotters—for $700 a month. He went to Europe with the Globetrotters, where they performed in front of the Queen of England. After that, the "Chief" got the chance to play in the fledgling ABA for the Kentucky Colonels, making a cool $13,000—very good money for the time. "They paid me as much as they did Cotton Nash or any of them," he said.

Part of the display of Orb "Big Chief" Bowling outside the Elliott Country High School gym. JOHN FLAVELL/THE INDEPENDENT

But the experience turned sour. "We played twenty games and didn't win but four," he said. "They were ready to run us out of Louisville."

He gave up basketball, at least from a competitive point of view, after the ABA experience. "Chief'" landed a job with Union Planters National Bank and became a security bonds salesman in Tennessee and Kentucky. His legendary tales went along with him and the deals followed. It was a match made in heaven.

"We underwrote a bunch of bonds, all over Pike County—$50 million worth," he said. "I made a lot of money selling bonds on Rupp Arena, too. They borrowed about $25 million worth of bonds to build Rupp Arena. I sold them all over Kentucky and Tennessee."

Bowling also married well. Donna, his wife of forty-five years who met her husband while attending school at Tennessee, said her husband never minded poking fun at himself.

"He's a real down-to-earth person who doesn't mind people making fun of him," she said. "I guess if he had good sense, he wouldn't like it."

MARK MY WORDS
• • •

They raised two sons, Orb Jr. and Jason. The youngest son ended up 6'-10", like his father. He played basketball but ended up an outstanding volleyball player at Pepperdine.

Bowling loves keeping up with Elliott County basketball and knows the players by name. He talks about the Faulkner twins, Ethan and Evan, and Jonathan Ferguson, and how well the team is doing. If they return to the State Tournament, he even plans on making a trip to Rupp Arena for the game to watch them in person.

His dream would be "for one of those boys to get a scholarship to Tennessee. I'd give my eye teeth to see one of them at Tennessee."

There's a reason for that, too.

"Big Chief" played for the Volunteers from 1960 to 1963, becoming known throughout the South for his country wit and wisdom and an uncanny ability to block shots and rebound. He once scored thirty-one points against Vanderbilt—"They took me out with five minutes to go. I was hot. Could have gone for fifty," he said.

The prankster of high school that was Orb Bowling was also the prankster of college. Campus police once arrested him for throwing snowballs. "He said he only threw one," his wife said. "Being big and tall like that, who are they going to see?"

Donna remembered another time when Tennessee played a team in Texas, near the Mexico border. The coaches decided to take the team across the border as an educational experience. They told the players when they re-entered the United States to tell the border guards they were American citizens and everything would be fine.

"Orb told them he was a Russian," she said. "It was a big mess and the coaches nearly killed him. That is very typical of Orb."

Orb had a couple of auditions in front of Adolph Rupp in Lexington. The basketball was fine but the grades weren't good enough.

"I'll be honest with you," he said. "I didn't have the grades. I didn't have the As and Bs. They looked at that."

And besides, Rupp had his pick of All-Americans to choose from and Orb didn't fit the mold. Rupp did take one of Orb's teammates, Bobby Rice, but passed on the gentle giant.

Orb was courted with letters from Tennessee, South Carolina and some others. But after his high school days were over, he appeared to have settled on going to Eastern Kentucky. Living in the basement of the gymnasium and working a summer job in Richmond, Orb was thrown in with some other athletes in his cramped living space. A couple of them were football players from Tennessee who were trying to get grades up. They talked glowingly about life in Knoxville and gave Orb some reason to rethink his decision.

"I thought 'Why didn't I look into that?' They gave me a number and I called the basketball office and Ralph Patterson, an assistant coach, answered. I asked if they were still interested in talking to me about a scholarship. They said 'We sure are. We thought you'd already signed with somebody or were going to go to Kentucky. They said 'You go home because we cannot come out to that campus and talk to you. We'll send somebody up there to get you.'"

As the story goes, Orb went home and was working in the tobacco fields with his father when the Volunteer coaches came driving up. They spotted Orb and his father in the field and asked them if they knew where Orb Bowling lived? Orb pointed to his house and the car drove off. They later met up with Orb and his father when they got in from working the field.

Bowling went back with them to Knoxville and a deal was worked out. Orb would be a Volunteer. "I found a home," he said. "Best thing ever happened to me."

He said he loved playing against Kentucky and usually had a good game against the Cats, even though UK typically came out the winner. He remembers a game when he battled the great Cotton Nash.

Orb Bowling at the YMCA in Collierville, Tennessee, after a pickup game of basketball in February 2008. Bowling once played for the University of Tennessee and now plays daily at the Y. GREG CAMPBELL

"Dad asked him once 'What was the greatest moment in your whole sports career?'" said Roger Davis, whose father was a longtime superintendent in Elliott County schools. "He said it was against UK, defending against one of the highest scorers in the history of UK basketball. Every time Cotton Nash put up a shot, I put it back in his damn face."

Well, maybe not every shot.

Bowling had fifteen points and fourteen rebounds in a 1962 game against Kentucky but in that one anyway, Nash scored 30 in a 95 - 82 victory for the Wildcats. Orb outscored Nash 21 - 15 in a 1961 game that UK won 96 - 69 in the UKIT. Bowling also had a double-double—thirteen points, ten rebounds—in a 1962 loss to the Cats. He averaged a respectable nine points and six rebounds in six games against UK.

"I was a very devout basketball fan at that time and was, in fact, his English teacher," said Roger Davis, seventy-seven, and a 1947 graduate of Sandy Hook High School.

So what kind of student was Orb?

"Let's not go there," Davis said. "There wasn't anything wrong with him but he had an unfortunate background in one of those little country schools. They didn't hold him down as tightly as they should. At that time we were in the social-pass mode rather than the academic-pass mode."

Orb himself admits he wasn't the, well, studious type. He'd much rather pull a prank on somebody than study for a test. He was in a one-room schoolhouse for the first six years of his education before coming to Sandy Hook High School as a seventh grader—a very tall, 6'-5" seventh-grader. That's when he first had a basketball put in his hands.

"They didn't furnish no tennis shoes back then," he said. "My first pair of tennis shoes I bought from Sears and Roebuck."

He may have worn them out walking to school.

"They didn't have no bussing back then," he said. "I had to walk to school. Me and my first cousin, we'd walk five or six miles one way."

Bowling started mastering some of the basketball skills that would be his ticket later in life. He played on some of Sandy Hook's all-time great teams and with some of its greatest players, like Roy Fannin and Bob Rice.

The Lions played in the 15th Region at the time and were highly ranked in the state. When Bowling was a senior though, Oil Springs stung Sandy Hook 71 - 60 in the first round of the district tournament in West Liberty. That team finished 24 - 5, but left disappointed at the end.

Sandy Hook played in the Ashland Invitational Tournament in December of 1957 and shocked the host Tomcats 61 - 56 in the opening round.

The previous season, the Lions couldn't handle Wheelwright in the regional tournament.

"Orb was a good ballplayer in high school but developed a lot better when he went to Tennessee," Fannin said.

Fannin said "Chief" had a temper, too. When colorful official Sid Meade once called a foul that Orb didn't agree with, he threw the basketball down hard on the floor and it bounced high into the air. "Meade T'd him up," Fannin said. "Orb said 'What'd you do that for?' Sid said because you threw the ball down. Orb said 'That was just a normal bounce for me.'"

The stories about Orb Bowling are never-ending, like a fountain of "pokeberry" juice. Which leads us to the nickname.

While many in Sandy Hook only call him "Chief" even today, most don't know how he picked up the nickname. Orb said when he was fifteen-years old, he and a cousin decided to have some fun on Halloween. They doused themselves in the juice from the red berries of a pokeberry bush and rode two horses into town screaming like Indians.

"They didn't arrest us, but they ran us out of town," he remembered. "Ever since then, they nicknamed me 'The Big Chief.' We were redmen. It wasn't a pretty scene the next morning. It (the juice) was poured out in the street and everything."

Orb said the pokeberry juices were once used for ink in quills, a red dye that wasn't easy to wash off either.

"Chief" often spoke about home while he was at Tennessee, keeping anyone who would listen laughing.

Most of the stories were on him. "Unfortunately," his wife said, "most of them are true. Of course, he's been creating new ones ever since he was in the limelight."

He once said Sandy Hook was so far away the Saturday night Grand Ole Opry didn't arrive until Tuesday. "Chief" also knew some history of the town, like when Sandy Hook changed its name to Martinsburg in 1872 to honor John Martin, only to find out there was already a Kentucky community named Martinsburg. The forefathers quickly

Orb Bowling searches for a teammate after pulling down a rebound during a basketball game at the YMCA in Collierville, Tennessee, in 2008. Bowling plays basketball every weekday at the Y. GREG CAMPBELL reversed the decision and the town located in the bend of the Little Sandy River has been called Sandy Hook ever since.

"When he first went to Knoxville from Sandy Hook, I'm sure there was plenty of opportunity for him to be embarrassed," Donna said. "Everybody we meet seems to have an Orb story."

The tales of "Big Chief" are so legendary around Sandy Hook that when state representative Rocky Adkins—an Elliott County legend himself—met Bowling for the first time, he felt like he was meeting a friend.

"I was either in sixth grade or middle school and it was actually in the gymnasium," Adkins said. "I was playing ball and this big fella walked in. He was a tall guy and looked like an athlete. Other people were there in the gym and they said 'There's Chief Bowling.' Even though I'd never met him, I felt like I knew him. I'd heard that much about him."

Bowling followed Adkins' career through high school and on to Morehead State and became friends.

Even today, at the age of sixty-eight, "Chief" plays basketball five days a week at the Schilling Farms YMCA near Memphis with a group of businessmen. But instead of the inside game, Bowling now specializes on the three-point shot.

"I'll hit two or three out of five from three-point range," he said. "It's almost like a foul shot once you get your rhythm. Like my golf game, it's strictly for exercise."

Bowling comes back to Sandy Hook at least once a year to visit his sister Sarah Jane Ison and take in the tobacco festival and visit with his many friends. And wherever he goes, the name "Chief" is sure to be heard. The stories are endless from anybody who knows him. But everybody always remembers him.

Legends are like that.

THREE MEN STANDING
September 2007

• • •

It has been seventy years since Ralph Felty, Bun Wilson, and Charles "Doc" Stanley were part of the Ashland Tomcat football team that christened Putnam Stadium in September of 1937.

For a night, they will be young again, remembering the day when they pranced onto their new turf with a twinkle in their eyes and nothing but playing football on their minds.

The only living members of that '37 team will be recognized as part of the Tomcats' proud tradition. It is a program that has recorded 596 victories—No. 7 on the state's all-time win list—with many of those coming on the hallowed grounds of Putnam Stadium.

This trio remembers the time before Putnam Stadium became a staple—and the home of the Tomcats—in South Ashland. They played during an era that had no equal in the annals of Ashland football history. It was rock em-rock-em football with leather helmets, no facemasks, and no mouthpieces.

"It was like playing in Ohio State's stadium," remembers eighty-six-year-old Bun Wilson, a 140-pound junior guard that season. "It was so overwhelming...the cheerleaders, the supporters. We always had good crowds."

Felty said the Ashland football game on Saturday was an event for the town. "They closed up the city of Ashland (on game days)," he said. "On Saturday night after the game, everybody would meet up downtown."

When the stadium first opened, the only dressing room was on what is now the visitor's side of the field. The Tomcats stood on those sidelines but after the first couple of games, the fans moved to what is now the home side because of the blinding sun.

"The students were looking right into the sun," Felty recalled. "I don't know if they moved after that first game, but it wasn't long (afterward). We stayed (on what is now the visitor's side) because of the dressing room."

Felty lived on Crooks Street, just a few blocks from where Putnam Stadium would be built. He was able to watch as the pieces came together to the historic stadium. The architect of the stadium "was a high school teacher named Brown," Felty said. "It was all hand and shovel. When they laid the foundation, the corners of the stadium were equal. That was quite a feat."

Felty, eighty-eight, said he played many sandlot games at the site where Putnam Stadium now stands. It was called Dicky Adams Field but it was more of a pasture actually. "It had cows on it," he said.

Meanwhile, the Tomcats were making a name for themselves away from that home. Ashland was the king of the hill, rolling off a 60 - 0 - 4 record from the last two games of 1925 to the fourth game of 1932 when Erie East, Pennsylvania, defeated the Tomcats 19 - 13 at Armco Park to snap the sixty-four-game unbeaten streak in a game that left Ashland fans stunned and heartbroken.

Ashland's 1930 team was a 10 - 0 juggernaut that scored 591 points for a 59.1 per game average, a record that still ranks No. 1 in state history and isn't likely to be toppled. The Tomcats had thirty-five consecutive victories from 1929 - 31 under coach Paul Jenkins.

Felty was a utility lineman on one of the Tomcats' most fabled teams in 1935, one that was coached by Fayne Grohn and went 10 - 0, outscoring opponents by a ridiculous 365 - 2.

"I was a scrub on that team," said Felty, who subbed on the line for Howard Hall.

Felty said when the Tomcats played Huntington High, the "scrubs" went into the game in the fourth quarter and the Pony Express threatened to score. The fans were calling for Grohn to put the first-team back in the game but he wouldn't.

On fourth down inside the ten, Felty was on his knees when the great Jackie Hunt came running at him. He grabbed Hunt's legs as the powerful back plowed into him and Felty wrestled him to the ground, keeping Ashland's scoreless streak intact.

"He ran over me, but I grabbed him and held on," Felty said.

But that was before the stadium that has housed eleven state championship teams—the last one coming in 1990—was built with Works Progress Administration (WPA) funds.

A $15,000 bond was issued in 1935 to build the stadium and furnish Putnam Junior High School (which is now George M. Verity Middle School), located adjacent to the stadium. The cost for the stadium was $6,500. It took nearly two years to complete construction but the Tomcats began playing games here in 1937.

Wilson's father, also named Bunyan, was on the Ashland school board when the stadium was being built. "He was very impressed with the workmanship," Bun said. "What he was really proud about was the wooden seats that had been treated for weather."

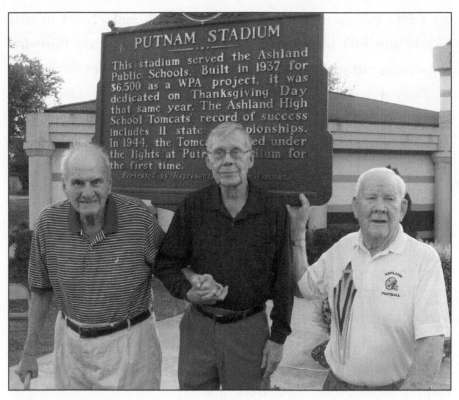

Bun Wilson, Doc Stanley, and Ralph Felty pose in front of a historic marker at Putnam Stadium. The three were on the first Ashland High School team to play at the stadium in 1937. MARK MAYNARD

Bun's father was also on the school board when the old Ashland High School basketball gym was built on Lexington Avenue.

Wilson said Felty, who later went on to earn All-State and All-America honors with the Tomcats, was a fierce blocker and one of the best player of his era.

"He was strong, quick and smart," Wilson said. "He was the best."

Wilson said he remembered running a "sucker play" toward Felty during one practice. Center Red Miller hit him high and Wilson hit him low. "They practically broke my back," Felty said. But on the next play, revenge was sweet.

"They said 'Let's run it again,'" Wilson said. "I thought, oh boy. The center and I both hit him but did he ever hit us. You talk about seeing stars."

Felty went on to play for Duke University and was on the 1938 Rose Bowl team. He eventually went on to serve his country in the Marines, earning a Purple Heart.

"He played in a Rose Bowl, was a high school All-American, and a Marine hero," Wilson said. "You can't get much better than that."

Wilson was also a Marine hero. They are two of a handful of area men who served during World War II and were all at the battle of Okinawa.

Felty didn't hesitate about a comparison between today's players and the players of his era.

"These guys today couldn't carry our helmets," he said. "The difference between us and now, we had to be tough. We didn't have the weight and we didn't always have the ability. But we were tough."

The leather helmets were little more than "a sock hat with holes in it."

"The joke was they put the holes in the side (ear holes) so when the helmet got twisted around you could see out of them," Felty said laughing.

Wilson said during practice, assistant coach Dopey Meade offered to buy players milkshakes if they could cause a bloody nose from one of their teammates.

"Somebody hit me with a fist and I was seeing stars," Wilson said. "They got a milkshake and I got to see Doc Stanley's dad (who was a dentist)."

Wilson described himself in high school as "one hundred forty one pounds of shimmering beauty."

The late Ernie Chattin was the first head coach to walk the sidelines at Putnam Stadium. Ashland went 3 - 3 - 3 in that debut season in the stadium, including 2 - 2 - 2 at home.

"I've never heard of another team doing that (going 3 - 3 - 3)," Stanley said. "That was something."

The first victory, a 22 - 0 blanking of Ceredo-Kenova, West Virginia, came in early September of 1937. The stadium was officially dedicated on Thanksgiving Day that same season.

Until the stadium secured lights in 1944, the games were played on Saturday afternoons and usually to full houses. Football in Ashland in the 1930s was a big event, often outdrawing the professional teams in Ironton and Portsmouth. The popularity of the Tomcats may have actually led to the demise of professional football on this side of the river.

It wasn't unusual for a Tomcat football practice in Central Park to draw a crowd of hundreds, Felty said. "We scrimmaged on Wednesday and there would be people lined up everywhere to watch," he said.

The Tomcats played in Armco Field before calling Putnam Stadium home.

It was Felty, along with Victor Rucker, who helped spring Oliver "Moose" Zachem for the first touchdown in stadium history, a 16-yard end around, during the victory over C-K. Zachem also booted the extra point, giving the Tomcats a 7 - 0 halftime lead.

The second touchdown was scored by Stanley, a fleet-footed running back, to give the Tomcats some breathing room.

The first year, the stadium was actually known as Tomcat Stadium. It later came to be known as Putnam Stadium, named after Donald Putnam, a longtime educator in Ashland schools.

"They told us the first Tomcat to score a touchdown would have the field named after him," Stanley said. "Moose thought it was going to be Zachem Stadium. But it didn't happen."

Charles "Doc" Stanley, Ralph Felty, and Bun Wilson, the three remaining members of the Ashland Tomcat football team that christened Putnam Stadium in Sseptember 1937 were recognized as part of the Tomcats proud tradition before a game in September 2007. KEVIN GOLDY/THE INDEPENDENT

Stanley didn't really make his mark until late in the season, first with some outstanding defensive play against Huntington High and then with a four-touchdown performance against Belfry in a 69 - 0 victory on a muddy Tomcat Stadium turf.

Stanley said the grass really wasn't that great even from the start because everything was so new.

"The field itself wasn't in the best of condition," he said.

Stanley did have a healthy respect for teammates, especially the physical Felty.

"One shoulder is lower than the other," he said. "That's from the only time I tried to block him."

Even today, at 86, Stanley is sleek looking. Wilson said he and Felty would be ashamed to ride around the field with Stanley because he was "still such a good-looking fella."

Stanley lives in Roswell, Georgia, near his two sons.

Putnam Stadium has been a multi-purpose facility for the Ashland community throughout the years, too. It has been the site for revivals, band festivals, concerts, graduations, and other events. In the mid-60s there was even college football played at Putnam Stadium with the Shrine Bowl games that once even played host to a battle between Morehead State University and Eastern Kentucky University.

The Kiwanis Bowl, which for years pitted Ashland junior highs Coles and Putnam against each other, was always played at Putnam Stadium. When those junior high schools consolidated, another Kiwanis Bowl game was born between Russell and Ashland. That game is also always played at Putnam Stadium. Throughout the years, Ashland Junior Football League and high school boys and girls soccer have called Putnam Stadium, too.

Once the stadium was able to put up lights in 1944, winning the first night game with an 80-6 thrashing of Huntington Vinson, the Friday night lights have been burning brightly.

In 2003, Putnam Stadium was recognized as a Kentucky Historical Society landmark. It became the 15th historical marker in Boyd County. It is the first stadium in Kentucky to have that distinction.

OH WHAT A NIGHT
February 2008

• • •

For Dan Cornett, the years haven't faded the memory of his greatest night as a high school basketball player.

It was a November night in 1964 when Cornett, a skinny senior guard for Breckinridge Training School, had the most amazing individual scoring performance in 16th Region history. Cornett scored eighty-seven points—still the third-best total in Kentucky high school history—during a 118 - 57 victory over Carter City at Button Gymnasium on the campus of Morehead State.

"I can still see it vividly in my mind," he said. "I was in the Twilight Zone. I was out there."

If the three-point line had been in play, Cornett's eighty-seven points could have easily turned into a 100-point game. He was thirty-six of fifty-six from the field and most of his baskets came from beyond nineteen feet. Jim Webb was a junior guard for Carter City that season. He remembers Cornett bombing shots in from everywhere, including some while falling out of bounds.

"If we had the three-point shot, he'd have scored 120," Webb said.

Cornett couldn't believe his eyes either. Whatever went up, went in.

"I surprised and amazed myself that some of the shots went in," he said. "I would shoot it and be like, dang, that went in. I was making everything. I couldn't miss."

While Cornett shot an incredible 64 percent from the field in that game, it could have been better if not for fatigue. "I was shooting a better percentage than that, but I started getting tired in the fourth quarter," he said. "I started missing free throws. I was something like fifteen of twenty-one (from the foul line). I remember one of my former coaches came up to me, patted me on the back and said 'Dan, look here, you missed six foul shots.'"

But he didn't miss much else. Jim Webb was a junior guard for Carter City that year and on this night he had the forgettable task of defending the high-scoring Cornett. "I started off trying to guard him," Webb said. "I didn't have any luck. Sid Meade officiated the game. I had three fouls in the first quarter. Sid would call a foul, look at you and grin. That's the way he did everybody."

On this night, Webb said there was no stopping Cornett.

"The shots he was taking were from twenty-five feet and it was nothing but net, every shot," Webb said.

The game was sparsely attended, at first, but once word spread that Cornett had scored forty-four in the first half, it quickly became filled to capacity.

When it started, fraternities were running pledges through the paces at Morehead State. For one frat's hazing, the pledges were to attend the Breck-Carter City game but turn their backs to the game and face the wall.

"They turned around the second half," Webb said. "The place was so full the second half you couldn't get in. News got around campus about what was going on."

There was a college dance at the student center across the street. Cornett, who went on to play for Morehead State, had several friends who were MSU players at the time. "People had gone across the street and started talking about it," he said. "Before you knew it, the gym was packed. They were yelling sixty-eight! Seventy! Because they thought I'd broken King Kelly's record."

What they didn't know was that King Kelly Coleman's record of sixty-eight points came during the State Tournament, not during the regular season. But it didn't matter. They were enjoying the show.

Breck Coach Edgar Warner had decided to leave Cornett in the game to see how many points he could score.

Paul Webb, who was Jim's cousin, was the Carter City coach and a bit of an intimidating figure. He looked at the scorebook at halftime and saw where Cornett had scored forty-four points. "We went to the

Dan Cornett with Breck coach Edgar Warner.

locker room at halftime in the old PE section of the auditorium," Jim Webb said. "We had to go down three flights of stairs. When we got there, he (Paul Webb) had the book with him. He told us 'I'll make you all a promise right now. If Cornett scores forty-four the second half, I'll kick every one of your (butts).' I got to the locker room after the game and I asked the scorekeeper 'How many did he get?' They said forty-three and I breathed a sigh of relief."

Jim Webb was a high scorer himself and once had forty points in a game against McKell when Don Gullett was a sophomore. "Forty points was a lot but think about eighty-seven," Webb said. "Unbelievable." Cornett followed up the eighty-seven-point performance with thirty-nine points in a loss against Grayson when Jerry Holbrook scored forty. That gave Cornett 127 points in two games.

The game against Carter City was on a Saturday night and came

Game ball from a game in 1964 when Dan Cornett scored eighty-seven points. JOHN FLAVELL/THE INDEPENDENT

after Breck had played the previous night in southeastern Kentucky against Albany. Cornett said he'd scored "in the twenties" that game. He woke up the next day feeling sick and told his mother he wasn't going to play on Saturday night but she encouraged him to go to the game.

"I told my mother, I don't think I'm going to the ballgame," Cornett said. "I wanted to stay in bed. But she said you need to try and play. Once I got there, the adrenalin started flowing a little bit and it happened." Cornett couldn't remember his highest game beyond the eighty-seven-point eruption. But he said during a game against Walton Verona, he'd scored more in the first quarter than he had in the Carter City game when he came down on the side of an opponent's foot and twisted his ankle.

"It absolutely killed me," he said. "Worst injury I had in my life."

Dan Cornett in front of Button Auditorium on the Morehead State University, where he played basketball in the 1960s. JOHN FLAVELL/THE INDEPENDENT

It also limited Cornett's playing time in the next few games and brought down his scoring average considerably. He still finished the season with a twenty-seven-point average but, if not for the injury, it would have been much higher, Cornett said.

Cornett had a brilliant career at Breck, even starting on the 1963 regional championship team that defeated Olive Hill in the finals. It would be a bitter defeat for late Comets Coach Jack Fultz who later would call Dan his son-in-law. Cornett married Fultz's youngest daughter, Andrea.

"We kept them from going to the State Tournament and, of course, he never let me forget it," Cornett said. "He made the statement he couldn't believe he let his daughter marry that Breck Brat."

For one November night in 1964 though, that Breck Brat was the king of Kentucky basketball.

LIVING LARGE IN RENO
September 2008

• • •

Eighteen years ago, he was terrorizing opponents on the football field for the Ashland Tomcats before embarking on a fourteen-year minor league baseball journey.

Today he's into landscaping, coaching youth baseball in Reno, Nevada, and expecting a child in February.

Life is still good for Juan Thomas.

"I did everything I was supposed to do," he said. "I couldn't do anything else. It was fun. I had fun; I traveled and had a lot of experiences." Thomas was a career minor leaguer with Crash Davis-like numbers. He bashed 291 home runs, clubbed 303 doubles, and drove in 1,019 runs from 1992 to 2005.

He was a 2001 Triple-A All-Star for the Tacoma Rainers, hitting forty home runs and driving in 152 runs during a two-year period. But despite those mega power numbers, the parent club Seattle Mariners never gave him a call.

Thomas isn't bitter. Not one bit.

"You make the best of what you have," he said. "Life gives you lemons, you make lemonade. I've made a lot of lemonades."

Juan Thomas was drafted by the Chicago White Sox in 1991. THE INDEPENDENT

Thomas moved to Reno in 2005 after taking his last swing in professional baseball.

"I moved not knowing exactly what I wanted to do," he said. "I had offers to play overseas. The owner of the Outlaws (youth baseball) organization got me hooked up. He made me an offer I couldn't refuse. It was one of the turning points in your life (decisions)."

Thomas is coaching two teams—a fourteen-under and an eighteen-under squad—in the Reno area. The experience has been exhilarating for him.

"The way I look at it now, in my life, I'm where I'm supposed to be," he said. "I had great coaches from football to baseball, from Vic Marsh to French Harmon, who were my mentors. What they did for me is what I'm doing now."

Thomas said the lessons he learned from those coaches—and many others—are what he's passing on to these young players.

"I look back on my career, all the way back when coach Marsh grabbed my facemask for the first time, I can think back to that time," Thomas said. "What he taught me, what coach (David) Arthur taught me, what Bill Blake taught me was to always go hard on the field. These coaches put into me discipline, team and how to go all out for teammates. I had a great football career but I couldn't have done it without (Chris) Hutt, (Charlie) Johnson, (David) Brown, Jim Bentine, Dwight Walters, Stu Hackworth...We did everything as a team.

"Everybody kept saying how good I was. Not, that's not it. The other kids made me good, they made me stand out. That leadership and learning on the field helped me to go on to better things in life. It helped me be a better person off the field and on the field."

Thomas said what he misses most about professional baseball is the camaraderie with teammates.

"People ask me 'Do I miss playing?' I don't miss it. I do miss the locker room. You don't miss waking up sore, red-eye flights across the country, things like that."

When Thomas isn't working with his baseball teams, he's helping manage a landscape and concrete company of which he's a partner. He's also a part-time scout for the Chicago White Sox, the team that first drafted him in the summer of 1991. He also likes to play golf— "I'm a thirteen-handicap," he said—and snowboards.

"Oh yes," he said. "You should see me."

Thomas and his new wife, Dixie, are expecting a girl in February.

And Thomas can still swing a baseball bat.

He said his younger players were taking batting practice recently and a couple of them hit home runs. "One of them said 'Coach, don't you wish you could still do that?' I told one of the kids to go get my bat. I said 'By the time you guys are done, count up how many home runs you hit and I'll match it. As a matter of fact, I'll double it.'"

The players took him up on the challenge and belted six home runs.

"I took a couple of warm-up swings and then said, 'OK, give me fifteen pitches.'" He then proceeded to hit thirteen home runs as the players stood with their mouths open.

"I said 'Now go pick up the balls,'" Thomas said. "They were like 'Man, coach can still rake.' I was hurting the next day. My back was so hurt but I wasn't going to let them know it."

Want to feel old? Thomas is thirty-six. It seems like only yesterday that he was playing for the Tomcats with the world ahead of him.

Time certainly has a way of marching on, even for the legends.

GULLETT WELCOME
IN TOMCAT TERRITORY
September 2008

• • •

Don Gullett's appearance at the CP-1 Reunion last Saturday in Central Park was a special moment and gave further proof, as if any were needed, about how magical that place was in the 1950s and '60s.

Gullett, one of the best all-around athletes in northeastern Kentucky history, was a hero to many of my generation who grew up with the Big Red Machine. Gullett is much like Arizona's Brandon Webb has become today, a role model in the truest sense of the word.

Everybody liked and respected Gullett, just like they do Webb today. You could see that at the reunion when Gullett's mere appearance created a buzz among those assembled at the park.

Gullett was invited to the CP-1 Reunion because he had some outstanding moments in the park as a youth league pitcher and a high school pitcher for McKell, and because of his lofty status in the eyes of so many in the area.

One of Gullett's most memorable high school games came against Ashland, but it wasn't played in the park. It was the regional finals in

Don Gullett, left, and Larry Conley, right, share a moment at the CP-1 Reunion in August 2008. Paul Conley is in the middle. MARK MAYNARD

1969 and the three-time defending state champion Tomcats mustered only one hit but still won the game 1 - 0.

While most remember the game, the place where it took place and the Tomcat pitcher who threw against Gullett are usually wrong. The game was in Morehead and Gullett was outdueled by Tim Huff, not Bobby Lynch, who had already graduated and was playing basketball at Alabama. Ashland would go on to the state tournament where it fell just short of a fourth consecutive title, losing 1 - 0 to Owensboro in the championship game, also in Morehead.

Nevertheless, that 1 - 0 game when the Tomcats beat Gullett is one that Ashland fans will always remember as much for the outcome as the who and the where.

About a year after that game, Gullett was pitching for the Cincinnati

Reds and embarking on a career that had Hall of Fame written all over it.

Gullett must still wonder what if? He was only twenty-seven-years old and one of the best pitcher in the major leagues when his left rotator cuff gave out on him in June 1978.

Had he continued on the pace that he had set from his first nine seasons, he would easily be a Hall of Famer. Gullett was 109 - 50 with a 3.11 ERA when his career ended. His .686 winning percentage would be the fourth best in history if he had enough decisions to qualify.

Gullett is often compared to Whitey Ford, the Hall of Fame pitcher with the New York Yankees whose career winning percentage was .690.

By contrast, the twenty-nine-year old Webb is 84 - 60 with a 3.18 ERA while pitching in his sixth season. He has been a three-time National League All-Star and won the 2006 NL Cy Young Award. Webb has his sights set on another Cy Young Award, certainly being among the leading candidates with a 19 - 5 record and 2.96 ERA with seven starts remaining.

Gullett was already two years out of the game by the time he was Webb's age. If he had pitched into his late thirties, he may have put up Hall of Fame numbers.

When healthy, Gullett averaged a 13 - 6 record. He could have added another 130 victories or so with ten more seasons.

Timing in life is everything. The same injury that curtailed Gullett's career could be repaired with today's medicine. But it was career-ending for him.

Gullett grew up in Lynn as a Reds' fans and often imitated pitchers like Jim Maloney and Joey Jay. It had to be a dream come true when the Reds signed him. He only pitched eleven games at Class A Sioux Falls in 1969 and was invited to spring training the next year.

Not expecting him to make the team, Gullett threw so well the Reds had no other choice but to take him north. He was mostly pitching out of the bullpen and appeared in forty-four games as a rookie in 1970. He went 5 - 2 with a 2.42 ERA but was even more dominant in the postseason, pitching ten 1 - 3 innings and allowing only one run on six hits in the National League playoffs and World Series. He saved two of the three wins over the Pittsburgh Pirates in the NL Championship Series.

The following season Gullett was put in the rotation and went 16 - 6 with a 2.65 ERA.

Of course, the Reds went to the World Series again the year after that, in 1972, losing to the Oakland Athletics in seven games, and then won back-to-back World Series titles in 1975 and '76 with Gullett as the ace. He went to the Yankees as a free agent the next season—the Reds didn't get into the bidding—and was on world champions there in 1977 and '78. That meant he played on four World Series winners in a row, a feat few anywhere can match.

Around these parts, Gullett has always been a sports legend. Besides being picked first in the 1969 draft, he did some incredible things in all arenas. He once scored seventy-two points in a football game, a 72 - 0 victory over Wurtland in 1968, and threw a perfect game against (Portsmouth) Clay High School where he struck out twenty of twenty-one batters.

Gullett's name still commands attention, even thirty to forty years after some of his greatest achievements. He received a warm greeting when introduced to the nearly 180 who gathered in the park.

I know some of Ashland's all-time greats, including many who went head-to-head against him, appreciated Gullett taking the time to come to the reunion.

CONLEY'S TOMCAT LEGACY
October 2008

• • •

If the Putnam Stadium restoration committee wanted to erect a statue that embodied the spirit of Ashland Tomcat football, then square-jawed and tough-as-nails Herb Conley would be the perfect model.

Preferably, a statue of him running over somebody.

Nothing could be better.

Conley has played it, coached it, and admired it. He's one of the names that keep the tradition going.

On Friday at the grand 'ol stadium, the 1958 Tomcat team that Conley was part of will be honored.

The '58 Tomcats, a bruising, battering, bludgeoning team, finished 10 - 0 - 1. Conley and Dick Fillmore, Mr. Inside and Mr. Outside, ran behind a physical offensive line that punished opponents.

They were a nightmare for foes to defend.

Just ask a coach who would know.

Conley, who coached the Tomcats to state runner-up finishes in 1972 and 1975, knows a good team when he sees it. He got his hands

Herb Conley from his Ashland playing days in 1958.

on some DVDs from the 1958 season and graded them as a coach would do.

"I tried to watch it as a coach, to try to do a scouting report as if I were preparing a team to play them," Conley said. "I tell you what, it's pretty frightening. I'd hate to be playing us when I was coaching."

Defenses that tried to take away the outside, got an inside dose of Conley, Joey Layman, or quarterback Ken Bocard. Gang up on the inside and Fillmore would burn you on a long run. Ironton would know about that. Fillmore's eighty-six-yard run in the closing minute provided the Tomcats with a 28 - 22 victory at Tanks Memorial Stadium in the fifth game of the season.

Even though the Tomcats didn't pass much, Bocard was effective when they did—nine touchdown passes out of fourteen completions. And, oh yes, Bocard may have been one of the most physical players on the team. He and Conley were the linebackers on defense.

Twelve players from the 1958 team eventually earned scholarships to play in college, including five to the University of Kentucky.

Conley has been a Tomcat institution almost since his playing days. His reputation comes mostly from his toughness both as a player and a coach and both on and off the field.

Conley grew up watching Tomcat stars like Don and Ralph Clere, Jim Graham, Buffalo Bill Hopkins, Ace Bowman, and Gilly Layman.

"I mimicked a lot of those guys," he said. "We'd be playing in somebody's yard and one time I'd be Don Clere, the next time I'd be Buffalo. That's how the tradition got going."

Conley burst into Tomcat camp as a sophomore in 1956 and earned a starting position on the varsity, a rarity in that day. It was so rare that the sophomores didn't even dress in the same place as the juniors and seniors.

"We dressed in the little hole down in the gym," Conley remembered. "I'd be down there by myself."

Before the first game, Conley dressed himself and put on the long maroon socks. Because he'd never worn them before, he didn't know to tape up the socks so they wouldn't fall down when he ran.

"I got on the bus and we went out on the field to warm up," he said. "My socks would keep falling down. It embarrassed me to death. One of the juniors on the team said 'Herb, I know you don't know how to do that.' He showed me how to tape them up."

Conley then proceeded to knock the socks off everybody he came in contact with the rest of his career.

His playing style became his coaching style as well. He learned under Harrison County's Bill McKee, Ashland's Jake Hallum, and Roy Kidd, his college coach at Eastern Kentucky University.

But Conley had a style of his own that translated into seventy Tomcat victories in nine seasons. He retired from coaching early and became an administrator in the Ashland school system. He stepped away from coaching to raise his family with wife Janice, who he calls "my inspiration."

Conley was an assistant on Ashland's 1967 state champions and became head coach the following year when Hallum went to Morehead State.

Herb Conley, right, and Joe Fleming share a conversation in August 2009. MARK MAYNARD

At the end of his third season in 1970, the Tomcats were struggling to a 2 - 7 record and the offense had scored only four touchdowns in six games. Fans were grumbling, even calling for a change in coaching.

On the eve of the last game against Ironton, a column by then *ADI* assistant sports editor Mike Reliford supporting Conley, helped turn public opinion and the Tomcats unveiled a wishbone offense and beat the Fighting Tigers 7 - 3. It probably saved Conley's job and the rest, as they say, is history.

The wishbone became the offense of choice and Ashland had six consecutive winning seasons, including years of ten, eleven, and fourteen victories.

Conley's legacy, both as a player and a coach, makes him one of the most memorable and most important figures in Tomcat history.

OLIVE HILL LEGEND PASSES
December 2007
• • •

On Wednesday afternoon, the area's best sports links to the past and a friend to this region for a lifetime, passed away.

The death of Andrew Jackson "Jack" Fultz leaves a void, an emptiness in our landscape that will not be replaced.

Jack was eighty-one. He lived a good life, one filled with adventure, and love, and few regrets. We all should be so fortunate.

You learned from Jack by listening. He was a true storyteller whose uncanny memory could bring out the most wonderful and sometimes unexpected detail. It was always the kind of detail that made the story come to life. Listening to him was like watching a history book come to life.

For the past five years, on an average of about once a month, I was fortunate to break bread with Jack and his sweet wife, Jean. He'd call me up, say we needed to go to lunch and we'd set a date. We met often at Rajah's, where Jack loved a heaping portion of the kielbasa and sauerkraut. We'd eat and talk, share some laughs, and then he'd share some stories. When he got wound up during an account, his voice would go high and a big grin would come over his face. His facial expressions

Jack Fultz, a former Oliver High School basketball coach and longtime educator, was the honoree for the 33rd annual Ashland Elks Sports Day. JOHN FLAVELL/THE INDEPENDENT

were priceless and his tales everlasting. They were stories I've tried to pass on in print whenever the opportunity presented itself.

There were so many times during my thirty years working for this newspaper's sports department, that Jack Fultz was my source for things that happened before I started working here. He liked getting the phone calls because it usually opened up the door for another tale. He'd talk and I'd listen. That's how you learned from Jack.

We were friends for many years, but it wasn't until the last five years, during those once-a-month lunches, that I truly began to understand what a giant of a man he was. And his heart was bigger than his stature. He grieved for every one of the Olive Hill High School players he coached who died before him. They were his boys and he loved them unconditionally.

A true stature of a coach isn't just what happens between the lines— although Jack Fultz knew how to get the best out of his players—it's what happens after the last whistle has blown. Jack Fultz never forgot his players after they graduated. He kept up with them, mentored them and, too often for him, stood by their caskets.

A coach is a father figure and he was that to many in Olive Hill, a place he called home for a lifetime. Jack was good enough to coach anywhere, but he chose to stay in Olive Hill. He loved the Comets and they loved him back.

His family and Jean, his wife of sixty years, were first in his life. He was a caregiver to Jean and so kind, patient, and loving to her. He loved his school, too, a place he worked for sixty years. Jack became a Christian late in life and he was proud of his faith. He'd share it with anyone, including former players, whenever an opportunity presented itself. Shy, Jack was not.

Charlie Baker, who coached East Carter's basketball team for many years, was one of the smart ones. He took advantage of being around Jack Fultz, often sitting and listening to him for hours on end. He learned not how to attack a 1 - 3 - 1 zone; he learned how to attack personalities. And that, more than the X's and O's, is what coaching is all about. Learn what makes the players tick and how to handle situations and coaching can be made easy.

Baker and Jack Fultz go way back, back to when Baker's family moved to the Carter County area. Baker was a shy third-grade farm boy student when he first encountered this giant of a man. He was in gym class watching from the stands as others played basketball and other games around him.

Jack came up to Baker and asked him why he wasn't playing. Baker pointed down to his feet. Baker wasn't wearing tennis shoes. "He said 'Is that all? Well, we'll take care of that' and he gave me a pair of shoes," Baker said. "They were huge on me. It was a pair of Converse and I wore them out. He didn't know me and didn't have to do that. Jack was always the guy who would do the right thing."

I'm sure one wouldn't have to look far to find other similar acts of kindness when it came to Jack Fultz. Baker never forgot that generosity and later in life developed a coach-to-coach relationship with Jack that served him well in his chosen profession.

Jack Fultz, center, talks with Charles Chattin, left, and Paul Boyles during a reception at the Ashland Elks Club. Fultz, a former Oliver High School basketball coach and longtime educator was the honoree for the 33rd annual Ashland Elks Sports Day. JOHN FLAVELL/ THE INDEPENDENT

Jack Fultz led three Comet teams to the State Tournament in 1955, 1956, and 1959, even reaching the semifinals of the Sweet Sixteen in '59. But his legacy isn't so much about winning as giving. He gave us the Comet Reunion, an event that brings Olive Hill High School graduates together again. He gave us the Comets' Tale, a 794-page history of Olive Hill High School athletics and he gave us the stories.

Oh my, those wonderful tales of yesterday. That's what I'll miss most of all.

Rest in peace, my friend.

Tragedy and Triumph

November 2007

• • •

Championships are supposed to be celebrated.

But in 1967, the joy that the Ashland Tomcat football team gave its community with a state championship victory was replaced with sorrow.

It was a night of triumph after a day of tragedy.

Forty years later, the emotions of the eventful night still weigh heavily on the players, coaches, and fans. Ashland defeated Elizabethtown 19 - 14, capping a 13 - 1 season with the school's first state championship since 1942. That was the triumph. The tragedy happened earlier in the day when an automobile accident took the life of Joe Franklin, a promising junior basketball player who was popular with classmates. Franklin and four other students—three of them basketball players— were going to Frankfort for a basketball scrimmage on the morning of the football championship. He volunteered to drive his yellow sports car to Frankfort when an original driver didn't show up as planned.

Unlike today, there were no legal ramifications to consider. The bus wasn't available, so the players piled in cars. Seat belts were optional— not just for those in the cars but the cars themselves.

Ashland's Joe Franklin was killed in a tragic automobile accident while going to watch the 1967 state football championship.

The five boys were planning on traveling on to Louisville to watch the Tomcats in the championship after the scrimmage. It was going to be a night to remember.

But three miles outside Morehead, Franklin lost control of his car and crashed into a tanker truck. He was killed and the other four boys injured in a horrific crash that mangled the car. It was a time before cell phones and e-mail. News traveled much slower in 1967 than it does today.

Ashland's football team had a midday meal before boarding the bus and heading to Louisville for the state championship. Interstate-64 wasn't completely finished, so the trek to Louisville went through towns, and one of those was Morehead.

As the bus passed through town, Tomcat players Johnny Radjunas and Les Lyons noticed a mangled yellow sports car and commented to each other about how much it looked like Franklin's. They agreed, shrugged and went on with other conversation. Of course, they didn't know that it was Franklin's car and had no reason to suspect it was.

As the bus neared the rest stop in Mount Sterling, the plan was for the players to "eat an apple and stretch their legs." Radjunas said they noticed a couple of Ashland cars making the stop, too. "Some girls got out of the car and they were crying," he said. "We were just like 'I wonder what's wrong with them?'"

The coaches told the players there was a change of plan and they'd just eat their apples on the bus and head on to Louisville. The coaches had heard the horrible news but chose not to tell the players, fearing the reaction when learning that one classmate was dead and several others were in critical condition.

As the bus rolled into the Fairgrounds in Louisville, the players were funneled directly to the locker room under the stadium. Again, it wasn't the plan—the players were told they would watch part of the first game and then get ready for their game—but the coaches wanted to keep them as isolated from the news as possible. There was a slight drizzle that night and the coaches told the players they didn't want them to get wet. The players only knew, or even cared on this day, what the coaches told them.

Joe Franklin was more than a promising basketball player, too. He had been the quarterback on the junior varsity team as a sophomore and decided to quit football to devote more time to basketball. Everybody understood why. His future was bright in basketball.

As fate would have it, Ashland was on the visitor's side of the Fairgrounds, with no stands behind them. They were insulated from everything outside of football that night. The game was about the only thing that went according to plan for the coaches that day. The Tomcats bulldozing running game had built a 19 - 0 lead at halftime.

Elizabethtown quarterback Gary Inman rained twenty-eight passes down on the Tomcats' secondary in the second half. He almost brought the Panthers back, but Ashland held on for a hard-earned victory. After the game was over, the celebration started. Players were chanting, cheering and soaking up the moment.

Some of them found out about the accident then and others learned what happened from Hallum in the locker room after the game. It became a subdued celebration, to say the least.

Ashland stayed in Louisville that night and came back home on Saturday. Fire trucks were waiting for them at the city limits and Tomcat fans had lined the street holding signs and cheering.

Riding the firetruck had become an Ashland tradition. The '60s was a great time to be a sports fan here. Players on the 1967 football team grew up watching celebrations: the 1961 Tomcat basketball team rode the fire trucks after winning the state championship, the Tomcat baseball teams won three consecutive state titles from 1966 - 68, all complete with fire truck rides. Little League and Babe Ruth state champions were treated to the victory ride, too.

But the 1967 Tomcat football team never got their ride.

When the bus was about to Grayson on the way home, Hallum went back and spoke with co-captains Paul Hill and Radjunas and told them he thought it would be best if they didn't celebrate or ride the fire truck, out of respect to the Franklin family. The players were disappointed but agreed, knowing it was the right thing to do.

Jake Hallum led Ashland to the 1967 state title.

As they reached the city limits, the bus didn't stop where the fire trucks were sitting. Instead, the fire trucks followed them back to campus. When the team got off the bus, there was some polite applause. Everybody knew and understood why the celebration was muted.

Ashland's '67 champions never got the celebration or recognition they rightly deserved. It was a team built on strength by Hallum and his staff, which included Herb Conley. They worked tirelessly in the weight room and became one of the greatest champions in school history.

Harrison County, the team that was supposed to rule Class AA that season, demolished the Tomcats in a preseason scrimmage. But in the first game of the playoffs, Ashland shocked the state by upsetting Harrison County in Putnam Stadium.

The Tomcats almost didn't make the playoffs, which, at the time, were based on a complicated point system ranking called the Dickinson System. They took a 9 - 1 record into the last game of the regular season against Raceland and handily defeated the Rams 36 - 6. But the only way Ashland would be in the playoffs was if Campbell County beat Fort Thomas Highlands—an unlikely prospect since it hadn't happened in a dozen years. But as fate would have it, a downpour in northern Kentucky made for some horrible playing conditions and Campbell County stunned Highlands 6 - 0.

It was a team that relied on the running game with 1,000-yard rushers Paul Hill and Steve Scott. Les Lyons, a tackle who was moved to the backfield at midseason, gained 400 yards. Radjunas, the senior quarterback, was the consummate leader. He called about half the plays but knew the Tomcats' game was run, run, run.

Ashland's only loss came against Stonewall Jackson 13 - 3 as a 3 - 0 lead disappeared in the fourth quarter.

McKell, behind Butch Timberlake and Don Gullett, put a scare into Ashland, too. The Bulldogs weren't bad either, reaching the Class A state semifinals that season before losing to Mount Sterling in what most considered a major upset.

The Tomcats trailed McKell 20 - 14 late in the fourth quarter. The Tomcats began marching and called the second timeout of the game. Radjunas came to the sideline and told Hallum to hold onto the last timeout so Hill would have time to tie up his shoe to kick the extra point.

In '67, there were no two-point conversions. Radjunas was confident the Tomcats were going to score, which they did. Ashland took the timeout, Hill tied back his shoe and kicked the game-winning extra point in a 21 - 20 victory.

Ashland's Paul Hill lowers his head and shoulder on a run.

(Top) Ashland's Steve Scott found some open running room during the regular season.

(Left) Ashland quarterback Johnny Radjunas holds up the state championship trophy in 1967 in Louisville.

(Above right) Coach Jake Hallum and Ashland's players celebrate after winning the Class AA state football championship.

Jake Hallum, coach of the 1967 Tomcats state championship football team, waves as the team is recognized in October 2007. KEVIN GOLDY/THE INDEPENDENT

One of Ashland's biggest victories came early in the season, a 16 - 0 triumph over rival Boyd County. The previous year, Hallum's first at Ashland, the Lions beat the Tomcats for the first time—in any sport. They were red-faced over that loss, even though Boyd County's program was obviously on the rise. The win in '67 over Boyd showed them how far they'd come.

These Tomcats knew how to win—that was obvious. But they never truly got to celebrate, in Ashland style, their greatest victory. The fire trucks are still waiting to take them for a ride around town.

Herb Conley (left) and Dick Fillmore were Mr. Inside and Mr. Outside for the 1958 Ashland Tomcats. DON McREYNOLDS

1958 Tomcats Remembered
September 2008
• • •

It's been 50 years since Ashland had a football team go through a season without a loss.

The 1958 Tomcats—the last undefeated team in school history—will be recognized on its golden anniversary Friday night at Putnam Stadium.

The calling card for Ashland's '58 team was pretty simple: It was pound and ground.

Led by a Mr. Outside (Dick Fillmore) and Mr. Inside (Herb Conley), these Tomcats were built for running the football. Fillmore was also Mr. Excitement, averaging 41.9 yards on his twenty touchdown runs.

Perhaps his biggest TD run was an eighty-six-yard scamper against Ironton in the closing seconds of a 28 - 22 victory.

Fred Anson, an assistant who coached the running backs, remembers that game and that play well

"It was right at the end of that game and I was up top (on the press box)," he said. "There was only about two minutes left and I came down. I was satisfied with a tie."

With less than a minute remaining and Ashland on its own fourteen, a timeout was called. Quarterback Kendall Bocard huddled with the coaches and then came back with the play. It was going to be an off-tackle run by Fillmore.

"He broke a couple of tackles and was gone," Anson said.

Fillmore said the players were surprised with the call, but loved the outcome.

"We thought it was going to be a pass play," Fillmore said. "We ran it and Warner Caines got the last block on the halfback (defensive back) just as he was reaching for me."

Fillmore said an Ironton assistant coach, Charlie Kautz, who later coached at Marshall told Fillmore he was so close to the sideline he could have brought him down himself. Kautz was one of those killed in the 1970 Marshall plane crash.

Duke Moore, who had three interceptions in the Ironton win, remembered Caines and Bobby Lee delivering key blocks on Fillmore's electrifying run.

"He had a couple of key blocks and there may have been another one or two, but those two (Caines and Lee) stand out in my mind," Moore said. "He (Fillmore) probably got hit six times. You could never get a solid lick on Dicky. I tried my best (in practice) to get a hard hit on him and couldn't do it."

Moore, a starter at defensive halfback who finished with eight interceptions, was a speedster, too. But he couldn't nudge a starting spot on offense.

"I was teasing Dicky when I met him at the park (two weeks ago). I said 'You know who the best player yards per carry we had?' He said, 'I think I was.' I told him it was me but I didn't carry it but about eight times."

Ashland didn't make it through the season completely unblemished.

Huntington East tied the Tomcats 18 - 18 in the fourth week of the season.

"We let that daggone Huntington East tie us," Moore said. "Our kicker, Terry Collins, was feeling real bad after that one because he missed four extra points (including two after one TD because of a penalty). After the game he said 'I wish I had a gun, I'd shoot myself.' I told him 'It wouldn't matter if you did because you'd miss anyway.' We could tease each other. That's how this team was. I can't describe how close we were."

Of course, even after going 10 - 0 - 1, that was the end. The Kentucky High School Athletic Association hadn't instituted a playoff format.

Ashland went 9 - 0 - 1 in the regular season and then played Richmond Madison-Model, led by future UK quarterback Jerry Woolum, in the Recreation Bowl. The Tomcats led only 14 - 13 at the half but outscored Model 20 - 0 in the second half for a season-ending 34 - 13 triumph.

While there wasn't a state playoff, there were two polls—one from state coaches and another from *The Courier-Journal*. St. Xavier was No. 1 in the CJ poll and Ashland in the coaches poll.

"We wanted to play St. X," Fillmore said. "It didn't work out."

Bocard shrugs off the idea that there wasn't a playoff in place.

"That's the way the system was then," he said. "But we were a helluva good football team. We were not finesse. We ran the belly series. I'd put the ball in Herbie's belly and we'd sometimes run ten yards before I'd pull it out. It was a good, physical football team. Kind of like that 1961 (Tomcat) basketball team."

Fillmore's shifty running accounted for 1,223 yards and twenty touchdowns, averaging 11.4 per carry. Conley was the inside power and ran for 906 yards and sixteen touchdowns with 7.2 per carry.

Bocard (491 yards rushing) and Joey Layman (459) also did their

Ken Bocard was the quarterback for Ashland's undefeated
1958 football team. MARK MAYNARD

share of running. Layman scored on runs of fifty, eighteen, and seventeen against Model, which kept Fillmore out of the end zone for the only time all season. Fillmore scored 124 points and was second in area scoring that season to Catlettsburg's Jim Lee, who finished with 146 points.

As for passing, well, it just wasn't that kind of team. Bocard completed only fourteen passes all season—nine of them going for touchdowns. Monte Campbell had thirteen catches for 373 yards and eight TDs.

"We didn't have to throw," Bocard said. "We had a very good offensive line and with Herbie, Dick and Joey, why pass?"

Bocard was a hard-nosed runner himself and also teamed with Conley as inside linebackers in a wide-tackle six scheme. They were both punishing tacklers on a physical Tomcat defense.

Ashland rushed for 3,691 yards and outscored opponents 424 - 97.

The late Rex Miller was the head coach for the Tomcats in the '58 season.

"We began to see it develop the year before that," Anson said. "It was about halfway through that season when everything started coming together. We got off to a bad start that year."

RELIFORD'S DEFINING MOMENT
July 2008

• • •

If Charlie Reliford has a defining moment during a brilliant nineteen-year umpiring career, it came in 2000 during the Subway World Series between the New York Mets and New York Yankees.

Reliford, working his first World Series and behind the plate for the first time, helped defuse a potentially explosive situation between Yankee pitcher Roger Clemens and Mets slugger Mike Piazza.

"It is absolutely incredible," said Reliford, who will be honored by the Ashland Elks on Sports Day this weekend. "I still get asked about that. For an umpire's career, you have a couple of moments that stand out in people's minds. Fortunately, it turned out pretty well for me."

The now-famous incident occurred in the first inning of Game 2, when Piazza shattered his bat into three pieces fouling off an inside fastball. Clemens fielded the jagged barrel of Piazza's bat and fired it at the feet of the unsuspecting New York Mets catcher as he trotted down the first baseline.

Piazza, still clutching the splintered handle of the bat, immediately turned toward the mound to accost Clemens, who claimed innocence.

Both dugouts emptied, but no one was ejected.

Reliford stepped between the angered players and restored order quickly.

None of the umpires considered Clemens' actions intentional.

Once play resumed, Piazza grounded out on the next pitch to end the inning.

Clemens trotted off the field, tapping his chest and said, "My fault, my fault," to home plate umpire Charlie Reliford.

"I came back into the dugout and I said I've got to get control of my emotions and calm down," said Clemens at the post-game press conference.

"I told Charlie, the umpire, I didn't know Mike was coming out. I guess it came close to him. That was my emotions."

Clemens came back out and was overpowering. He threw eight innings of two-hit, nine-strikeout baseball before departing with a 6 - 0 lead.

The Yankees held on for a 6 - 5 victory and a 2 - 0 lead in the Series.

"I'm sure the Met fans wished I'd unloaded on him," Reliford said. "But baseball officials agreed it was the right decision (to not eject Clemens)."

Baseball did fine Clemens $50,000 for throwing the broken bat, saying he engaged in inappropriate conduct.

For Reliford, as an umpire, it's still what many fans associate him with even eight years later.

"There are a lot of baseball fans who hold out things coming on and off the field (for umpires) to sign," he said. "I've signed that picture more than anything else I have signed."

Reliford, who also called the 2004 World Series when Boston swept St. Louis, said umpires are often remembered for that one defining moment instead of what happened throughout their careers.

Major League Baseball umpire Charlie Reliford shows off a photo made with his daughter, Logan, during a fundraiser for Ashland American Little League. JOHN FLAVELL/THE INDEPENDENT

As an example, he said Don Denkinger was a "fabulous umpire with twenty-five to thirty great years" but is most often remembered for making the wrong call in Game 6 of the 1985 World Series between St. Louis and Kansas City. Denkinger's safe call on a bang-bang play at first base was clearly wrong and eventually cost the Cardinals a series-clinching win. The Royals went on to win Game 7 to take the series.

"He was one of the greatest umpires in baseball, just fabulous," Reliford said. "But he's remembered for one play in a World Series."

Bobby Simpson, left, and Reecie Banks point different directions during an interview about Central Park. MARK MAYNARD

"IT WAS LIKE FAMILY"
August 2008
• • •

Reese Banks and Bobby "Buns" Simpson never thought about the color of their skin while playing baseball here in the 1950s.

But they essentially broke the color barrier when they were allowed to join an Ashland Babe Ruth League team with white players in 1957.

"Fortunately, one of the good things to happen is we were ballplayers," Banks said. "The guys we played baseball with we had no problems whatsoever; some of the parents had a problem with us being on the team."

But between the lines, it was pure baseball, they said.

"It was like our family, in essence," Simpson said. "We never felt downgraded by our teammates or by our opponents. It was all a big happy family. Some of the parents were obstacles. They didn't like us."

There were some real racial tensions in Ashland, much like the rest of the country. Before teams were integrated, Banks remembers being asked by Eddie Smith to join a Pony League team he coached.

Banks agreed and was penciled in to play right field against a team from Ironton.

"One of the league officials came onto the field and said 'He cannot play.' The game was held up," Banks said. "Eddie and the official got into an argument. He came over to me and said 'I'm sorry Reese. Next year, this is not going to happen.' He fulfilled his promise."

Once Banks and Simpson were allowed to play with white players, they proved themselves to be worthy competitors. Their outstanding play helped open doors later for other blacks in Ashland. Banks and Simpson were essentially role models by being the pioneers.

"The responsibility we had to the black community was to do our best, to excel," Banks said.

"I would say it did open doors," Simpson said. "Some of the kids weren't going to play baseball. We'd tell them 'You play baseball. You can do it. We did it.'"

Banks said the overwhelming majority of the time there were no racial problems with baseball. They were ballplayers, no matter what the color.

Because of the way life was in the 1950s in Ashland and other towns like it, the black community knew what it was allowed to do and what it wasn't allowed to do. Sometimes they even knew better than their white teammates, who would make plans to do things after the game, like going downtown to watch a movie.

"We'd come up with some excuse," Banks said. "We knew more than our teammates knew. It was the law of the area. It was segregation."

But Banks said they never looked at it as being discriminated against.

"We didn't look at it like that," he said. "We knew where we could go and where we couldn't go."

Simpson said part of the "conditioning" was walking from Seventh

Street to Central Park nearly every day to play baseball. They were both proud of their uniforms.

"You were color-blind with that uniform on," he said. "I was so proud."

Simpson and Banks were selected to the Babe Ruth All-Star team in 1957, a team that advanced to the state level in Middlesboro behind coach Marvin Hall.

Simpson played on the team but Banks had a different commitment. He had been selected to attend the National Boy Scout Jamboree in Valley Forge. His parents decided that there would be a lot of baseball games in the future, but few scouting opportunities like this one.

"Scouting was an important part of my life also," Banks said. "We were involved in a lot of things besides baseball."

Simpson played on the All-Star team, although he was afraid he wouldn't be able to do some of the things his teammates did.

"My family didn't have a lot of money," he said. "I thought 'How do I afford things?' My teammates said 'Don't worry about it. You'll be covered.' And I was. That made me feel so much better. I could play ball."

As for Simpson's nickname, he said it came because he was always telling people to "Kiss my buns!" His teammates starting calling him "Buns" and it stuck.

Banks and Simpson were remembered as outstanding players.

J.D. Browne listed Reese Banks as one of the better hitters—along with Eddie Joseph, Jim Speaks, and Harold Sargent—he faced as a pitcher. Banks and Browne became close friends, a friendship that carries over today.

"J.D. Browne was one of the toughest pitchers," Banks said. "He didn't throw that hard but he was hard to hit. I remember getting him once though. I put him to the trees."

Browne said "you had to be careful how you pitched to Reese. Various guys were good hitters depending on the wind and the stupidity of the pitcher."

Banks said many of the white players became close friends over the years.

"Our friendships were expanded," he said. "When we got with the team, we were home. Not only during the games but after games. It was always a fond greeting. We'd swap stories, go to each other's homes."

Jim Stephenson said there was a black coach, Henry Tarter, who provided a lot of opportunities for players. He had an all-black youth league team before they were integrated.

Later, he started a semi-pro team with a lot of young men in their twenties and some much younger.

"He recruited Reese and me out of high school," Stephenson said. "The Ashland Redlegs. We'd travel to West Virginia and Ohio, and they'd bring teams here. That was a real experience. I won't say Reese was over his head, but I was."

Stephenson said Banks had a cannon arm. "He could throw the ball on the fly from the sidewalk to home plate on a line," he said.

Banks, who lives in Washington, D.C., and Simpson, who lives in Cincinnati, were in town for the CP-1 Reunion on Saturday in Central Park. Both players were still receiving those warm greetings from former teammates.

"It's good to be home, it sure is," Banks said.

A NOSTALGIC VISIT
August 2008

• • •

If you looked close enough, it was almost as if it were the 1950s and 1960s all over again.

On a hot and sticky Saturday afternoon—the kind most of them remembered from their playing days—many of Ashland's proud baseball past and even some of their rivals gathered on the main diamond in Central Park.

But now, instead of being primetime players wearing flannel uniforms, most of these players were admittedly well past their prime and in comfortable clothes.

While their best days are behind them, the stories shared made it seem like it all happened yesterday.

For one more day, they were kids again.

In their glory days, many of these players were the best of the best, multi-sport athletes who defined an amazing era of sports in Ashland

They came from thirteen different states and as far away as California to this impromptu reunion. Ashland great Larry Conley drove up from his home in Atlanta and Don Gullett, the former Cincinnati Red great, came to the outing and received a warm welcome from appreciative fans.

The reason for the gathering was to reminisce and to take a peek at the renovation of Ernie Chattin Field, formerly known as CP-1— the home to youth league, high school, and legion baseball games for decades.

The dugouts and press box that had stood for years has been torn down, paving the way for a beautification project that's been one year in the making. When it's finished, organizers are hoping the shiny diamond will be the showplace of the area, another gem in picturesque Central Park. The catalyst for the fix-up was a generous donation by Ashland native Gary Wright, who plunked down $125,000 to get the ball rolling. Much more funding is needed to complete the project, although Wright's donation took care of the first of three phases, including the new brick press box and matching retaining walls that will lead to the dugouts.

Wright, who lives in Florida, smiled as he gazed around the field that was once his personal summer playground.

"The turnout was fantastic and we're still just scratching the surface," Wright said. "We had a lot of last-minute cancellations. I know Jim Host, Larry Castle, and Herb Conley all wanted to be here. They're kind of bleeding because they couldn't come here today."

Wright's late father, T.R. Wright, was a youth league coach and mentor to many youth in Ashland in the 1950s. Gary Wright only asked that the press box be named in memory of his dad.

Conley said those who should be remembered were the adults who provided organized youth sports for the players of that era. "The Bob Hatchers, the Cecil Bushes, the Windy Kazees, and the George Conleys, people like that are the ones we should be thanking," he

Gary Wright put the CP-1 movement in motion. MARK MAYNARD

said. "They gave us such a great foundation. If we're going to thank anybody, those are the ones that need to be thanked."

Conley said one of his fondest memories of playing in the park was hitting a three-run home run in the City Little League championship game on the American League field, the one that bumped against right field on the big diamond. "It was a three-run blast that barely cleared the fence but I'll never forget it," he said.

Gullett, the fireballing left-hander who is considered one of the greatest athletes ever in northeastern Kentucky, remembered the battles with Ashland.

"It was a rivalry, if you will," he said. "Like me being down at the lower end of Greenup County. It was a David vs. Goliath kind of thing. We looked forward to it. It was great games. In baseball and football, we held our own very well."

Gullett said it was the first time since his high school playing days that he'd stepped onto the Central Park diamond. "It's changed a lot, a lot for the better," he said. "What they're doing here is a great thing."

Wright set up the mini-reunion of Central Park alumni to help others share his vision. City Recreation Director Sean Murray provided updates on the project but the day was mostly for sharing memories of days gone by.

"This is more than we expected, considering all the hurdles (red tape)," Wright said of the work done at the field. "The workers are triple-timing it. They're taking pride in what they're doing. They said they'd never seen this diamond looks this good ever, ever, ever."

Lawrence Humphrey rebuilt the pitcher's mound himself and did much of the infield manicuring, all to major league specifications.

"They're so proud of it they're going to make a call to Marshall University to play a game or two there next spring," Wright said.

The press box will be two stories with a storage room, a changing room for umpires, a level for scorekeepers and media, and a second level for scouting. It will be a split-face block structure. Also, there will be a matching retaining wall that connects the press box to the new dugouts.

Phase two of the project will include rebuilding the dugouts and phase three includes landscaping and bleachers. Instead of permanent bleachers, concrete pads will be laid and portable aluminum bleachers used during the season. They can be moved for other events when baseball isn't being played.

There will be added green space at the park when the revamping is finished, Murray said. A concept for participants to purchase memorial or honorary bricks that would add to the new look has been discussed. That would still need approval by the city.

The park's field has quite a history, including being the home field for major league players Brandon Webb and Drew Hall and major league umpires Charlie Reliford and Greg Gibson.

Webb, the 2006 National League Cy Young Award winner and a nineteen-game winner with the Arizona Diamondbacks this season, honed his skills on Chattin Field as a player in Ashland's youth leagues and in high school with the Ashland Tomcats.

Reliford and Gibson cut their umpiring teeth on the same field, starting careers that have carried them to the top of their game.

Many others who didn't make it to the major leagues played professional baseball for several seasons in the minor leagues also built their careers around Central Park.

Bobby Lynch, a star pitcher on Ashland's three-peat baseball champions from 1966 - 68, lost only one time in Central Park through his Babe Ruth League, high school and legion playing days.

"I think it's fantastic," Lynch said. "It will certainly revive the use of this park. When we were playing, the field was so overused. If it got watered during the day, it was an amazing thing. It's what we did."

David Carter has also started a PBS-type documentary on the field's history, and there's a Web site—cp-1.org—devoted to the park field. Carter interviewed dozens for the documentary on Saturday.

Banks Part of
BTW Sports Lore
August 2008
• • •

Marshall Banks played on one of Booker T. Washington High School's best basketball teams in 1958.

Banks was a senior that season and one of the area's top scorers at 22.9 per game. He was listed No. 1 among Boyd County scorers but finished behind South Portsmouth's Bob Kouns' 24.3 average in the Eastern Kentucky Conference.

Before the season, BTW was listed as one of the top three teams in the 16th Region. Powerhouse Clark County, which would eventually win the regional title behind coach Letcher Norton, was practically untouchable.

Banks eventually landed a scholarship at Morehead State, the first black athlete to receive financial aid from the university.

"It helped me at Morehead because I was considered a local guy because of the Ashland paper," Banks said. "(Former Sports Editor John McGill) followed me and he really played it up. If we had been in Lexington or Louisville, we'd have really gotten some major, major coverage."

As it was, playing in northeastern Kentucky, BTW was plenty tough. The Hornets entered the postseason that year with a 21 - 8 record.

Back then, the district tournament was a crowded affair. It took two victories to even make it to the district semifinals. And through the luck of the draw, BTW's path seemed loaded for the tournament that was being played at Russell.

First up was defending district champion Russell and the Hornets dispatched the Red Devils, 69 - 64, as Banks scored twenty-two. Next came Ashland. While hardly a dominant Tomcat team, it was still Ashland. And this turned out to be the first meeting between Booker T. Washington and the Tomcats.

The players knew each other well from hours and hours on the playgrounds. They played at Bayless Elementary. "Gravel Gardens, that's what we called it," Banks said. "We played against players from Holy Family and Ashland High School. It was no big deal for us. The only issue was, we didn't go to school together. All summer we'd play until it got too dark."

The game was a big one but Banks wasn't around long. He was thrown out of the game for "deliberate tripping" in the first quarter. With the Hornets' star out of the game, it didn't look good for BTW.

Banks said his feet got tangled up on a rebound and when the players fell to the floor, he was ejected.

Even after the shock of the ejection, BTW recovered and went on to defeat Ashland 54 - 46 on a Thursday night.

"That meant we had to go to school on Friday," Banks said. "Everybody was cheering for us at school. We'd never played Ashland and we beat them. We didn't have much transition time."

Wilbert Barrow, Don Keeton, Tyrone Fitzpatrick, and James

Banks, along with Marshall Banks, were some of the most underrated players in the region, McGill wrote after the win over Ashland.

The next night, BTW played Holy Family, which it had beaten 79 - 63 during the regular season. But the Irish, behind big Dan Stephenson, eliminated the Hornets 65 - 54 in the semifinals. Although scoring twenty-one, Banks had a woeful shooting night, going 8-for-32 in his last high school game.

"We were spent from the night before," Banks said. "We couldn't recover."

Ashland in the 1950s was segregated and Banks said the blacks "knew the rules in regard to the segregated situation." Downtown was off limits and so were the movies and department stores. Dental appointments and medical checkups were done after hours.

Banks recalled the Capitol Theater having a Christmas show with cartoons and movies and "all the kids in town" were invited to come with admission being a can of food for the Ramey Home.

"My mother (Flora) snatched me and Reece up, gave us a can of goods and took us to the theater," Banks said. "They challenged us but she said 'You said any kid with a can of food.' So they let us in."

He said the blacks were allowed to sit in the balcony at the theater in Catlettsburg. They could also go to Ironton and watch movies.

"This was fifty years ago and we grew up that way," Banks said. "We had a really strong black community, good families, a good church. I went to New Hope Baptist. My father (Lawrence Banks) was on the deacon board. When the church doors were open, we were there—Monday for Boy Scouts, Wednesday for midweek prayer service, and Sundays for church. It was a good place to grow up."

Bert Greene poses while coach Jack Fultz holds the 1959 regional championship trophy. Jim Harrison, former Morehead State University center, is pictured right. Harrison served as an usher for the Comets throughout the tournament that year.

LEAVING HIS MARK
July 2007
• • •

Jack Fultz has always had a way of leaving an impression on people.

Whether it was with teammates, players, coaching rivals, or just admirers, the former Olive Hill High School basketball coaching great has always had a giant's presence in life and on the sidelines.

On Friday and Saturday, the Ashland Elks will be honoring Fultz during the thirty-third annual Sports Day festivities at the Elks Lodge on Carter Avenue.

Freddie Simpson, the Sports Day honoree in 2004, said it's an honor long overdue.

"I asked somebody once 'Where's Jack?' and was told this is kind of an Ashland thing. Translated: a Tomcat thing," Simpson said. "With Jack, the guy is in the Kentucky (High School Athletic Association) Hall of Fame. I'd say he should have been one of the top ten guys."

Fultz coached the Comets from 1951 - 68 and dueled some of the best basketball teams in Ashland history. Of course, during that time Clark County was also a state powerhouse and Russell had its share of good teams.

Fultz still managed to win the 16th Region championship three times—1955, 1956, and 1959. His '59 Comets went to the state semifinals before injuries to both guards sent them to a disappointing defeat.

Simpson, a star player at Holy Family High School, said you were in for a battle against the Comets every time.

"I remember what a relentless coach he was," Simpson said. "His teams were always so well-prepared defensively. He had them playing defense."

Ashland Mayor Steve Gilmore, who is on the Sports Day selection committee, has always admired Fultz both as a coach and educator. He worked in the Carter County school system for sixty years.

Gilmore remembers watching Holy Family-Olive Hill games when he was a young boy in grade school when Fultz was coaching.

"He was an intimidating factor from the bench," Gilmore said. "I can remember a couple of games, he had one of the loudest stomps I ever heard.

"To me, Jack was a purist as a coach. There are so many things you can do now. Jack's strong suit was he knew kids. He demanded much, at least that's what some of the old-timers who played for him say. They were intimidated by him. He was just trying to get the very best out of them."

Gilmore also remembers some of the pure shooters who played for Fultz, like Bert Greene and J.D. Kiser.

Bob Wright, who led Ashland to the 1961 state championship, went against Fultz not only as the Tomcats' coach but also at Vanceburg.

"He was a coach in full charge," Wright said. "His teams were always strong fundamentally. He had his own things that he did and he did them well."

Fultz lost more than he won against the Tomcats in his coaching career, going 7 - 20, but he wasn't without some memorable moments.

Olive Hill defeated the Tomcats 58 - 56 in double overtime to win the 1955 regional title in Winchester. That would be the first of three championships for the Comets during that decade.

In 1963, Olive Hill upset Ashland 59 - 57 in the opening round of the regional tournament. The Tomcats had won the state title in '61 and was runnerup in '62.

But perhaps the most memorable game he coached against Ashland was a loss in 1953 when the Comets held the ball. The final score was 25 - 19, a game that infuriated Tomcat fans who were used to getting it up and down the floor.

Fultz remembered H.V. Ellis, Ashland's principal at the time, coming up to him after the game.

"He said 'Jack, they won't come out and watch that kind of ball,'" Fultz said. "I told him 'I'm coaching to win.' The next year, when we played them in December, you couldn't get in that gym there were so many people there."

Truth be told, that may have lit the fuse on the Olive Hill-Ashland rivalry over the next decade or so. There were some fierce battles, to be sure, with both schools producing standout athletes and teams.

Despite a glowing record and reputation, Fultz never left his hometown despite many opportunities to coach elsewhere. Home was always Olive Hill and it has been his entire life, including a sixty-year marriage to wife Jean. They have two daughters, Suzanne and Andrea, and have three grandchildren.

"Jack was a close-knit person to Olive Hill," Wright said. "He had something there. It was a connection in his mental makeup. He didn't want to go anyplace else and that speaks well of him. He did the community a great favor."

Gilmore said Fultz deserved the Sports Day recognition that will come his way this weekend.

"He's kind of the epitome of 16th Region basketball," Gilmore said. "He's had such a high respect for Ashland all his life and it has been vocal. He's part of that 16th Region history we're a part of here. He's dedicated so many years after coaching to children and the school district itself in Carter County.

"Jack epitomizes all that's good about being in the coaching profession for the right reason."

Even at the age of eighty-one, Fultz was loyal to the Carter County school district, where he was still working. If it were up to him, he'd keep working there, too.

"The superintendent presented me with a letter that my services would not be needed after June 30," he said. "It just floored me. For sixty years, I got up every morning to do some function for the Carter County Board of Education. It kind of got started that I was retiring, but I'll never retire. This has really been hard on me."

LEGEND OF COBBIE LEE
October 2008

• • •

Cobbie Lee, who died earlier this week, is one of those names that I heard about for years while working the sports beat at this newspaper. Regretfully, I never met the man.

I knew he was from Catlettsburg and played football on some of the great Catlettsburg Wildcat teams of the 1930s. But I didn't know just how big a star this guy must have been in his day.

Football was different during that great era...from equipment to style of play. But Lee apparently played a brand of football that separated him from his peers.

Marvin Meredith, who also made his mark as a great Catlettsburg athlete and then a legendary basketball coach at Russell High School, remembers watching Lee play in high school.

"I was small at the time," Meredith said. "Cobbie was a great athlete, one of the best around here. They played on old Lee's Field. That thing was like concrete.

"There was a house at one end and they broke a woman's window out several times (kicking extra points). They finally decided to always go to the opposite end to kick."

That's where Cobbie Lee, and others, made their mark.

Lee would go on to Murray State Teachers College where he earned fame as a multiple-sports star with the Racers, earning an incredible twenty letters while there. He played a little bit of everything at Murray and was even drafted by the Cleveland Rams—that's right, the Rams—in the 1941 NFL Draft.

Meredith said he remembered Lee as an outstanding boxer who once won a Golden Gloves competition, too. He also recalled a story where those fists were put to protective use.

"We went up to Paintsville to play one time and some guy came out there and he was cussing Cobbie up and down," Meredith said. "Cobbie said to him, 'Listen, you need to behave yourself.' But the man kept it up and then he got in Cobbie's face. Two licks, and Cobbie knocked him colder than a wedge. I've never seen anything like that."

Lee was protective of his players and his teachers when he was an administrator at several high schools in the area, including Boyd County, Raceland, and Rock Hill. Meredith and Paul Reliford, who worked with Lee in three different school systems, said he was loyal to his friends.

"If you went to war, he'd be the man you wanted to take with you," Meredith said.

Cobbie coached Catlettsburg for one season in 1943, when Meredith was a freshman with the Wildcats. It was a long year, Catlettsburg finishing 1 - 6 - 2.

Meredith remembered a time when Lee, ever the competitor, lined up against the high school players in practice.

"He was scrimmaging with us and broke his ribs," Meredith said. "Of course, he was tough and didn't want to let on, even though it was about to kill him."

Maybe that's why years later Lee had some sympathy for Reliford, who while a teacher at Boyd County, was part of a group of older players who went against Tom Scott's varsity in the mid-1960s. Scott had asked Reliford to gather up a team and Reliford told him "I'll not only coach the team, I'll play."

Reliford, who was an outstanding football player at Ashland High School, said he'd always wanted to be a quarterback. He got his wish and, as the saying goes, you should be careful what you wish for.

Reliford, who was twenty-seven at the time, hadn't been hit on a football field in about ten years. He took some punishment and ribbing from the football players—"Getting up kind of slow, aren't you Mr. Reliford?" they would say.

The next day, he practically had to crawl into work.

"I came to work, swollen up bad," he said. "Cobbie looked at me and said 'I got you a substitute. Go on in the whirlpool the rest of the day.'"

Cobbie probably remembered how he felt twenty years earlier when he scrimmaged against the Wildcats.

With legendary area sports figures like Cobbie Lee come some of the greatest tales. My regret is not hearing some of those from the man himself.

Billy Ray Cyrus, shown here playing the Paramount Arts Center in 1992, was a member of Russell's 1978 state champions. KEVIN GOLDY/THE INDEPENDENT

LESSONS LEARNED FROM '78 CHAMPIONS

September 2008

• • •

State championships of any kind should never be taken for granted. Ivan McGlone learned that lesson in 1978.

That was the year Russell won the Class AAA championship with a 17 - 7 victory over Woodford County at Hanger Field on the campus of Eastern Kentucky University.

It took twenty-seven more years for McGlone to taste that sweet elixir of state championship tonic again.

"I was young—well, I was forty—and just thought this is what you're supposed to do," he said of the victory in '78. "I probably appreciated the second one (in 2005) more. The first one, I was like, 'Well, it's about time.' We played pretty good football. I thought surely every four years we'd get back there."

McGlone was only in his third season at Russell in '78. The first year the Red Devils went 4 - 7 and his second season they reached the state semifinals, losing a 13 - 7 heartbreaker to Fort Thomas Highlands.

"That '77 team was awfully good," he said. "Fort Thomas beat us

13 - 7 and they scored on fourth down late in the game. We came back in '78 and the confidence is up. That kind of carries you."

What Russell was in the midst of was a three-year stretch from 1977 - 79 of very good football. If not for an early season loss to Belfry, when only the district champion advanced in the playoffs, the '79 team may have well given the Red Devils back-to-back state championships.

But the stars aligned right in '78 for a Russell team that knew how to win.

Brent Muncy was the quarterback and is the name most equated with the '78 champions. Even though he was one of the better passing quarterbacks around, the Red Devils did then what they do now—run, run, run.

In the state championship, Muncy threw only three times, completing one to Mitch Julien that set up Mike Keen's field goal that put Russell ahead 17 - 7 in the fourth quarter. McGlone said he walked over to assistant coach Grady Walters on the sidelines and told him they were going to run the bootleg pass. Walters, a proponent of the passing game, was shocked.

"Grady was always harping we need to throw the ball more," McGlone said. "When I told him that, he wouldn't even talk to me. He just walked away."

But the bootleg completion was a big one, albeit the only one, in the finals.

"Obviously, we could throw the ball," McGlone said. "We didn't throw much in the playoffs but we did throughout the season."

The leading receiver for the Red Devils was Bill Cyrus, who was later more commonly known as Billy Ray Cyrus. The country music star was also the holder for kicker Mike Keen, who was a weapon that McGlone called upon often in the '78 season.

"We were pretty good defensively. It was back in an era where you

106

didn't have to score forty points. We were happy to have seventeen points. We always felt back then if we got a touchdown lead, we're going to win it."

It wasn't an offensive juggernaut, but the same Wing-T that McGlone runs today was efficient. It got first downs. It ate the clock. And it put the defense in position to finish off teams.

Linebacker Greg Allen, Jeff Roy, Scott Hester, Muncy, Mike Peffer, and Scott Boyd were some of the other defenders. Andy Rayburn, the fullback, was knocked out of the game with a hip-pointer. The Red Devils scrambled, moving Bill Jenkins to fullback and Boyd, who had over 100 yards rushing in the game, to left halfback.

Rayburn was blasted by a stunting Woodford County linebacker and it made the coaching staff change the blocking assignment on the play. "We call it the Scott Boyd rule to this day," McGlone said.

Russell wasn't supposed to be in the finals in '78. Lloyd Memorial was a powerhouse from northern Kentucky that Jessamine County upset in the playoffs. The Red Devils then defeated Jessamine County 18 - 0 to reach the finals for the first time.

"It was a big upset," McGlone said of Lloyd's loss. "I know we had scouts down there and somewhere in the fourth quarter they decided to start scouting Jessamine County."

Jessamine County and Russell were in a scoreless tie in the first half. The Colts had driven inside Russell's 10 but the defense made a stand. The Red Devils then drove it down the field and kicked a field goal in the closing seconds for a 3 - 0 lead. "They were kind of dominating us throughout the first half," McGlone said.

But the Red Devils survived and then finished an 11 - 3 season like it started, with a win over Woodford County. Russell defeated Woodford County 28 - 7 in the Recreation Bowl season opener.

The Devils three losses came to Huntington East, Huntington High, and Greenup County.

McGlone has since coached the sons of many former players. This year he has three sons of fathers who were members of the 1978 championship team—Will Rice (Greg Rice), Zach Smith (Jeff Smith), and Tanner Locey (Denny Locey).

"I told them I'm not coaching their grandkids," McGlone said. "I'm not going to do it...unless they're really good."

YELLOWJACKET MEMORIES, LAUGHS ABOUND
May 2008
• • •

The names and faces were the same, but the years had, well, changed some of the bodies.

When Prichard High School's 1959 baseball team knelt for a team picture on Monday morning at Princess Chapel, knees cracked and joints popped. It wasn't a pretty picture.

"Hurry up, dadblameit,"one of them shouted as the photographer, who was also the Yellowjackets star pitcher in '59, steadied the camera.

"Somebody's going to have to help me up after this one is over," another one chortled.

Everybody laughed. Age may have taken some of their athleticism, but not the senses of humor or the memories of some of the best times of their lives.

Clell Lucas, the pastor at Princess Chapel and a '59 Prichard alum, set up the reunion to honor one of the players who couldn't be there.

They held signs for Phil Hammond, the team catcher and leader, during the impromptu team picture.

Hammond lives in Pima, Arizona, and is suffering from cancer.

"I'd like to be there," Hammond said via cell phone from his Arizona home. "The baseball team in '59, with a couple of breaks, could have gone to the state tournament."

The Yellowjackets did make it to the regional finals in '59, losing 10 - 0 to McKell. Prichard workhorse Stanley Dyer finally ran out of steam after pitching game after game in the postseason.

"We pitched him almost until his arm dropped off," Hammond said. "Our way of taking care of him was thirty-nine cents to buy a bottle of Absorbine Junior at Brown's drugstore. That was it."

Dyer didn't have much left for McKell in the championship. Harold Holbrook, Prichard's coach, said he was hoping for rain after the Yellowjackets made it into the regional finals.

Dyer was the photographer on the scene during a picture-perfect Monday morning. His wife, Carolyn Wilson Dyer, said her husband has been dabbling in some filmmaking as well. He is working on a documentary about Prichard High School that he hopes to finish in time for the fiftieth reunion of the '59 class next year, Carolyn said.

This day was for the players. Twins Bill and Beryl Satterly were outfielders and easily the team's best two hitters. Beryl batted .428 and Bill .378. Both of them were there, tossing the baseball around on the grounds.

Other Prichard alumni were there, too, including Larry Boggs of West Sunberry, Pennsylvania, He didn't play baseball but followed the team closely. "I went to the games to get out of class," he said with a sly grin. "They were a good team. They just needed one more pitcher."

Prichard's defense was anchored by Jack Calhoun, who was

Prichard High School 1959 baseball team members gather for a photo during a reunion in May, 2008. Kneeling in front are Beryl Satterly, Kenny Applegate, and Jack Calhoun. Standing in back are Stanley Dyer, Bill Satterly, and coach Harold Holbrook. KEVIN GOLDY/THE INDEPENDENT

recognized by *The Courier-Journal* as the best shortstop in the state in preseason.

"He was our Roy McMillen," Boggs said, referring to the former Cincinnati Reds shortstop of '59.

Hammond was the catcher, Kenny Applegate played second base, Jim Felty third base, Dick Damron and George Waggoner first base, Bill Nash left field, Bill Satterly right field, and Beryl Satterly was in center.

"Every time they hit the ball in the outfield, if those guys ran into each other there would be a fistfight in the outfield," Boggs said of the twins.

Dyer and Waggoner were the pitchers, although the ball was mostly in Dyer's hands.

Most of the players on the team grew up only a street apart, living on Second and Third Streets in Grayson. While there wasn't organized youth baseball in the summer, the players in this neighborhood played together from daylight to dark.

"They were a bunch of good athletes," said Holbrook, who later became superintendent of Carter County schools. "They'd played together for some time and it showed."

Applegate, a leadoff hitter who batted .320, said the team's tight-knit relationship made them hard to beat.

"We all grew up together playing basketball and baseball," he said.

Jack Strother, a sophomore on the '59 team, also joined in during the summer games.

"We'd have car washes and buy either a bat or ball," he said. "We'd play until either we broke the bat or lost the ball."

Prichard also had an outstanding basketball team that season but was still no match for another Carter County school. Olive Hill High School's '59 team was one of the best in the state, losing in the semifinals of the Sweet Sixteen.

Prichard's basketball season came to an unceremonious end with a loss to Vanceburg. Almost immediately after the game, as the team shared pimento-cheese sandwiches—a longtime food tradition for away games—on the way back to Grayson, the attention turned to baseball.

Hammond told anyone within earshot that the baseball team was going to make it to the state tournament. He also had some advice for the team's pitcher.

"Dyer, you are going to throw strikes," he said. "You about killed my shins with all those balls you threw in the dirt last year."

Prichard High School's 1959 baseball team reunion shirts made up in May 2008. KEVIN GOLDY/THE INDEPENDENT

Hammond laughs about it today. "We didn't have anybody else on the team who knew where home plate was," he said. "We had nobody else who could pitch."

Dyer remembered Hammond telling him to plunk the first batter.

"The strategy was always to hit the first batter," Dyer said. "Then we had them psyched out."

Bill Satterly, who lives in Lexington, said the reunion brought back some precious memories for him.

"Something like this brings you together," he said. "I haven't had a ball glove on my hand since high school."

But he did remember a home run he hit at Boyd County that went over a hill and out of sight. "That ball may still be rolling," Satterly said.

Stories like that were frequently being told on Monday to anybody who would listen. The Yellowjackets were in their heyday again, complex with yellow-and-black T-shirts and ball caps provided by Lucas.

"I'd love to be there," Hammond said. "If I can beat this cancer, I'll be there for the fiftieth (reunion)."

SPINNING THE WEBB FROM 1990
July 2008

• • •

Long before Brandon Webb was a three-time National League All-Star and the 2006 Cy Young Award winner, he was a spindly eleven-year-old All-Star pitcher for Ashland American's 1990 state champions.

It was the last Little League state champion from the area and just making that team as an eleven-year-old was quite an accomplishment. As it turned out, it was partly because of Webb's clutch pitching that Ashland American won the state championship.

We knew even then that great things seemed to be in store for Webb although nobody could have envisioned what's transpired. He's a true inspiration for anyone who ever played Little League or Babe Ruth League baseball in the area.

Webb honed his pitching skills right here, not in some elite academy with professional coaches and high-tech training techniques and gadgets.

Even as a young boy, the big stage never frightened him.

Webb wasn't the No.1 or No.2 pitcher on the Ashland American staff during that All-Star campaign—most eleven-year-olds aren't. But it was his relief pitching in the district championship against Russell-

Flatwoods and then in the state championship against St. Matthews that eventually sent the Ashland team to St. Petersburg, Florida.

The game with Russell-Flatwoods was most memorable. Ashland American won the game 6 - 5 in ten innings with Webb pitching six shutout innings of relief. He retired the first fifteen he faced and drove in the winning run with a grounder.

It wasn't Webb's patented sinker—his bread-and-butter pitch with the Arizona Diamondbacks that he learned in the minor leagues on the way up—but a sharp-breaking curveball that had Russell's potent hitters tied up in knots. He struck out nine and didn't walk a batter.

Casey Sparks pitched masterfully for Russell, working the maximum allowed nine innings while striking out seventeen.

The day before, in a must-win game, Webb was one of four players who belted home runs in a 12 - 5 victory over Russell. The others were Tony Barrow, Omar Henry, and Travis Hignite.

During the State Tournament, the coaching staff of Steve Moore and Marvin Childers turned to Webb again in relief during the championship game.

Webb pitched two-hit baseball over three 2 - 3 innings, allowing only one run while striking out ten in an 8 - 6 win in Hazard.

Ashland American had to wait out a sixty-eight-minute rain delay just to get that last out. Webb fittingly struck out St. Matthews' best hitter to end the game with a runner on first base.

The next week, Ashland American played Florida in the Southern Regional and dropped a 14 - 11 slugfest. Ashland had a three-run lead in the sixth inning and needed only one out to defeat Dunedin before its foe erupted for six runs, creating a heartbreaking defeat.

Ashland's starting lineup from the All-Star season included Brian Strader, Hignite, Barrow, Henry, Casey Davis, Robbie Francis, Gary

Brandon Webb pitching in an Ashland American All-Star Game in July 1990. KEVIN
GOLDY/THE INDEPENDENT

Holland, Josh Leadingham, and Webb. Barrow and Davis, like Webb, eventually were professional prospects.

I'm sure even today all those players remember well their playing days with Webb, along with playing on one of Little League's grandest stages as part of a state champion.

When Webb takes the mound in Yankee Stadium on Tuesday as part of the National League All-Star team, be it as the game's starter or in relief, he'll have plenty cheering for him in this neck of the woods—especially a group of Little Leaguers from eighteen years ago who carry their own special memories.

ME AND THE MICK BACK IN 1989
November 2009

• • •

One great thing about this job is the chance encounters we have with the celebrity world.

For me, it has been the sports celebrity world.

The list goes on and on of sports heroes that I've been able to interview—Muhammad Ali, Pete Rose, and Michael Jordan to name a few.

And, oh yes, Mickey Mantle.

The story of my five-minute interview with The Mick is much better than the interview itself.

Mantle, the baseball idol of the 1950s and 1960s, is a name that everybody knows.

It was back in 1989, long after Mantle had retired from baseball as one of its all-time home run leaders. The Mick didn't just hit home runs, he hit them out of sight. His legend was unprecedented.

While browsing through a magazine at work one day, I began reading an article about the Mickey Mantle-Whitey Ford Fantasy Camp in Fort Lauderdale. At the bottom of the article, there was a number to call. It had a 606 area code and a 474 exchange. That said one thing to me—Grayson, Kentucky.

The curious reporter in me made the call to the number and on the other line was Wanda Greer, who was the camp director. David E. Carter, who produced the "Ashland's Field of Dreams" documentary, was actually the one who had a hand in starting the fantasy camp many years ago.

I set up an interview with Wanda and she asked if I'd like to speak with Whitey and Mickey.

Well, uh, absolutely, I told her.

So the wheels were put in motion. She actually gave me Ford's number and I called him about a day later. We spoke for fifteen or twenty minutes about the camp, about Mickey and about Wanda. It was a good interview but The Mick would be what could turn the article from good to great, at least in my estimation.

Wanda said Mickey would be a little harder. She wasn't going to share his number, which was understandable. And besides that, Mickey was always on the go, flying here and there, doing autograph signings or whatever. He was Mickey Mantle and that was job enough.

Wanda took my home phone number—these were the days before cell phones—and told me when Mickey was available she'd give me a call.

That was good enough for me. So I waited.

One Sunday night, my wife, five-year-old son, two-year-old daughter and I were at church. My wife wasn't feeling well, so she told me she was taking the kids and going home. We'd driven separately, so that would be fine.

On the way home from church, my wife drove by the Oakview Elementary playground and Stephen, being a five-year-old, begged her to stop.

"No," she said, "if we were anywhere right now, it would be in church. The only reason we're going home is because Mommy doesn't feel well."

So that was that. Stephen wasn't happy about it but understood as much as five-year-olds understand these things.

Well, lo and behold, when Beth arrived home she got a phone call and Wanda Greer was on the other end. She asked for me and Beth told her I was at church. She told Beth that if there were any way possible, could she have me at the phone in fifteen minutes because Mickey Mantle was going to be calling.

Mickey Mantle!

My wife knew I was working on the story and didn't want me to miss the opportunity. She hurried back to church, with Stephen and Sally in tow, and told someone in the back of the church, in our sound room, to let me know.

He came down the aisle—I was sitting near the front—and told me. I jumped up and walked out of church and headed for home, excited about the opportunity that awaited.

In the other car, Beth was posed with an interesting question by our five-year-old: "Mom, is Mickey Mantle bigger than God?"

Wow! What a zinger. Always quick on her feet, Beth said, "Well, no, but this is different. It's Daddy's job. That's why we got him out of church."

It turned out, that wouldn't be when the interview with The Mick happened. Mantle was at an airport and didn't have time to make the call. Wanda called me and apologized and promised that Mantle would call me at work on Saturday.

That was fine with me. I was working on a Saturday morning—the paper was afternoon back then—with Tony Curnutte. Nobody was a bigger baseball fan than Tony. When I told him The Mick was calling today, he was giddy.

I told him that we needed to make sure one of us was always near the phone because I didn't know when the call would happen. Well, naturally, The Mick called when we were both away from the desk.

Our switchboard operator at the time didn't look for me because she thought it was a bogus call.

"Somebody saying he was Mickey Mantle called but I knew it couldn't be him," she said. "So I hung up on him."

"What?" I screamed. "That *was* Mickey Mantle!"

I quickly called Wanda back and told her what had happened. She didn't know if The Mick would call back but told me to sit right by my desk. I'm sure she had to do some explaining but whatever she said worked.

I told Tony what was happening. He begged me to let him answer the phone so he could say he talked to Mickey Mantle. I agreed.

Ringggggggggg! Ringggggggggg!

Tony, in his most proper and professional voice, cleared his throat and then answered: "Sports, Tony Curnutte."

The countenance on his face dropped immediately. In subdued tones he said "Yes, uh, I guess. Hang on a minute."

"It's not The Mick it's The Rick," he said. Rick Greene, a sportswriter for us at the time, wanted to know if I wanted him to cover an American Legion game in the park that afternoon.

"Get him off the phone!" I said.

We both sat quietly. Tony stared at the phone, poised like a cat getting ready to pounce on a mouse.

Ringggggggg! Ringggggggggg!

Tony answered again in professional voice. "Just a minute," he said firm and proper. This time it was The Mick. He transferred the call to me and on the other line was none other than Mickey Mantle.

The first thing he said to me, in his thick Oklahoma drawl, was: "You sure are a hard guy to get ahold of."

We both laughed. I was as professional as I could be and we had a brief interview that was cut off when I asked him about Pete Rose and gambling.

"I'm not here to talk about that," he said.

Good enough. I mean, it was Mickey Mantle.

I hung up the phone and the journey had ended. After plugging in Mantle's quotes in the story, the job was done. The feature ran the following day and Wanda, being so classy, was kind enough to get me an autographed Mickey Mantle baseball. It had "To Mark, best wishes, Mickey Mantle" on it and it still sits today on my mantle at home.

Autographed baseballs that are personalized are worth less on the open market than those that just have the name. But I liked that it was personalized and wouldn't sell it anyway.

To me, it serves as a reminder of a story worth telling.

Mickey Mantle's photograph sits behind the autographed baseball on the Maynards' mantle, a memento of a 1989 interview. MARK MAYNARD

Jeep Clark Honored as Great Player, Coach
July 2006
• • •

Eugene "Jeep" Clark may be best remembered in the area for building Boyd County High School's basketball program into a 16th Region powerhouse.

But Clark's roots are pure maroon and white.

Clark will be honored this weekend during the 32nd annual Ashland Elks Sports Day festivities at the downtown lodge.

Clark, who grew up on 32nd Street, was a terrific basketball and baseball player for the Tomcats in the late 1940s. He was an All-State basketball player as a senior on Ashland's 1949 region runners-up.

That Tomcat team fell to Clark County 46 - 33 in Winchester in the regional finals. Clark County was the No. 1 team in the state.

"Jeep was all right," said Jim Graham, a former Tomcat teammate in baseball and 1950 graduate. "He was all business and played to win."

Graham said he followed the Tomcat basketball team in Clark's senior season, including a trip to Winchester that he thought gave Clark County an unfair homecourt advantage.

"They (Ashland) had a good basketball team back then," Graham said. "Ashland had the best team (in the region). I went out there (to watch the game) thinking 'This is not right having to play them on their home floor for the right to go to the state tournament.'"

The game ended with coach Letcher Norton's team clutching the championship trophy, just as it had the previous year when Clark County defeated Ashland 39 - 38 in Ashland.

Joe Slone was a senior captain that season, a four-sport star with the Tomcats. He was the second-leading scorer with a 10.5 average behind Clark's 12.9.

"Jeep did his job, like the rest of us," Slone said. "He was behind me one year. I went on to Ohio Wesleyan and he went to Southern Mississippi. I really lost contact. He went south and I went north."

As a senior, Clark averaged 12.2 per game with 6 - 1 junior Bob Lowe's 9.4 average the next highest.

But it was Clark's ballhandling skills that separated him from the rest, Graham said.

"He was such a good ballhandler, he could control the game," Graham said. "Jeep knew the game, too. Nobody was surprised when he became a coach."

Even before Clark went to Southern Mississippi, he played a year at Ashland Junior College and was the leading scorer in seventeen of twenty-seven games. Clark's teammates there included Marvin Meredith, Charlie "Stick" Stewart of Olive Hill and Jim Highley, a high school teammate. Clark eventually landed at Southern Miss where the team went 76 - 31 during his time there. He later came back to coach his alma mater from 1971 - 76 before he came to Boyd County.

Clark had several high school coaching stopovers, including a couple in Kentucky at Montgomery County (1954 - 59) and Paris

Eugene "Jeep" Clark poses in the Boyd County Middle School Gym, where he coached the high school team 1976 - 1982, building the Lions into a 16th Region powerhouse. He won the titles in 1981 - 1982. JOHN FLAVELL/THE INDEPENDENT

(1954 - 62). He was the basketball coach at Boyd County from 1976 - 82 and retired after seven more years as the school's athletic director.

It was at Boyd County that Clark made his mark, using a suffocating man-to-man defense that dominated opponents and put the Lions on the state map as a basketball power. He won back-to-back regional titles in 1981 and 1982 before handing the baton to Roger Zornes, who took the program to even greater heights in a twenty-year run.

"He was a mastermind of the game," said former East Carter coach Charles Baker, who was breaking into coaching when Clark came to Boyd County. "The way he carried himself with so much confidence but no arrogance. He makes you feel so at ease when talking to him.

"Here I was, up and coming, trying to make it, and this guy has been around the world in the coaching area. It was so humble."

Baker said Clark's philosophy of aggressiveness and hard-nosed defense took the program to great levels.

"It was nothing dirty," Baker said. "He had his players take your space away. They would bang on you and bang on you. They (the referees) would get tired of blowing the whistle. It proved out and it carried over. He had his stamp on it."

Zornes was an assistant under Clark for seven years. He said there was plenty to learn.

"The big thing on Jeep was just the way he handled people," Zornes said. "He had a knack of getting things out of kids without the fussing and hollering at them.

"I really liked the way Jeep did things. I picked up a lot from him."

Zornes said Clark was also good at giving his assistant coaches responsibility.

"Jeep would listen to his assistant coaches," Zornes said. "I had a lot of ideas. Of course, he was going to make the final decision. But he allowed me to do a lot of things."

Clark was 118 - 51 in six seasons at Boyd County.

"He got that program off the ground, just like the other Ashland guy (Jody Hamilton) did with the baseball program," Graham said.

Baker commended the Sports Day committee for the selection of Clark as the honoree.

"The Ashland people, they recognize the people that do quality work," he said. "They like sports. He's the man that brought Boyd County to statewide recognition and then Roger added to that."

Bob Sparks, another one of Clark's longtime assistants at Boyd County, said the Elks honor is long overdue.

"Jeep's a great man," he said. "He just did things the right way."

GRAYSON MOURNS
LOSS OF FRIEND
October 2008

• • •

Steve Clay was a mountain of a man, both inside and out.

And East Carter High School, along with the Grayson community, never had a better friend.

Clay, forty-nine, died on Sunday from cancer complications. Those who knew him and those who were touched by him—which were usually one and the same—will never forget his big ole heart and his passion for life.

"He was a role model in the community," said Charlie Baker, the longtime East Carter boys' basketball coach. "A lot of people look for Christ when they're in trouble. He's had Christ all along."

Clay was one of the founders of Freedom Baptist Church where he was a deacon, taught Sunday school and was the Sunday school superintendent.

His other passion was East Carter football. He coached at practically every level for twenty-six years, including high school where he was a defensive coordinator on the staffs of Joey Cecil and Donald Damron.

"Steve was just a giant of a man and more than just his size," said Damron, who is now East Carter's principal. "He was a Christian role model for young people and an avid sports person. Everybody loved playing for him. He was an in-your-face motivator but he didn't use any profanity or anything like that to do it."

Clay wasn't a teacher at the school. He coached and was an insurance salesman for Kentucky Farm Bureau. He was also a dedicated family man. Steve and his wife, Rene, had two sons—Mark and Tyler—and a daughter, Lauren.

When Clay learned there wasn't much more medically that could be done to help him, he loaded up the family for a memorable six-week trip this summer. Family was always most important.

"They broke the mold when they made him," Damron said.

Clay began coaching right out of high school and worked his way through JFL, middle school and then high school. His spirit played out on the field when he was coaching.

A few years ago, when East Carter was playing a highly regarded Estill County team, Clay was having a kidney stone attack.

He was literally lying on the ground and throwing up, Damron said. "The whole team turned their attention to Coach Clay," he said.

"They pulled ahead of us at the beginning of the fourth quarter and he couldn't stand it anymore. He pulled himself up and ran out there on the field after having a kidney stone attack. Those kids thought he was Superman. We came back and won the game. Honestly, 999 out of 1,000 would have left in an ambulance from the field. But not Steve."

There are those in communities who make a difference with their attitude, their spirit and their kind hearts. Those are the kind that are toughest to lose. Steve Clay was one of them.

"He was a man who had his priorities right," Damron said. "He was in it for the kids win, lose or draw."

THE EARLY ORGANIZERS
October 2007

• • •

T.R. Wright and other similar men made it possible for Ashland to be part of the organized youth baseball world in the 1950s.

Wright, who died in 1992, was instrumental in establishing the first Babe Ruth League and the first American Legion teams in Ashland.

He will be honored when a new press box is built as part of a $125,000 renovation made possible through a donation from Gary Wright to renovate the main diamond in Central Park.

Gary Wright is one of T.R. Wright's sons who benefited from his father's giving spirit.

Don Frailie, a classmate of Wright's, said a lot of youth in Ashland during that time were the beneficiaries of a lot of volunteer time from fathers and other men throughout the city.

But he said T.R. Wright was much more than just someone who volunteered his time to coach.

"He epitomized what a good Christian daddy should be," Frailie said. "Anybody can be a father but not everybody is a daddy. There's a difference. There was none better than Mr. Wright. He was awfully good to all of us."

Frailie saw later in his adult years what a good father T.R. Wright was. During a time when Frailie was teaching at Coles Junior High, Wright's wife died while some of the couple's younger kids were in school.

"Mrs. Wright had died when a couple of those kids were at a fairly tender age," Frailie said. "I was always so impressed with how Mr. Wright was like a father and a mother both."

Frailie said he and his late wife, Karen, attended church with the Wrights for years at Old Orchard Church of Christ.

T.R. Wright also had a passion for baseball that he passed on to his sons. He coached in the old YMCA Midget, Junior, and Pony Leagues in the 1950s. What Frailie remembers about that was the team Wright coached, Ballard's TV, was the only one in the league with full uniforms.

"We never had things like that until we played Little League and then they couldn't get them off us," Frailie said. "Everybody wanted to play for Ballard's because Mr. Wright was the manager and because of those uniforms."

He said the other popular team was Miller's Funeral Home because of the blue caps the sponsor supplied to the players.

Gary Wright was thirteen and a few months too old to participate in Ashland's inaugural Little League season. He did play in the first Babe Ruth season, which his father helped established. Gary Wright was a good player, Frailie recalled.

"When Gary was in ninth grade, he started at shortstop for Ashland (High School)," he said. "They'd bring him over from (Putnam) junior high. Gary was a dandy shortstop."

Men like George Conley, Stan Radjunas, and Ellis Johnson, whose sons were all about the same age, were other men who helped get Ashland established in the nationally recognized baseball leagues.

Gary Wright's donation to renovate the park field, now known as Ernie Chattin Field, came out of his love of playing during that era and the love and respect for his father, Frailie said.

"All of us kids called it CP1," he said of the main baseball field in the park. "There is no CP2 (formerly the softball field in the park where soccer is now played). But we lived down there. We not only had baseball but there was fast-pitch softball (to watch). We'd get there early and they'd turn off the lights around 10:00. You were as safe as you could be down there. It was as much a part of us as our homes were, really."

Frailie said the upgrade being proposed is a salute not only to T.R. Wright but the many other men who made organized baseball a reality in Ashland.

"It's a way of honoring all of our fathers who were so active back then, especially to do it for a bunch of snotty-nosed little sneakin' kids like we were," he said.

Dr. Marshall Banks at the Booker T. Washington School, in front of the historical sign on Central Avenue. JOHN FLAVELL/THE INDEPENDENT

A Long Journey
August 2008

• • •

Ashland native Marshall Banks never considered himself a pioneer. He was just a basketball player.

But Banks, an African American who starred for Booker T. Washington in high school in the late 1950s, was the first black scholarship athlete at Morehead State University in 1958. As might be expected, it came with its frustrations and unfairness.

Banks had the temperament—and the courage—to make it work. He went to Morehead knowing a little of what was ahead of him, but probably never understanding the full scope of what was to come.

"It was mentioned that I'd be the first, but it didn't really register," Banks said. "It was not even an issue."

It wasn't until many years later—nearly forty years after the fact— that Banks actually came to grips emotionally with the racism he experienced at Morehead.

He had been working on a project and collecting data about the first black athletes at predominantly white colleges and universities, of which he was one, and what they experienced. Banks was presenting the information at Howard University, where he is a professor, to a group who had called for research ideas.

"Midway through, I just broke down and cried," Banks said. "It was such a delayed stress piece. I thought, I cannot believe this. It was that emotional. I never put a handle on it at all. I'd blocked out a lot of that nonsense."

Now, Banks, who is sixty-seven, has revived the project and hopes to author a book, giving details and stories about what happened to these pioneer athletes when they began attending the white colleges and universities. His tentative title is "Order On The Court" and the research is never-ending, although the clock is ticking because of the age of those who are the subjects. He hopes to possibly receive some funding from the NCAA for the project but doesn't have a timetable for completion yet.

Banks was one of only ten blacks on campus when he started school at Morehead in September of 1958. There were rules to follow, too. For instance, blacks weren't allowed downtown. And dating outside your race, while not specifically addressed, was not acceptable either, he said. His fellow students, teammates and professors treated him fairly enough, though, during a time when racial feelings were tense.

Academically, he had been prepared well at Booker T. Washington. "I had no problem competing in the classroom," he said. The youngest of ten siblings, Banks was bright and determined, a young man dedicated to learning and earning a college degree.

It was through the advice of his parents and C.B. Nuckolls—his principal at Booker T. Washington—and the invitation from Morehead President Adron Doran that Morehead even became a possibility for Banks.

"I was scheduled to go to Kentucky State or Marshall," he said. "Everybody had gone to Kentucky State. I was pretty much pegged to go there. I had this conversation with C.B. Nuckolls, the school principal, who asked if I'd ever thought about going to Morehead. One of the (Morehead) board members lived up the street."

Much like Banks' idol, the great Jackie Robinson who had been handpicked for the assignment of breaking the color barrier in major league baseball, Banks was chosen to do the same at Morehead. He was a superb athlete and student—qualities that would help him rise above situations that were bound to occur.

Banks said he and his brother, Reece, were enamored with Robinson. When the Brooklyn Dodgers would ride the rails back to New York, after spring training before the start of the season, they would come through Ashland. "Having the C&O Railroad here, they'd travel through," he said. "My father worked for the railroad. He'd get me and Reece up to see their train pass at the station. We'd be so excited. We could swear he (Robinson) waved to us."

Banks played on the freshmen team his first year at Morehead (freshman were not allowed to play varsity at the time) and had what he called "a fairly decent season."

He began working out with the varsity players in the summer and after a few practices liked his chances of getting playing time for coach Bobby Laughlin's Eagles the following season. "I thought it was OK coming back my sophomore year," he said.

When he came back to school that fall, though, a few things had changed. "We officially started practice October 15," he said. "I was ready to play.

"They took the team picture in mid-November or so. Everybody lined up and got their uniforms. They took one picture and then Laughlin says 'You step out.' They took another picture without me it. The official team picture came out on our first game and I wasn't in it."

Banks said anytime Morehead played a team from the South, that was the picture that was used in the program.

Years later, during Banks' induction into Morehead's Athletic Hall of Fame, he was presented with a team photo from that season that included him in it. Last spring, Morehead honored him on Founder's Day for his contributions to the university.

There were more injustices, including not allowing him on a road trip to Bowling Green because there were no accommodations for blacks. "I'd go through that process over and over and over again," he said.

By the time Morehead played at Ohio University in December, Banks said he had worked himself into being one of the team's top six players. But Laughlin played him only about sixty seconds, Banks said. It was a clear sign that he wasn't welcome or wanted.

"The players were all great," he said. "They didn't understand."

In practice, there were times when Banks would strip the ball from other guards coming up the floor and Laughlin would get upset, claiming it was only happening because Banks "knew the plays." He told Banks to "let the players pass by." The late Steve Hamilton, who later would become MSU's athletic director, shared Banks' frustration. "He said, 'We knew Laughlin would never play you,'" Banks said.

The final straw for Banks came when Morehead was playing Mississippi at home and not only was Banks not allowed to suit up for the game, he also had to sit in the stands. "It put the other black students in an uproar," he said. "This was a home game. I went home that weekend and told my parents I was not going to return to the team. I told them I didn't feel it was a comfortable situation."

Banks returned to Morehead after the Christmas break, but he was finished with basketball. As a means to keep the scholarship, he was assigned to the training staff, including working with the basketball team. "That was somewhat humiliating," he said. "I contemplated transferring but decided against it. I was going to stay there and graduate."

It turned out, Banks' niche came in the classroom and on the track. He ran track during his freshman year, even winning the 220 dash in the Ohio Valley Conference meet.

Earl Bentley, an assistant football coach and the track coach, urged him to run again as a sophomore and promised there would be none of the unfairness he experienced in basketball. So Banks agreed, and won the OVC's 220 again as a sophomore and junior. He eventually won the 100-yard dash his senior year.

There were still racial moments even with track, including one time in Murfreesboro, Tennessee, when Banks had to eat in the kitchen and not the dining room of a restaurant. But his experience overall, with Bentley's support, was a good one.

So was the rest of his experience with Morehead, including in 1965 when Doran again called on Banks to be a pioneer. Doran hired Banks as the first black faculty member at Morehead State. He taught and coached track there from 1965 to 1969 before moving on in a brilliant higher education career.

Banks wants to tell the stories of other athletes like himself who were the firsts at their respective universities. He's taken on the project of writing a book about that time between 1954 and 1970 when black athletes began entering predominantly white colleges and universities.

The study focuses on the college student/athletes and not the first black athletes in professional sports nor the first to participate at colleges prior to 1954. It was the Brown v. Board of Education decision in 1954 that opened the door to integration for the black athletes to attend predominantly white colleges.

Banks was in junior high school in 1954 but he eventually benefited from the decision by being able to attend Morehead.

"In reference to the '54 decision, they were talking then of including the idea of all deliberate speed," Banks said. "All deliberate speed for Ashland was (integrating) one grade at a time. Starting in 1956, they integrated the first grade. The intent was to integrate one level at a time and then the entire school system."

According to his research, Banks was only the second black athlete in the United States to be put on a scholarship at a predominantly white university during that era. The first was Prentiss Gault, who went to play for coach Bud Wilkinson at Oklahoma in 1956. Banks was able to speak with Gault before he died a couple of years ago.

"He was kind of like me," Banks said. "As a freshman, nobody knew he was there because he couldn't play on the varsity. Then, in the fall of '57, he was a starter."

Banks hopes to find many other athletes who were "firsts" at their respective universities and for them to relate those stories to him so the milestone in U.S. history can be told and shared to others through the book. "If you look at the NCAA records, there's no documentation of that transition," he said. "I would like to fix that."

A Cy of Relief
November 2006

• • •

Life couldn't get much sweeter for Brandon Webb.

Arizona's sinkerballing right-hander finished a momentous year by winning the National League Cy Young Award in only his fourth season.

It's been quite a year for the Ashland native. Brandon and his wife, Alicia, who were high school sweethearts, had the birth of daughter Reagan Lucille in March. That joyous moment was followed by his best season to date.

Webb made the All-Star team for the first time, sitting down David Ortiz, Derek Jeter, and Alex Rodriguez in a sterling sixteen-pitch performance—and he became one of baseball's most consistent starters on the way to a 16 - 8 record and 3.10 earned run average.

"I can't believe it," said Webb, only minutes after receiving a call from the Baseball Writers Association of America notifying him of the award. "I didn't want to get my hopes high; I've been disappointed before."

After Webb's rookie season in 2003, he was a top contender for

Brandon Webb holds the 2006 NL Cy Young Award he won while pitching for Arizona. KEVIN GOLDY/THE INDEPENDENT

the NL Rookie of the Year honors but finished behind Florida's flamboyant Dontrelle Willis.

This time would be different, although Webb had no idea on Tuesday morning. An avid hunter, he was unloading rifles with his father, Phil, when Alicia came out and told him somebody from the Baseball Writers Association of America was on the phone.

"He said 'This is such and such and I wanted to let you know you're the 2006 National League Cy Young Award winner,'" Webb said. "I said 'Are you serious?' I couldn't believe it."

Phil Webb, who has been instrumental in his son's development from an early age, was overcome with emotion about the announcement.

"We're all in tears here," he said. "You know me, I'm the eternal pessimist. I think I do that so I won't be disappointed, even though I would be disappointed."

Brandon's father wouldn't allow himself to believe that it could even happen.

And then it did.

Webb received fifteen of thirty-two first-place votes and 103 points in balloting by the BBWAA. San Diego closer Trevor Hoffman, who broke the career saves record this season, got twelve first-place votes and seventy-seven points.

St. Louis Cardinals ace Chris Carpenter, last year's winner, finished third with two first-place votes and sixty-three points.

"All three of us probably were deserving of it and probably a couple more guys, too," Webb said. "I knew that I had a pretty good chance."

Houston's Roy Oswalt, who led the NL with a 2.98 ERA, got the other three first-place tallies and came in fourth.

Webb was listed second on seven ballots and third on seven others. No other pitcher was included on every Cy Young Award entry.

"It was pretty big emotions. We were very excited for it," Webb said. "It's with you forever. To have that title go along with you means a lot."

Webb's victory total was the lowest for a starting pitcher who won the Cy Young Award in a full season. The previous low was seventeen wins, by Pedro Martinez of the Montreal Expos in 1997 and Randy Johnson for Arizona in '99.

Fernando Valenzuela of the Los Angeles Dodgers was honored with a 13 - 7 record in 1981 and Atlanta's Greg Maddux went 16 - 6 in '94—but those seasons were cut short by players' strikes.

"A lot of the wins pitchers can't control," Webb said. "You can give up one hit and still lose the ballgame."

Webb was fearful that his last start of the season—a 7 - 6 loss to the San Diego Padres when he allowed a season-worst seven earned runs in

Brandon Webb smiles as his Little League and Babe Ruth coaches are
introduced during a ceremony to retire his high school jersey number.
JOHN FLAVELL/THE INDEPENDENT

four innings—would haunt him. That was the same day the Cy Young
Award ballots were due.

"I talked to one of our PR guys on the phone and he said that
last game made it a lot closer than it could have been," Webb said.

"Hoffman had recorded his 400th-some save and I have a game like that one."

Webb went into the game leading the league in ERA and he ended up finishing third, the ERA soaring from 2.88 to 3.10. He is the first NL winner to have an ERA above 3.00 since Philadelphia's Steve Carlton had a 3.10 mark in 1992.

Webb's season was full of highlights. He posted a thirty scoreless innings streak over three-plus starts from May 20 through the fifth inning of his June 5 start against the Phillies.

Webb went unbeaten in his first thirteen starts while posting an 8 - 0 record with a 2.14 ERA during that span.

Before Webb, Johnson was the only Diamondbacks pitcher to take home the award, winning four straight times from 1999 - 2002.

Webb threw a career-best 235 innings, which ranked second in the NL. The twenty-seven-year-old also tied Carpenter for the league lead with three shutouts and both had five complete games, good for second in the NL.

"I was pretty surprised that Carpenter didn't get as many first-place votes," Webb said. "I thought it would be between me and Carpenter."

Voters select their top three choices and points are tabulated on a 5 - 3 - 1 basis.

"I think it's an honor well-deserved. There was some concern that his last start would have an effect on the voting," Diamondbacks pitching coach Bryan Price said. "One start doesn't make or break a season."

Webb tied for fifth with twenty-three quality starts—pitching at least six innings and allowing three or fewer earned runs. He tied for the league lead in victories and also led the majors in groundball-to-air out ratio at 3.64. His 400 groundball outs ranked second only to the

Brandon Webb during an autograph session in Ashland in January 2008. KEVIN GOLDY/THE INDEPENDENT

Yankees' Chien-Ming Wang.

Webb, who walked a major-league high 119 batters in 2003, has worked to regain his control. He cut that walk total in half in 2005 and surrendered only fifty bases on balls last season while also getting more help from Arizona's improved infield defense.

"Basically, I just tried to do what I've done the last three years, which is throw a lot of sinkers," Webb said. "Early in my career, even in the minor leagues, if I had a bad inning or something went wrong, I'd show emotion out there and let that get to me. Every year, I've tried to improve on that."

Webb agreed to a $19.5 million, four-year contract with Arizona in January. For winning the Cy Young Award, the buyout of his $8.5 million option in 2010 doubles from $500,000 to $1 million.

"When you look at No. 1s in baseball, and every team has one, a legitimate No. 1 will look like Brandon Webb," Price said. "He replaces the strikeout with the double play. That defines a No. 1 pitcher in the big leagues to me."

GULLETT'S 72-POINT OUTBURST TURNS 40

November 2008

• • •

Steve Crum remembers trying to tackle Donnie Gullett.

"It was like all knees up in your jaws, like a thrashing machine," said Crum, who played against Gullett in high school at Wurtland during one of the most amazing feats in area history. It all happened forty years ago.

On Nov. 8, 1968, the McKell Bulldogs trounced the Wurtland Warriors 72 - 7 and Gullett scored all 72 points. He rushed for 410 yards of the 564 total that McKell piled up on Wurtland in the last regular season game that year.

Gullett's 72-point game curiously followed him throughout his major league baseball career. It was one of those notes on the back of a baseball card and the kind of tidbit that announcers used to fill the time. You'd hear it time and time again

It's no wonder. How many times does a player score 11 touchdowns and kick six extra points in one game?

Gullett's scoring outburst broke the previous mark of Herb Phelps, who had scored sixty-eight points when he played for Old Kentucky Home.

Gullett, the perfect blend of power and grace, scored two touchdowns in the first quarter, missing both extra points, and then scored 20 points in each of the second, third, and fourth quarters.

His touchdowns were runs of 1, 2, 8, ten, seventeen, thirty-six, forty-three, fifty-five, sixty-five, seventy, and eighty.

"One thing I remember, my jersey was ripped off me completely," said Crum, a defensive end, for the Warriors. "I had cleat marks on the back of my jersey. They ran three plays: Gullett up the middle, Gullett off tackle, and Gullett around the end. I met Roger Marshall, one of the best pulling guards in the area, and he tattooed me every time. He would have made (Russell coach) Ivan McGlone smile."

McKell, which finished the regular season at 7 - 3, made it to the playoffs but bowed out to Lynch 28 - 13 in the opening round. The previous year, McKell eliminated Lynch 24 - 0 in the playoffs.

Ed Miracle, the coach of that eventual state champion Lynch team, made sure his players knew of Gullett's astounding feat—and reminded them of that previous season loss to the Bulldogs, too.

The '67 team is regarded as one of the best in McKell history. Those Bulldogs appeared headed for a state championship but got derailed 21 - 13 by Mount Sterling in the semifinals.

McKell was 10 - 3 that season and lost a 21 - 20 heartbreaker to Ashland, which went on to capture the Class AA state championship. That was Tom Simms' last season as McKell's coach, compiling a 49 - 11 record. Jim Hastings followed for the '68 season before C.A. Noble took over for the last four years of McKell's existence from 1969 - 72.

Of course, Gullett was a star on that '67 team as well. One of the most well-rounded athletes in area history, Gullett was a star at whatever he did—football, basketball, and especially baseball.

Bob Kouns, who coached Gullett in baseball, described him as "muscular, hard, a farm boy" with natural skills.

"It was like a man playing with boys," Kouns said. "He punished people when they tried to tackle him. Notre Dame and Alabama recruited him in football, if that tells you anything about how good he was in football."

However, most who watched him play say he could have played in college in whatever he chose.

But when you're left-handed and have a blazing fastball, who could blame him for taking the fast track to the major leagues?

If not for a career-ending injury, he'd probably have his bust in Cooperstown.

Gullett's seventy-two-point game still has a place in the record books but, believe it or not, it only ranks seventh on the list of most points scored in a single high school football game.

Elvin McCoy of Haven, Kansas, scored ninety in a game in November, 1927. Eddie Byrge of Huntsville, Tennessee, scored seventy-eight the same year as Gullett's feat and Ernie Perea of Los Lunas, New Mexico, scored seventy-seven in November, 1967.

There was also an eighty-eight-point game from Don Wile in 1943 in Salem, Illinois, and an eighty-point outburst from Frank Greene in San Diego in 1929.

But around these parts, Gullett's seventy-two-point game will probably stand forever as one of the most remarkable individual feats ever.

"It stands out that he did break the Guiness Book of World Records at that time," Crum said. "It was kind of embarrasing in a way but kind of cool in a way, too, to think 'I was in that game.'"

Crum said he remembered Gullett being in the area scoring race and assumed that's why he was left in for the touchdown barrage.

Gullett attended Wurtland schools in junior high before transferring to McKell.

"Wurtland and McKell were big rivals and Donnie had gone to Wurtland like as a seventh- and eighth-grader," Kouns said. "That may have been a little factor in there, too."

Maybe there was something between the coaches—the late Bill Robinson at Wurtland and Hastings. Nobody seems to know the answer.

"Bill Robinson told us after the game 'You guys played hard, I'll give you that.' I would have run through a wall for that man," Crum said. "We just played a far superior team."

I'm not sure there would be many coaches today who would even allow a player to score that many points by himself, especially considering twenty of Gullett's total came in the fourth quarter with McKell holding a 52 - 7 advantage.

It wasn't Gullett's decision to run-it-up against the Warriors. That wasn't his nature. While he was a competitor on the field, he was humble off it.

"He didn't let everybody know he was probably the greatest athlete ever in our area," Crum said. "He never let it known he was better than anybody else. His talking was all done on the field."

Nevertheless, on this night forty years ago, Gullett did what he was told to do—run like the wind and into the end zone time after time after time. It's a night and a feat not likely to be repeated.

WHERE WERE YOU WHEN UK BEAT LSU?
October 2007
• • •

It's already in the books—and the memory banks. Instant classic? You betcha. My guess is the good folks at Kentucky will have a highlight video—"The Day the Cats Put the 'L' in LSU"—ready for Christmas.

Kentucky's 43 - 37 triple-overtime thriller over No. 1 Louisiana State will be a night this state will never forget.

Ten, twenty, or even thirty years from now the question will come: Where were you when Kentucky defeated top-ranked LSU?

I've already heard from some who were in Commonwealth Stadium (that number will probably grow as the years progress, much like the New Yorkers who say they were at the Polo Grounds when Bobby Thomson hit the "Shot Heard 'Round the World" in 1951; the stadium held 34,000 but three times that many claim to have been there that historic day). I've heard from some UK fans who were in cars on the way home from fall break, some who were at weddings and even one poor tortured soul who found himself trapped at the airport.

These games don't come along often. The last time it happened for Kentucky was 1964 against Ole Miss. That's forty-three years ago. Before that it was the 1951 Sugar Bowl against Oklahoma and we had the great Bear Bryant coaching the Wildcats then. That one couldn't have been as big a shocker as this one.

The Associated Press has been releasing polls since 1934. The odds of even playing against a No. 1 team are not good. The chances of beating them? Slim. I enlisted some help from my sister-in-law, a math teacher at Blazer, to track the odds for me (since journalists are pretty much forbidden from doing any math equations). So here you go, compliments of the Blazer math department:

- The odds of UK playing a No. 1 team (based on 767 games played since 1934 and eleven of those against No. 1 teams): 1:69. That translates into about once every seven seasons.
- The odds of UK beating a No. 1 team (based on 767 games played since 1934 and three wins against No. 1 teams): 1:255. That translates into about once every twenty-five seasons.

That's why if you watched this game, you'll remember where you were for years to come. You may be telling your grandchildren, even great grandchildren, about the time 'ol Rich Brooks and the Wildcats took down the No. 1 team in the land on the second Saturday in October of 2007.

It's reminiscent of the classic Duke-Kentucky basketball game in 1992. It's been fifteen years since that one. (I was fortunate enough to be in Philadelphia covering the game for this newspaper). But I bet you remember where you were, too.

Those in Commonwealth Stadium on Saturday should savor the moment, even if they had to stand up the entire game. The joint had to be jumpin' after this one. Kentucky is regarded as a "basketball state" but that's only because football hasn't been nearly as successful. Kentucky fans love to win be it basketball, football, or horseshoes. As the fans like to tell the coaches: We're with you, win or tie.

Some were making the trek back home after a week at the beach or some other vacation destination. It was the end of fall break for most schools in the area. Many of those were either forced to call a friend for updates or maybe dial in on the radio, listening to Tom Leach call the game and hearing his trademark "TOUCHDOWN, KENTUCKY!" more times than they could have ever imagined.

Another told me about being at a wedding reception downtown where there were no televisions. Luckily, the Ashland Plaza Hotel was nearby and its lobby did have TVs. Many from the wedding reception crowded around for the exciting finish.

Another longtime UK fan from here was in the Atlanta airport when the game was being played. He was about to board his flight home when the third overtime was starting. He was able to delay getting onto the plane until hearing the final stop that clinched the victory. He then proudly proclaimed to those on the flight that UK had just beaten LSU. Most of them cheered. Half of them probably didn't even know why.

Like many of you, I was at home watching every pulsating second. It was five hours of fantastic football.

My wife was at a wedding shower for much of the game but she kept calling the cell phone for score updates—and then passing that score on to those at the shower, proving it's not just a guy thing—until making it back in time for the fourth quarter and three overtimes.

So many times UK's tortured fans have been teased. So many times the Cats have played a great team close, only to find some way to lose in the end.

Was it going to be like that again?

When the last stop was made and the victory preserved—and No. 1 had been beaten—there was a giant gust of wind in Kentucky from all of us who were finally able to exhale.

A special moment had happened in UK sports history. Biggest win ever for the Wildcats' football program? Maybe so, given the circumstances.

This much is for sure: You'll always remember where you were the day Kentucky defeated LSU.

COMMUNITY HELPED SANG FIND PASSION
September 2008

• • •

Rick Sang credits the Ashland community and the youth coaches who made it strongest when he was growing up here, in the 1960s and 1970s, for leading him to his passion.

The roots of any successful person start with community.

It starts with having people around you who care not if they're going to win the city championship, but if their players are going to find their way in life.

Some make it as athletes and some don't. But all should have the experience of finding out if they could. Sports are supposed to teach many lessons and only a few of them have to do with winning and losing.

"We had great coaches in our community—Tom Gates (JFL), Charlie McDowell (Babe Ruth), and Glenn Judd (Little League) were three that helped shape me. Then I go to high school and there's coach (Herb) Conley and Bill Tom Ross. Then in college, it was Roy Kidd. Coach Conley, when you know him, he's real. He sold me—no, he oversold me—to Roy Kidd at Eastern Kentucky University. I didn't know how great his (Conley's) reputation was statewide."

Sang was a late bloomer himself. He went to Coles Junior High but "only played about eleven seconds in the Kiwanis Bowl." But Sang would make his mark as a punter and sure-handed receiver on one of Ashland's all-time greatest teams, the 1975 JAWS Class AAAA State At-Large champions. He said teammates from that team, like U.S. Army Gen. Chuck Anderson, who was the Tomcat quarterback and middle linebacker, made an impact on him as well.

Sang's other influence came from home through his parents. His father, Bob Sang, spent a lifetime coaching football in Ashland and Huntington.

"I learned about passion early on," he said.

Sang's passion is a niche in football—specialty teams and all that goes with it. He's the director of American Football Specialists/Ray Guy Kicking Academy, a highly successful kicking camp that is developing a reputation nationwide. There are 150 players starting on college football teams who have been through the program. There are ten active players in the NFL who experienced the kicking academy.

Sang runs the camp out of his home on 29th Street, although he's away from Ashland almost as much as he's here. He's directing forty-two kicking camps a year all over the country. They identify the best kickers, punters, and long-snappers in their camps and market them to college coaches.

"Ashland's a great community to grow up in," Sang told a recent gathering of the Ashland Breakfast Kiwanis Club. "(But) I never thought I'd come back."

Sang remembers the sandlots, like Stafford's Field, and the outdoor basketball courts, like the one at Jerry Henderson's house on Grandview Drive. "You always knew where they had the basketball court," he said. "Alan Mayo and I would go there and play Sheila Salyers and Birdell Fish and they'd wear us out."

Sang left Ashland at the age of seventeen when EKU offered him a full scholarship as a punter and receiver. He eventually played on

Rick Sang talks to a Kiwanis Breakfast group in Ashland. MARK MAYNARD

the Colonels' Division I-AA national championship teams in 1979 and 1982 and was an assistant coach there from 1982 - 86.

Through coach Larry Marmie, another Herb Conley connection, he went to Arizona State as the kicking coach on teams that won the Rose Bowl and the Freedom Bowl. Sang coached there with John Cooper, who later became Ohio State's head coach.

Despite being around some of the most successful programs in the country at the time, Sang found out coaching wasn't the life he wanted.

But that kicking niche always stayed in the back of his mind.

Sang switched gears and left the hectic life of college coaching to join sports marketing giant Host Communications in Lexington. The sports marketing education he received there would be put into practice with the kicking camps later.

Sang fell back on his college degree and became the athletic director at Greenwood High School in Bowling Green. But as the kicking camp grew, Sang wanted to make sure he put 100 percent effort behind it. So he left education to educate kickers fulltime.

"It was easy to make that decision like this when it's a solo act," said Sang, who wasn't married. That was in 1999 and the camp has seen steady growth ever since.

Sang had his first kicking camp in 1991 at EKU, but the academy really took off when he was able to put Ray Guy's stamp of approval on it. Guy, the first punter ever drafted in the NFL in 1973, played for the Oakland Raiders and is regarded by most as the greatest punter in NFL history.

Sang went to Guy's hometown of Thompson, Georgia, to try and speak with him. Guy's number wasn't listed in the phone book. Sang was persistent, going to a local car dealer and pleading his case. He told him why he wanted to speak with Guy, and asked if he could help. As fate would have it, the car dealer did have Guy's number and, after a short meeting, the persuasive Sang had talked the NFL great into making a punting video that they would market. It started a friendship that developed into a highly successful business friendship.

The rest, as they say, is history.

Sang's mother and father died within six months of each other in 2002. His father finished fifty years of coaching in 2000. A statue of his likeness stands outside the stadium at Huntington High School. Like most children, Rick Sang yearned for mom and dad's acceptance on anything he did. When he decided to leave coaching, his father never questioned the decision, Sang said.

"I always wanted their approval," he said. "Dad went to a camp at Notre Dame with me and he had a great time. The last thing Dad said to me was 'I love you and I'm proud of you.'"

Sang moved back to Ashland about a year ago. He says it's good to be home.

Next Win Historic for Lutz, Ohio
October 2009

• • •

Amazing doesn't do justice to what Bob Lutz has accomplished as Ironton High School's head football coach.

I don't like to throw around the legendary word but, in this case, it applies.

When you win like Lutz does, it's legendary.

On Friday night, Ironton's veteran coach could move into a tie as Ohio's all-time winningest coach with his 360th victory at home against Portsmouth. Most of those victories—339 to be exact—have come since he took over Ironton's program in 1972.

He coached three seasons at Ironton St. Joe before taking over the Fighting Tigers and turning them into a household name in a state where football most definitely rules the roost.

Lutz has done it all, including win a pair of state championships in 1979 and 1989.

Ironton is a perennial playoff team and a name that, frankly, commands respect in any football circle.

Lutz has had good players and he'd be the first to say that good players make good coaches. But to win with the consistency that he has won in forty years of coaching shows that he knows what to do with good players. Lutz has had great teams with good players and that is coaching.

Teams on this side of the river haven't experienced many victories against Lutz since he started coaching at Ironton.

When they do, they know they've done something special.

That's why Ashland's fans were so deliriously happy over the Tomcats' victory against Ironton last month—the first in the series since 1990. If you can beat Ironton, or even be competitive, then it's likely you have a good team that can make a deep playoff run.

Even Ashland's 1990 team that won a state championship had one of their toughest games of the season against Ironton, a 15 - 10 victory at Tanks Memorial Stadium.

Just like Ironton's football team, you get what you see from Lutz.

He's never been someone to play the media or dodge the media.

I'll never forget his summation walking off the field after a heartbreaking 16 - 14 loss to Sandusky Perkins in the 1999 state finals when he went for a fourth-and-inches instead of punting deep in his own territory. Lutz said: "The team didn't lose this game. Their dumb-ass coach did."

Lutz calls it like he sees it. He always has.

It's fitting that the crowning victory could come against Portsmouth. The Trojans and Tigers will be playing for the 113th time, which is one of the longest running series in state history.

Lutz wouldn't want any fanfare over becoming Ohio's all-time winningest coach either. If anything, he tolerates the media and doesn't want to be in the headlines. He always respects his opponent, too, in word and actions. His expression and mannerisms hardly ever change, win or lose. Stoic would describe him well.

But when you reach a milestone like Lutz is on the verge of reaching, that of being the winningest coach in Ohio high school history, it's hard not to be a little excited for him.

Ironton High School is synonymous with great football. They can thank Bob Lutz for that.

Former Ashland standout Arliss Beach trots through the end zone during pregame warmups in Cincinnati. JOHN FLAVELL/THE INDEPENDENT

Beach Plays Waiting Game

November 2008

• • •

Arliss Beach waits.

And waits some more.

And then waits some more.

The sound of his non-ringing cell phone can be deafening at times. He knows he's good enough to play in the National Football League. There's not a doubt in his mind.

He's done it, at times, with three different teams—the Packers, the Cowboys, and the Texans.

Beach is on the edge. Not quite there, but almost. It's worse than being between the proverbial rock and a hard place.

"I'm kind of stuck between football jobs," he said on Friday at Ashland Sporting Goods, where he's working and hoping. "I'll try to wait it out."

Arliss Beach isn't ready to give up on the NFL dream. He knows it's still a longshot, yet he waits.

That's the hard part.

"This is frustrating," he said.

Beach has twice been invited to be on the practice squad for the

Houston Texans. Twice he's been cut. Neither time was it because he did something wrong.

"You can go there and do well and get released," he said. "It's all part of the game. You get on the practice squad and it's day-to-day, nothing guaranteed. You may go in one day and do great and the next day, a guy will tell you the coach or the general manager wants to talk to you."

By now, Beach knows how that conversation goes. It's not fun.

Everybody likes Arliss Beach. The coaches like him, the players like him, the ownership likes him. What's not to like? He's a team player, a hard worker, a good teammate, and a better person.

But he's still on the edge. That's life in the NFL. It's business, nothing personal.

The Packers signed Beach out of the University of Kentucky as a free agent in 2006. He was on the verge of making the team, playing well in Green Bay's exhibition games both on special teams and as a running back all the way to the final cut.

He was on a Monday Night Football game when the Packers played the Bengals in Cincinnati. Mom and Dad were in the stands cheering him on. In the fourth quarter, just when it looked like Beach was getting a career break and would be the Packers' main runner for the rest of the game, he suffered a high ankle sprain. Instead of carrying the football for the Packers and further solidifying a possible roster spot, he was left carrying some agony.

It wasn't just his ankle that was hurting either; so was his heart.

"I think I would have made the team," he said. "I was being pretty productive. I would have at least made the practice squad."

The Packers put Beach on Injured Reserve, which protected any other team from taking him but sidelined him for the season. He stayed in Green Bay, did things with the team, but never got the chance to play. Then the spring after the Packers had protected him, they released him, this time because of a nagging turf toe injury.

Beach was starting over again.

He had a two-day stint with the Cowboys, not really much of an audition, before being released.

The Texans signed him to their practice squad on Christmas Day 2007, and he jumped at the opportunity. This is how you break into the league. He was later released.

The last time he was with the Texans was when the hurricane rocked Houston. Beach slept through the storm in his hotel room.

"I heard it but there wasn't much I could do about it," he said.

That's kind of like his professional football career. It's out of Beach's control. He knows the NFL is a business. "In this league, it's what have you done for me lately," he said. "That's what it comes down to."

The pay is good when he's on the scout teams, but the practice can be brutal. He runs the opposing team's offense for the week. One week he may be Adrian Peterson, or maybe Reggie Bush. He tries to give the Texans a look at what they're going to see on Sunday.

"Being on the practice squad is way tougher than being on the team," he said. "The first-team defense may run ten plays. With the scout team players, there are no subs. After six or seven plays in a row, you're tired. It's hard, man."

The action is usually in helmets and pads, but there's still contact, he said. "Oh yeah, they hit you. They don't knock you down, but they hit you."

If a team has a personnel problem, it can be good or bad for the scout team player. An injury could mean the team needs another tight end and that could mean goodbye to a running back.

"You do what you can when you're on the scout team to impress them," he said. "Sometimes it doesn't matter."

All through his athletic life, Beach has been a go-to kind of person. He's not used to scraps when it comes to playing time. Now he's fighting for survival and for another chance. His agent, Keith Conrad, sends a sheet out to NFL teams on a weekly basis. He's working hard at selling Arliss Beach.

"I'm not ready to give it up," he said. "I know there's always a time and place."

Beach is twenty-four and the clock is ticking. But he also knows there's time left to make it in the NFL. He's not giving up on the dream. Not yet anyway.

"The Lord always has a plan," he said. "Maybe it's not playing football. I'm just taking it day to day."

All the while, Arliss Beach is praying for that one more chance. It's still his dream and he's not about to give up on it.

HELLO AGAIN TO DREW HALL
November 2008
. . .

On Thursday night at the El Hasa Shrine Temple, the Ashland American Little League will be recognizing four from the area who made their way onto major league fields.

Everybody knows Brandon Webb, the ace right-hander and perennial All-Star with the Arizona Diamondbacks. The 2006 National League Cy Young Award winner is baseball's winningest pitcher over the last four years.

Everybody knows umpires Charlie Reliford and Greg Gibson, who have made the area proud with their expertise and appearances in the playoffs and World Series.

But everybody may not remember the fourth honoree.

Say hello again to Drew Hall.

The lanky lefty from Ashland pitched for the Chicago Cubs, Texas Rangers, and Montreal Expos from 1986 - 90. He was the No. 1 draft choice of the Chicago Cubs—No. 3 overall behind Bill Swift and Shawn Abner—during the summer of 1984.

Hall was a Sporting News All American in 1984 after leading

Drew Hall when he pitched for the Rangers.

Morehead State to the NCAA Tournament where the Eagles lost 4 - 3 to a Michigan team that included Barry Larkin and Chris Sabo.

Hall made it to the twenty-five-man traveling squad of the U.S. Olympic baseball team in 1984. On the final cut to twenty players, he was cut—along with Norm Charlton and Greg Swindell—the only other lefties on the team. The team played without a left-handed pitcher on the roster.

Go figure.

Hall was mostly a journeyman in the major leagues, carving out a 9 - 12 record in his career.

But he made it. Played with Nolan Ryan, Rick Sutcliffe, and current major leaguers Jamie Moyer and Greg Maddux.

"Jamie's still pitching the way he always pitched," Hall said. "He hasn't changed much at all."

Hall was at The Show, too. How many can say that?

Today, the forty-five-year-old Hall is the pitching coach—and a student—at Morehead State University. He left Morehead in the spring of '84 to pursue his major league dream. Twenty-five years later he's back on campus—older and wiser.

"It's a different perspective now," he said. "These students have heard of (President) Reagan. I voted for him."

Hall looks back on his brief major league career with great fondness. He understands the odds of someone from Ashland—or Anywhere, U.S.A.—are long to make it to the major leagues. That's why he appreciates the experience.

His first victory was in Wrigley Field in 1986, defeating the New York Mets 8 - 2 in a complete game on September 24. He allowed six hits and struck out eight—Hall also was 1-for-4 at the plate—in front of only 6,428. Hall's debut came against the Pirates ten days earlier and he was the losing pitcher in a 9 - 2 decision.

Hall was pitching for Pittsfield, Massachusetts, in Double-A, when he got the call. Pittsfield had just lost to Burlington, Virginia, in the playoffs when Dick Pole—the current Reds pitching coach—called Hall and Rafael Palmiero into the office.

"He and the manager sat us down and said 'You're not finished playing, you're going to Chicago,'" Hall said. "It was almost unbelievable. To go from just losing in the playoffs to that...it hadn't crossed my mind."

Hall's first peek inside Wrigley Field was his first day as a Cubbie. It was a surreal experience.

"I'd been on the outside (of Wrigley Field) but had never been in," he said. "The first we did as soon as we got to the gate was look out on the field. There's so much history there."

Hall came up as a starter but his arm had good recovery to it so they moved him to the bullpen. His best season was with the Rangers in 1989 when he went 3 - 1 with a 3.70 ERA in thirty-eight appearances. The Cubs traded him to the Rangers along with Moyer and Palmiero for Mitch Williams, Paul Kilgus, Curtis Wilkerson, Steve Wilson, Luis Benitez (minors), and Pablo Delgado (minors).

Palmiero, who went on to collect 3,000 hits and 500 home runs, was a sure-fire Hall of Famer until the steroid investigations.

Hall was traded to the Expos the following season and he went 4 - 7 with a 5.09 while appearing in forty games before a bout with tendonitis cut short that season. He never made it back, eventually giving it up after not making the Pirates in the spring of 1995.

Hall has never looked back.

"The travel starts to wear you down (in the minor leagues)," he said. "I had two children who were very young and was moving them from one place to another. It's one thing competing in the big leagues, it's another competing in Triple-A."

Hall had some other big moments in the majors. He once struck out five of six Blue Jays in a relief appearance. "It wasn't until the next day that I actually thought about it," he said. "Striking out five of six major league hitters was pretty special."

He also pitched in the Crosstown Classic between the Cubs and White Sox in 1986. "I got to start that game," he said. "That was pretty exciting. I pitched seven innings in it. They'd try and save the starters."

Hall grew up on the Little League fields of Ashland. He played for the Red Sox in Ashland American. Webb did the same, playing for the Angels. Gibson played for the Twins and Reliford was a member of the Ashland National Phillies.

The point is, they made it. That's why the Ashland American Little League is renaming its complex in their collective honor with the name "Dreams Come True."

After all, these guys are living proof that sometimes dreams really do come true.

'88 Game History Lesson for Tomcats
November 2008

• • •

Ashland will go to Fort Thomas Highlands with an "I Believe" attitude on Friday night.

Coach Leon Hart won't have it any other way. I'm sure he's been preaching it to his players already.

But the Tomcats are certainly decided underdogs against the Bluebirds, the top-ranked Class 5A team and one that many say has no equal in Kentucky, at least in their classification. State ratings systems indicate it will be a one-sided romp of five touchdowns or more.

Ashland can take a history lesson from its own books for inspiration.

It was twenty years ago this month that the Tomcats and Covington Catholic staged one of the greatest games in Putnam Stadium history in the Class 3A semifinals.

Catholic was a prohibitive seventeen-point favorite, a northern Kentucky powerhouse who was ranked No. 1 and seemingly unbeatable. Sound familiar?

What happened on that cold November Friday night in 1988 was,

Ashland Tomcat football coach Leon Hart leads the team in 2003. KEVIN GOLDY/THE INDEPENDENT

well, chilling, the stuff of goose-bumps and legends. The Tomcats battled the Colonels to a scoreless tie in regulation before dropping a tear-your-heart-out 6 - 0 decision in overtime. While a haunting loss for the 1988 Tomcats of coach Vic Marsh, it's one of the classics of Putnam Stadium. It remains one the fans still talk about today.

Those Tomcats didn't listen to the "lunch-counter" pre-game talk. These Tomcats may want to stay off the Internet chat boards this week.

The game with Covington Catholic in '88 was supposed to be a mismatch. The Colonels were high-powered with quarterback Paul Hladon expected to make it look easy for the defending state champions.

If Ashland had any chance, it would be because of a battering-ram offense that had carried the Tomcats most of the season. It included running back Mike Johnson, who that season would become Ashland's all-time leading rusher.

But on this night, it was a defense designed by assistant coaches Don McReynolds, Steve Salyers, and David Arthur that befuddled the Colonels. It was a mix of zone looks and was predicated on a fierce pass rush. And it worked. Hladon completed only four of twenty-two passes for twenty-eight yards. It wasn't all Hladon's fault. Some of his throws were rushed but his receivers also dropped many passes after some jarring hits from Ashland's secondary, namely Jason Hall and David Hicks, who had two interceptions.

By the end of the game, the receivers were hearing the footsteps of Hall and Hicks when a football was thrown their way

That was the only way the Tomcats were going to compete with Covington Catholic. They weren't the more talented team so they had to be the more physical team (sound familiar?).

Hladon left the game with a healthy respect for Ashland football. "I'll tell you, Ashland Paul Blazer deserved to win," he said.

The game may be the most exciting scoreless football ever played in seventy-one-year-old Putnam Stadium.

Ashland put the past behind it that season. The Tomcats were 3 - 5 at one point and came into the state semifinals with six losses. The defense had allowed 209 points to cross the goal line going into the game against a 12 - 1 team that represented one of the best the Cincinnati area had to offer.

Zeros dominated the scoreboard but on the field there were blocked punts, blocked field goal tries, blocked linemen, a touchdown called back by penalty, long runs, big losses, passes dropped, passes intercepted, fumbles, a goal-line stand, critical penalties, great decisions, lousy decisions, and gutsy decisions.

The only score came on Dan Ruh's ten-yard run on a draw play in overtime.

Ashland had taken possession first in overtime and got to the four on two runs by Johnson before Hicks, the quarterback, was dropped for a two-yard loss. That left it up to Charlie Johnson's foot and Roger Werner blocked the sophomore's twenty-two-yard field goal try.

When Covington Catholic took possession for its overtime opportunity, Charlie Johnson chased Hladon back to the twenty-three and looked to have him corralled for a sack when the quarterback flung a pass out of bounds in the vicinity of a receiver.

On the next play, Ruh went up the middle, did some stutter steps to avoid the first wave of tacklers, cut left and went into the end zone.

Ruh, excited with the win, spiked the ball. The officials threw a flag, but unless it was going to be marked off on the kickoff of the state title game, it was meaningless.

Ashland's players stood frozen on the field and it wasn't because of the November chill. Their emotions were chilled. This roller-coaster ride of a game was over.

Ashland had its chances to win the game in regulation with only seconds remaining. Stopped at the Covington Catholic twelve with only nine seconds to play, the Tomcats called a timeout. Johnson tried a twenty-seven-yard field goal that was slightly to the left, but an illegal procedure penalty gave the Tomcats a five-yard setback but another try for the win, much to the protest of the Colonels' sidelines. Again Johnson's kick, this time from thirty-four yards out, was wide left and regulation ended 0 - 0.

Covington Catholic had a chance in the fourth quarter but a goal-line stand by the Tomcats kept the shutout. The Colonels had a first-and-goal from the three-yard line. The first two plays were one-yard gains and then fullback Chris Penn was stopped twice for no gain. Ashland's fans in the end zone went wild. Everybody who was at this game was into the game. For the Tomcat fans who had invested so deeply, that's what made losing so much tougher.

But the 1988 state semifinal game, even though a loss, will be forever remembered by those same fans.

Covington Catholic went on to repeat as state champions, defeating Paducah Tilghman 30 - 24 in overtime.

Two years later, the sophomores on this Ashland team, including Charlie Johnson, would win a 19 - 14 semifinal game with Bell County in Putnam Stadium on the way to the 1990 state championship.

Ask them today and they'll proudly tell you about both games, each considered an epic in Ashland's proud history.

GIBSON GETS ALL-STAR OPPORTUNITY
July 2008
• • •

Arizona Diamondback ace Brandon Webb won't be the only Ashland connection in tonight's All-Star Game in Yankee Stadium.

Greg Gibson will be part of the All-Star umpiring career when the National League and American League square off in the historic venue for the Midsummer Classic.

Gibson, a ten-year major league umpire veteran, lives in Catlettsburg and grew up in the area, graduating from Rose Hill Christian School. It will be his first All-Star umpiring assignment, and he's excited about the opportunity.

"It's rather exciting, to say the least," said Gibson, who was enjoying the pre-All-Star Game festivities in New York with his three sons—eight-year-old Kyle, five-year-old Cameron, and four-year-old Carter. "I'll have the boys with me on the field tonight (last night, during the Home Run Derby). This whole thing is an experience they'll never forget."

And neither will Dad, who will be the umpire on the left-field foul line tonight. While umpiring a foul line may not seem quite as

Major League Baseball umpire Greg Gibson at Brandon Webb's Baseball Camp in December 2007. KEVIN GOLD/THE INDEPENDENT

important as, say, behind the plate, Gibson knows the strange things that can happen in baseball anywhere.

"Fan interference (is possible) everywhere," he said. "You just hope everything goes well."

Gibson has followed in the footsteps of his good friend Charlie Reliford, a nineteen-year umpiring veteran, and the All-Star assignment is another example. Reliford's first All-Star assignment came in his 10th season, too.

"Our two careers have absolutely mirrored each other," Gibson said.

Reliford will be the honoree for the 34th annual Elks Sports Day celebration this weekend in Ashland. Gibson said his buddy is "quite excited" about the experience.

With Reliford in Ashland, Gibson will be the temporary crew chief for this weekend's four-game series between the Orioles and Tigers.

Gibson had three days off prior to the All-Star assignment which gave him some time with his boys in New York. They attended a broadway show and the All-Star Gala on Sunday night at the National Museum of History. He was at the Fanfest on Monday morning with his sons.

"The things the boys are getting to do and see are what it's all about," he said. "It's so great having them there and watching their eyes light up on everything. They'll look back on this in twenty years with some great memories and so will I."

While this will be Gibson's first All-Star assignment, he's been no stranger to the postseason. He's called both the Division Series and League Championship Series but is waiting for that World Series assignment.

"That's the only thing I have left," he said. "I'm hoping, but everything in time...Ultimately, that's my next goal."

Elliott County's Timmy Knipp drives for the basket during the 2008 State Tournament against Mason County. JOHN FLAVELL/THE INDEPENDENT

THE SEASON OF GREAT EXPECTATION
November 2008

• • •

Elliott County is the biggest 16th Region favorite in recent memory.

But is winning just a third consecutive regional title enough?

This once-in-a-lifetime team has some once-in-a-lifetime expectations.

"This team right here is the senior we've been waiting on," said senior guard Ethan Faulkner. "We've been playing together since fourth grade, working hard. We're not satisfied. We'll feel disappointed if we're not playing on Saturday night (at the State Tournament). We're not overlooking anybody. We know there's some team that can cause us problems."

As much as an expectation, it's a mission.

No matter what happens this season, this particular Elliott County group will be remembered. They have taken their fans on a four-year thrill ride, starting with a runner-up finish in the regional tournament in 2006.

Elliott County's Jonathan Ferguson puts up a shot against Mason County in the 2008 State Tournament.
JOHN FLAVELL/THE INDEPENDENT

The next year, the Lions finished that job, winning the first regional title in school history. The next week came an exhilarating win over Shelby Valley in the opening round of the State Tournament. The first taste of the Sweet 16 was sweet indeed.

Last year came another regional title and then a heartbreaking 66 - 62 loss to Mason County, the eventual state champion who had waxed the floor with the Lions in Maysville, 90 - 61, less than a month earlier.

Elliott County had the lead late in Rupp Arena rematch, only to watch the Royals' stars knock down the kind of shots that lead to state championships.

That's where Elliott County wants to be next March, clutching a state championship trophy.

There, I said it.

Winning the regional title won't be enough.

Winning a game at the state tournament won't be enough.

The pressure that comes with those kind of expectations can be like an 800-pound anvil. So much depends on staying healthy, staying insulated (Is that possible in today's Internet chatty world?) and staying focused.

Nobody in this region has more talent than the Lions. East Carter clearly comes closest, and the Raiders and Lions reside in the same competitive 62nd District.

Elliott County respects East Carter. It respects every opponent, as cliché as that may sound.

That's because the Lions respect the game, period.

Elliott County's Evan Faulkner puts up a jumper in a 16th Region tournament game. JOHN FLAVELL/ THE INDEPENDENT

If you've not watched these guys play basketball, do yourself a favor and make it to a game. Even if you have to drive to Sandy Hook, you'll come back smiling.

They play pure. They play with the heart. They play like it used to be played.

The pace is frantic, the defense superb.

"A lot of times people will say we're three-point shooters, and this and that," said coach Rick Mays. "What we are is hard workers who create situations. So many times I heard last year 'Defense! Defense!' They need to talk with the people that play. They're going to play hard.

Timmy Knipp slams a dunk against Boyd County when Elliott County scored 132 points in 2008.
JOHN FLAVELL/THE INDEPENDENT

They'll never upset me if they do that. If they don't play hard, I'll handle that situation."

The low-key Mays is enjoying the ride, too. What coach wouldn't like to be around players like this Elliott County team?

The classroom is never a problem. They are student-athletes in the truest sense, maybe as competitive with books as basketball.

They offer no excuses when failure comes (which isn't often). Opponents respect them, even like them.

Now they're trying to put that last happy ending on the joy ride of a lifetime.

Can it happen?

"So many people thought we'd never ever go (to the state tournament)," Mays said. "It's a dream come true. But it's not totally true yet."

The dream has changed. It now includes playing on the last Saturday night of the high school season.

It's time to get started.

THE NIGHT
BOYD COUNTY SCORED 170
December 2008

• • •

Elliott County's eye-popping 132 - 67 victory over Boyd County on Tuesday night has a buzz going in the 16th Region.

It was the second consecutive game that Elliott County cracked the century mark and the second consecutive game that Boyd County surrendered more than 100 points in a game.

Neither streak like those happen very often.

The 132 points scored against Boyd County is the most allowed in school history and the sixty-five-point losing margin the biggest.

Last year, Elliott County cracked the century mark four times, including scoring 132 against Greenup County, and reached the nineties six other times on the way to a 26 - 4 season.

But it was fifty-five years ago that Boyd County put up maybe the highest point total in 16th Region history when the Lions hammered Blaine 170 - 87.

That's right, 170.

It was one of nine games where Boyd County scored more than 100 points on the way to a 28 - 5 season in the 1952 - 53 school year under coach Delmis Donta, who later became the superintendent of schools in Boyd County.

While some may have thought Elliott County's 132 points was a bit extreme, just think about scoring 170 points with only six players reaching the scoreboard.

That's exactly what happened in the game with Blaine on February 24, 1953, in Cannonsburg.

Three players scored in the forties—Walter Lyons with forty-three, Gary Price with forty, and Frank Roberts with forty-one. Sam Renfroe scored twenty-six, David Phelps eighteen, and Jay Vanhoose had two points.

It was some kind of offensive season for the Lions, who scored 2,802 points and averaged 84.9 per game.

The other 100-point games came against Grayson (102 - 44 and 108 - 25), Erie of Olive Hill (112 - 60), Buffalo-Wayne (106 - 44), Blaine (106 - 65), Raceland (102 - 45 and 110 - 68), and Greenup (102 - 71).

Price, a six-foot-three senior center, scored 850 points and averaged 25.7 per game to lead Boyd County. Lyons (18.4), Roberts (17.3) and Renfroe (11.2) were also in double figures on the season.

Price had a forty-three-point game against Erie of Olive Hill and forty against Blaine.

Price, Roberts, and Lyons were all-Eastern Kentucky Conference selections and also all-EKC Tournament selections.

In the end, though, Boyd County's season came to an abrupt halt in the 64th District Tournament at Ashland.

The Tomcats, who had one of their greatest teams ever, whipped the Lions 94 - 49 in the district semifinals. Ashland did that to a lot of teams in '53 on the way to being ranked No. 1 in the state going into the Sweet Sixteen.

Paducah stunned the Tomcats 46 - 44 in the first round, a loss that almost fifty-five years later still sticks in the craw of Ashland fans.

TWO RECALL WATCHING WATERLOO WONDERS
December 2008
• • •

Not many remember the Waterloo Wonders.

Fewer watched them play and even less played against them.

But two from the area—Ashland's Herb Alban and Coal Grove's Lawrence Joseph—remember the Wonders, the remarkable basketball team from Lawrence County who won back-to-back Class B state championships in 1934 and 1935.

Alban, who is now ninety, was a seventeen-year-old teenager living in Columbus when he witnessed the Wonders win their second consecutive state championship at the Fairgrounds Arena.

"I was going to Columbus West and my team was playing in the Class A championship against Akron North," Alban remembered. "Waterloo played the first game for the B championship."

Alban said he got to the game early because seats were going to be scarce. It turned out, he got inside the gym but didn't have anywhere to sit.

"There weren't any seats because Waterloo was playing," Alban said. "They were amazing. I don't remember who they played, but they killed somebody. You had to see them to believe it. Their passing, I've never seen anything like it. They went behind-the-back, through-the-legs, and zipped that basketball around so fast you didn't know where the ball was most of the time."

While the game was the B championship, watching the Wonders play was an A-1 experience, Alban said.

"I remember their uniforms—black square here, white square here," he said, pointing to angles on his own shirt. "I knew all their names. To this day, I know their names."

Alban said Waterloo could have beaten either of the finalists in the A championship. "They could beat any high school team," he said.

Waterloo's two-year record is verified at 87 - 3 but Dick Burdette, author of "The Fabulous Waterloo Wonders," said the team probably won more than 100 games since all weren't reported.

Burdette, seventy-three, has expanded his original work, first published in 1961, to include more details about the town itself and the time frame in which the Wonders' magical seasons occurred. He received an 800-page history book from Gallia County historian Duane Null's family that helped bring the time era to life.

"It's amazing what they did and how they did it but when they did it adds real significance to the story," Burdette said.

Joseph had an upclose view of the Waterloo Wonders when he was a sophomore at Coal Grove in 1935. He sat on the bench as the Wonders dismantled Coal Grove in one game that season.

"When they would come to town, you were warming up on one end and you stood and watched them put on a show while they were warming up," he said. "They rarely dribbled. You couldn't guard them. They came in and destroyed us."

Joseph, eighty-eight, said he was only in the game for "two or three minutes" but he had the best seat in the house most of the night.

"I got to sit and watch them," he said.

He became a fan of the Wonders himself, traveling to watch them play.

"I went every place to watch them," he said. "They were absolutely the most amazing people that ever lived. They could play that game."

Waterloo actually played one game at the old Ashland High School gymnasium in the '35 season. The Tomcats weren't using the gym much that season after being suspended by the Kentucky High School Athletic Association for using an ineligible football player in the last four games of the 1934 season.

Ashland was the defending Kentucky state champion after going 30 - 2 in the 1933 - 34 season.

Waterloo played Piner, Kentucky, in the old gymnasium and recorded a 37 - 30 victory over the previously undefeated northern Kentucky powerhouse that had a team of players ranging from six-foot to 6'7".

The Wonders passed circles around Piner, which "lacked coordination," according to *Ashland Daily Independent* sports editor Brady Black's account of the game.

Even though there was a jump ball after every goal, Piner's size advantage wasn't enough. Waterloo's quickness usually led to the Wonders getting the ball after nearly every tip.

In Burdette's original book, there was a score of Waterloo defeating Ashland 30 - 27 but he said that he could not confirm it. He said it could have been an exhibition game.

Ashland played several independent teams and some West Virginia high school teams during the suspended season in 1935. Ashland actually defeated Williamson, a team regarded as one of the best in West Virginia, twice that season.

But the best team to play in the Ashland gym that season was the Waterloo Wonders, who played in front of a near-capacity crowd.

Bobby Lynch's Night
with a "Pistol"
January 2009

• • •

Like the rest of us, Bobby Lynch watched Kentucky's Jodie Meeks' amazing scoring display with awe.

Unlike the rest of us, Lynch knew what it felt like to try and guard somebody who is hotter than a, well, Pistol.

It was thirty-nine years ago this February—February 7, 1970 to be exact—that Lynch was a defensive ace for Alabama who had the misfortune of trying to stop LSU's marvelous "Pistol" Pete Maravich.

He didn't. The Pistol scored sixty-nine on the Crimson Tide—the exact same night Dan Issel set Kentucky's single-game record of fifty-three against Ol' Miss, which Meeks broke on Tuesday. When the ESPN cameras panned over to the Tennessee bench late in the game, one of the Volunteers' players just rolled his head and eyes after another Meeks' three pointer.

Lynch could probably sympathize with the Volunteers after a night of chasing Maravich all over the floor with little reward.

"The thing about Maravich, everybody was setting screens for him constantly," Lynch said. "That was their basic role. Sometimes they'd roll off the screens and he would pass it to them. He'd hit them in the head and the ball would go out of bounds because they weren't looking for it. Most of the time it went up."

The game looked a lot different in 1970 than it does today. For starters, there was not a three-point line. "Oh my goodness," Lynch said. "He'd probably had another eight or ten points in that particular game."

Also, in today's game, it's a more physical style. Players are allowed to fight through screens to defend the opponent. Not so much in 1970.

"Back then if you ran into somebody on the floor, you'd be called for a foul," Lynch said. "Nowadays they let you run over people. It's a much different game."

Meeks' efficient scoring night saw him take only twenty-two shots from the floor. He made fifteen of them, including a school-record ten from behind the three-point arc. There were also free throws. He made fourteen of them without a miss.

"To be honest, that may have been the greatest shooting game I've ever seen," Lynch said of Meeks' performance.

While the UK-Tennessee game was playing on Tuesday, Lynch said his daughter Sarah, son Robby, and wife Jo Etta were going through old pictures and information that Sarah was putting together for others in the family.

"It happened to be my Alabama years," said Bobby, who graduated from Ashland in 1968 after leading the Tomcats to three consecutive state baseball championships. But Lynch, who is the Elks Sports Day honoree this summer, was also an outstanding basketball player for the Tomcats and that's where he earned a scholarship.

He was starting his sophomore year at Alabama for coach C.M.

Newton. It was that year that he drew the assignment of guarding Maravich.

"If you look at some of the pictures I've got, I'm in pretty good defensive position, right there with him," Lynch said. "But he'd practically fall out of bounds making shots. It's a very helpless feeling when somebody gets on that kind of a roll."

Lynch knows because it happened for him as well. He scored a career-high thirty-four against Kentucky that same season.

"The whole game just slows down," he said. "I didn't have many of those kinds of games but it is true. Everything you do you feel like you know what's going to happen."

Lynch was better known for his defense with the Crimson Tide. He was even given the team's defensive award that season, named in honor of Guy Lee Turner.

But when you're going against the Pistol, there should be an asterisk. Maravich put up more shots in games than teams do today. He took fifty-five attempts from the field in the sixty-nine-point game against Alabama. Lynch estimated he guarded him "about half the game."

"Somebody asked me the other day if that was a record," Lynch said. "It was the NCAA Division I record for years and year and years. I believe someone out on the (West) coast finally broke it."

Meeks' performance broke the UK standard that was set 39 years ago: The very night that the Pistol never ran out of bullets against the Crimson Tide.

Mike Gregory heads up the Challenger Little League for Ashland National. KEVIN
GOLDY/THE INDEPENDENT

A Big Challenge
May 2008

• • •

There are no scoreboards or umpires necessary in this Little League.

The results of this baseball game come in the form of smiles, both from the participants and their parents.

Welcome to the Challenger League.

For the past nine years, Challenger League organizer Mike Gregory has given his time, talents, and even money to provide a baseball sanctuary for the disabled or handicapped in the area.

It also gives the parents of these children a chance to be, well, a Little League parent.

These Little League parents aren't typical. They don't chide the opposition; they instead cheer for their "opponents" on the field. Watching their children have a moment to be like other children is a rewarding experience.

"You see them blossom out here," said Tina Thompson, whose seventeen-year-old son Shelby is in the league. "At first, they don't respond. But a little at a time, they do a little more. They're capable of doing it.

"It's really encouraging. It's sort of like getting my battery charged."

Gregory, fifty-eight, has devoted his life to Little League baseball. He's been in the Ashland National Little League for twenty-nine years and manages the Cardinals, along with running the Challenger League since its inception nine years ago.

"Everybody bats, nobody loses," Gregory said. "If regular baseball were like this, it would be a lot more fun."

The Challenger League, for ages five to eighteen, is played a lot like T-ball, where lineups are set and everybody takes their swings. Players run the bases, whether the ball is caught or not. Fielders can try and make a play, but nobody is out—everybody's safe.

And the path around the bases doesn't always follow the correct pattern. Last Saturday, a young boy lined a hard grounder to the shortstop area and instead of running to first base, he sprinted toward the pitcher's mound.

He was then directed toward first base, with a smile that stretched from one dugout to the next.

Players in motorized wheelchairs also may step to the plate and take some cuts. Some may have trouble walking, or speaking. But everybody is welcome, regardless of the disability.

Paula Lambert of Louisa, whose son, Craig, has Angelman Syndrome and can't communicate verbally, said the opportunity for him to be a part of a baseball team has been a godsend. He's been part of the Challenger League since its inception here. "We started coming when he was about seven," she said. "It allows him to be part of a sport, and we love baseball. This shows the true meaning of sports. Winning or losing doesn't matter."

Paula's other son, Noah, is eleven and plays Little League baseball in Louisa. Paula said her youngest son usually participates in the

Challenger League activity although he was with the safety patrol trip in Washington, D.C., last weekend.

"Usually, Noah is right with us," she said. "I think it's made him a better kid."

There are many young helpers on the field with the Challenger League players, along with the parents.

"This is just a joy," Paula said. "A lot of times, Mike's Little League team comes over and helps."

Players come from Ohio to participate in the Challenger League.

"Last week was my first week and it was very humbling," said Wes Sites of Pedro, Ohio, who works with the Necco Center. "It made me thankful. I had a tough time watching. It brought a lot of tears to my eyes."

The Challenger League allows the disabled players to be part of an organized sport without the stares and whispers, Thompson said.

"This is where I'm accepted and I'm not accepted everywhere else," she said.

"Everybody's happy for a couple of hours. You don't have to worry about the looks and the comments."

On the field, parents and coaches are constantly in help-mode. From helping a player swing a bat to trying to throw a pitch in the sweet spot, the volunteers feel like they're part of something special, too.

A.J. Stadelmeyer's stepson, A.J. Rigsby, has played in the league for the past four years, Stadelmeyer said.

"This is a great, great thing for these kids," he said. "It lets them hit, run, and throw, be part of a baseball team. It's good for them physically and their self-esteem."

Stadelmeyer said the parents from the league he's encountered have been inspiring.

"Some of these parents are amazing," he said. "This is all about having fun, smiling, total joy, and no pressure."

Gregory normally pitches himself but shoulder surgery has limited him somewhat. He developed an aneurysm from the surgery and will have a heart cath on May 27, just a few days before the Challenger League will make its annual trek to Indianapolis on June 4th through 6th.

"I will make the trip," Gregory said.

The trip to Indy is a highlight for the players, but a financial burden on Gregory, Thompson said.

"He pays for so much out of his own pocket," she said. "We took the cookout away from him. He used to buy everything for that, too."

Gregory doesn't mind digging deep. When he was working regularly, anything extra he took in went to the Challenger League.

The Challenger League rents a bus for the trip to Indianapolis for the national Challenger League event. The entire trip usually surpasses $5,000, according to Thompson. "It's probably a lot more than that," she said.

Gregory said he's had some private donations and some help from Our Lady of Bellefonte Hospital. Of course, the league can always use more money for the expensive trip.

"It's the best game in town," Gregory said.

No First Downs
and a Victory
November 1977
• • •

The Paintsville Tigers hopes of a Class A championship ended in amazing fashion Wednesday night.

The Mountain Lions, despite not getting a first down, scored an improbable 8 - 6 victory over the Tigers.

Paintsville Coach Walter Brugh pointed to three pre-game situations for his team's downfall in the Region IV title:

1. The Wheelwright suit that delayed the playoff game for four days when a court order put an injunction on the region championship.
2. A steady downpour all day long in Pineville, dampening the field enough to put the quick Tigers' runners in slow motion.
3. And last, but not least, an injury that sidelined leading rusher B.J. Ward. Brugh reported that Ward was suffering from an abscessed tooth and didn't dress for Wednesday's game.

In Paintsville, they called Walter Brugh "The Blue Legend." THE INDEPENDENT

But the above was almost like a dream come true compared to what happened during the championship playoff for the regional title.

Paintsville's defense was spectacular, not even allowing a single first down. Yet the Tigers somehow still lost.

"This game just wasn't meant for us," admitted Brugh after the game. "I know one thing, we didn't get a break tonight. We really had our ups and downs."

The Tigers' defense was at its best, allowing only seventeen yards total offense and zero first downs. The Pineville offense would have made any dance teacher proud with its one-two-three-kick pattern. The Mountain Lions were forced to punt five out of ten possessions.

But the Mountain Lions did capitalize on one big Tiger mistake.

With the score knotted at 0 - 0 more than halfway into the second quarter, Paintsville's Don Jarrell was drilled by Darren Howard at the Mountain Lions' thirty-four and fumbled. Bill Bowling picked up the loose football and returned it sixty-one yards before quarterback John Simonton corralled him at the Paintsville five.

Even with the ball at the five, it took Pineville four plays to score and Mark Terry did the honors, going in from two yards out on fourth down with 2:35 left in the half. A pass from Tucky Woolum to Chris Van Bever, which turned out to be the winning points, brought the count to 8 - 0.

"They just took advantage of that one big break," explained Brugh. "Our defense played a great game, we just didn't have enough B.J. (Ward) tonight."

On the ensuing kickoff, Jarrell, who rushed for seventy-one yards, blasted up the middle for what appeared to be a seventy-five-yard kickoff return for touchdown. But a clipping penalty brought the play back and the Tigers were down at the half.

"We just couldn't get it in when we needed to," said Brugh. "Our offense did a real fine job for us tonight, too. But it all came down to not getting any breaks."

Paintsville did have a chance to go on top early in the game after Pineville punter Toby Zachery bobbled a snap on the game's initial drive and fell on it at the Pineville 20.

The Tigers drove to the one, but Mike Brown fumbled and the Mountain Lions recovered. Brugh also felt that was a key play.

"If we could have scored down there," he said, "it might have been a different game. You just never know though."

In the first half, the offensive stats were fairly even with Paintsville holding an edge in offensive plays (25 - 23) and first downs (4 - 0). But in the second half the statistics were anything but even.

The Tigers ran twenty-three more offensive plays, grabbed seven extra first downs, ran for sixty-nine more yards and passed for another thirty-three.

Following the second-half kickoff that gave Paintsville the ball on the Pineville 48, the Tigers mounted their only offensive drive that scored.

With Jarrell doing most of the groundwork, the Tigers marched downfield for their only score of the game. Jarrell gained thirty-nine yards in the thirteen-play drive that was capped by a one-yard Jarrell run with 4:15 left in the third period.

On the try for the game-tying points, Simonton spiraled a slippery football to fullback Brown in the end zone that sneaked through Brown's fingers and fell incomplete.

"Don Jarrell did a great job for us tonight," said Brugh. "And he was really hit hard on that fumble. He just played an outstanding game for us."

Following a Pineville fumble on the Tigers' 48, Paintsville looked to be headed for another score.

But that drive ended on a fourth-and-two when Jarrell was stopped short.

A David Lemaster interception gave Paintsville another good opportunity to score. But that drive ended on a fourth-and-two when Jarrell was stopped short. Another Lemaster interception gave Paintsville another chance to score, but a field goal try by Mark Stafford was partially blocked and fell short.

"It's been a great year for us," said Brugh, whose team finished 10 - 1.

Pineville, 10 - 3, faces Bellevue on Monday night to see who will play in the state championship in Richmond on November 26.

FIGHTING SPIRIT IN ESTEP'S CORNER
October 2009

• • •

For years, while growing up on Grandview Drive, one of our playing palaces was Greg Estep's yard.

Greg was my next-door neighbor, so it was always just a short walk to shoot some basketball in the driveway—even at night, because his father Emmanuel had fixed us up with some lights.

Many of our summer days were filled with playing Whiffle ball in Greg's side yard. It was usually two-on-two, double-or-nothing Whiffle ball. And we usually used wooden bats because swinging the lighter Whiffle ball bat was supposed to mess up your swing.

The trees served as the perfect backdrop, along with a row of bushes that rested parallel to Grandview Drive.

We'd keep statistics and standings, had our own league right there in Greg's yard.

Those days seem like so long ago.

I only bring it up now because of learning about Greg's illness. He was on my mind, along with his wife Pam and their grown children, Chris and Heather. Doctors have discovered what appears to be cancerous tumors in his esophagus as well as in both lungs and cancerous spots on his liver.

Greg and Pam are going to the Cleveland Clinic today to learn more about what Greg is facing and the course of treatment that will be taken.

Being next-door neighbors and the same age, Greg and I hung out a lot back in the day. He was always a good athlete and that translated well for him in high school where he played basketball and football for the Tomcats.

Greg was the starting quarterback for two years at Ashland in 1973 and 1974. During his senior season, which was also my senior year, he led the Tomcats to a 6 - 3 - 1 record.

Mike Gothard was the premier player on the team, but Greg was always a good leader and he had a knack for coming up with big plays at opportune times.

One of those six victories was a 14 - 13 decision over Ironton in Tanks Memorial Stadium when Estep threw a late ten-yard touchdown pass over the middle to Rick Sang and then again found Sang over the middle for the two-point conversion that turned out to be the winning points.

Estep completed all five of his passes for fifty-four yards in one of his highlight games that senior season. The victory snapped Ironton's twenty-one-game regular season winning streak.

The 1974 team had several underclassmen on it and that team went on to fame as the JAWS unit that finished 14 - 1 and lost in the Class 4A finals to Louisville St. Xavier in 1975. It is one of Ashland's mostly fondly remembered teams.

Estep played with those guys and others. He also played on a very good basketball team that was stunned in the 16th Region Tournament by Greenup County in the opening round after going undefeated against region competition in the regular season.

That would be the year that Fairview wound up going to the State Tournament—the Eagles' only trip to the Sweet Sixteen to date—as Ashland wondered what might have been.

The fighter in Greg Estep the athlete—his nickname was "Mad Dog" for goodness sake—is the same person who is in the fight for his life now.

Bill Hornbuckle, another of our gang on Grandview Drive, saw Greg in the hospital last week and said he was in good spirits and ready to learn more about what needed to be done. Greg would never be one to feel sorry for himself.

I hope and pray for Greg as he tackles this hurdle in front of him. I know he'll approach it head-on and with the same feisty spirit that made him a memorable athlete at Ashland.

John "Hop" Brown reacts during a game in 1994. West Carter's girls basketball coach won a state championship in 2000 with his daughter, Kandi, winning MVP honors. THE INDEPENDENT

Brown a Legend, but Also a Friend
August 2003
• • •

John "Hop" Brown's impact on girls' basketball reached far beyond the borders of Carter County. And the same could be said about his life.

Brown, who can count the 2000 state championship among his 514 victories at West Carter High School, died Wednesday morning after a courageous sixteen-month battle with brain cancer.

Hop's legacy is secure but his wit, wisdom, and positive approach to life will be forever missed. He touched lives not only from those whom he coached, but rivals who coached against him. And, yes, even sportswriters and sportscasters who covered his games. Trust me on this one: our area didn't have a better friend than Hop Brown.

"He was very, very competitive but very compassionate," said Francis Nash of WUGO radio in Grayson. "Those are two things that are hard for people to put together."

During the past sixteen months of Brown's life, Nash interviewed him countless times while putting together a book "The Hop Brown—

Lady Comet Story" that will be printed the first of November. He learned a lot about Hop Brown the man during interviews with others who know him best.

"I think I interviewed close to ninety people and everybody had a little different take," he said. "Everybody added something different with their encounters with Hop. All of it was so positive. I never heard a negative comment from anybody."

That's because Hop Brown didn't exude negative vibes. He was always an encourager, a trait that is never forgotten by those who are encouraged by him.

Anna Chaffin, the former girls coach at Russell, remembers receiving a handwritten letter from Hop during a difficult time in her coaching career. "He told me not to worry, that everything was going to be OK," she said. "At that point, I realized basketball was secondary."

What Brown did for his hometown of Olive Hill is another grand part of his legacy. The tiny town is known statewide because of the Lady Comet basketball program that he built practically from scratch.

"What he did for girls basketball in our region is unprecedented," Chaffin said.

Brown was born in Olive Hill, married his high school sweetheart and raised his family here. He never wanted to go anyplace else, even though his considerable coaching skills could have taken him anywhere.

Olive Hill was home and there wasn't a better place for him.

When Brown first started coaching the girls at West Carter there were some difficult times.

"They were awful a lot of those early years," said East Carter coach Hager Easterling. "All five starters quit one year a week before the season started. (But) He stuck it out. Kids can't see that today. They want that instant gratification. Hop was born there, grew up there, and played there. In today's day and age, especially the way kids move around, it's kind of refreshing to see that. He stayed and built something."

Whenever you needed a lift, Hop Brown was there. If you had even a brief conversation with him, it was a good one.

Many times, Hop would call the office just to talk. He wasn't fishing for publicity; he just wanted to talk.

We'd share some laughs—maybe even some secrets—before continuing our workdays. You always felt better after talking to Hop Brown if it was for five minutes or an hour.

Hop was a sportswriter's dream. If you walked away from a conversation with him after a game and didn't have a notebook full of unique and useable quotes, it was your own fault. Nobody ever tried to get out of covering a West Carter girls basketball game because they knew they were coming back with a good story. My biggest problem was always figuring out a way to share the wealth and not hog all the games myself.

Of all the many events I've been fortunate enough to cover here at the newspaper—including both of the Duke-UK epics, three Final Fours and a World Series—West Carter's state championship run is my favorite.

I shared that with Hop on many occasions. Maybe it was because a team from our area was shining on the state's biggest stage or maybe it was because of Hop Brown, a man I admired as a friend and a professional.

He began coaching girls basketball at West Carter about the time I was beginning my career here. Each of us matured a lot during the past twenty-five years and we developed a unique friendship. While it was always friendly, it was also always very professional. Hop wouldn't have wanted it any other way.

When he became ill with brain cancer, it paralleled with my life again. My father had been diagnosed with the same type of brain cancer only ten months before and would die two months later. My first trip to see Hop at the hospital after he was initially diagnosed was a surreal experience.

I knew what Hop and his family was facing, along with the amount of courage and strength it took to fight this disease. My heart ached for them, as it does today.

To his sweetheart of a wife, Sharon, daughters Kim, Karla, and Kandi, and son Kyle, I can only say that while the hurt never completely goes away, time does have a way of healing.

The good times you had will illuminate inside, giving you that warm feeling of his presence again and again.

And you can rest assured that your loving husband and father today is in a better place than he was yesterday.

"Hop" Brown
Leaves Behind Legacy
August 2003

• • •

John "Hop" Brown, one of the most successful and most popular coaches in Kentucky girls' high school basketball history, died early Wednesday morning after a sixteen-month bout with brain cancer.

Brown, who led West Carter High school to the 2000 state championship and 514 victories in a twenty-five-year coaching career, was fifty-three.

"He was quite an inspiration to many people," said Francis Nash of WUGO radio in Grayson, who worked extensively with Brown throughout the past year on a book that will be published in November. "He stayed so positive throughout the whole illness that kept everybody else positive. In the back of their mind, they knew what doctors were saying, and the history of the disease, but he was very positive about staying the course."

Brown was born in Olive Hill, graduated from Olive Hill High School in 1969 and put West Carter High School on the map with the 2000 state championship.

West Carter girls coach John "Hop" Brown points to wellwishers as he and Megen Gearhart take the stage at Lexington Catholic High School. Gearhart was named Kentucky's Miss Basketball 2003 by the Kentucky Lions Eye Foundation. JOHN FLAVELL/THE INDEPENDENT

As late as Tuesday afternoon, Brown was watching a video of the championship game with his daughter Kandi, who was the MVP of the tournament.

"They couldn't get him awake and when they put the video in, his eyes popped open just like that and he watched the game," said Von Perry, a close friend of the family and Brown's successor as the girls' coach at West Carter. Nash said he visited Brown on Tuesday afternoon as well.

"He was watching 'Andy Griffith' at the time but had been watching the championship game," Nash said. "He was trying to talk but some of the things he said you couldn't really understand."

Brown was diagnosed with brain cancer in April 2002 and doctors then removed a lemon-sized tumor. He fought courageously with the treatments locally and at Duke University's medical center.

The news of Brown's death, while expected, shook and saddened a tiny community that had come to love their coach.

"It's subdued and somber," said West Carter principal Jim Webb of the mood at school on Wednesday. "We knew it was coming, but it's still a shock. He was here at school last week."

Webb, who is also a close friend of the family, said it's been a sad time throughout Brown's tragic illness.

"It's been a difficult thing to try and deal with, knowing what the outcome was going to be and not being able to do anything to reverse it," he said. "It's been a helpless feeling for all of us."

Perry said the players on the girls' basketball team were having a difficult time dealing with Brown's death as well.

Brown's coaching legacy is well-chronicled. He accumulated eighteen 62nd District tournament championships, eight 16th Region tournament championships, twelve Eastern Kentucky Conference tournament championships, ten EKC regular-season championships, two All "A" Classic 16th Region championships, one All "A" Classic state runner-up trophy and the 2000 Sweet 16 championship.

He was an eight-time selection as The Independent's All-Area Coach of the Year, was The Independent Sportsman of the Year in 2001, was a two-time AP State Coach of the Year and a seven-time EKC Coach of the Year.

A collage of pictures and memorabilia were on display during John "Hop" Brown's funeral.
JOHN FLAVELL/THE INDEPENDENT

Brown also coached the Kentucky-Ohio All-Star team four times and the Kentucky-Indiana All-Star team in 2002. He also received the Silver Microphone Award from WGOH-WUGO radio of twenty-five years of service to girls' basketball.

"What he did for girls' basketball in our region is unprecedented," said Anna Chaffin, the former girls' coach at Russell High School.

Hager Easterling, the girls' coach at East Carter High School, said Brown meant more to the region than anyone would ever know.

"What he accomplished means a lot to this part of the state," Easterling said. "After he won the state title he said, 'This is the Carter County Championship. It belongs to everybody.'" Perry said Brown always remained the same despite the accolades.

"He's so humble in everything he does," she said.

The sculpture commemorating the West Carter High School girls basketball win in the 2000 state championship was decorated with a black ribbon during John "Hop" Brown's funeral at the high school. JOHN FLAVELL/THE INDEPENDENT

When there were students at West Carter who didn't have good tennis shoes to wear, it was Brown to the rescue, she said.

"He always took care of the kids at school," Perry said. "He was a shoe person. If somebody didn't have a good pair of tennis shoes, he'd go home and bring them some back. When he was growing he didn't have those things. He wanted to make sure nobody else did without."

Jack Fultz, the Hall of Fame coach at Olive Hill, said he knew Brown would be a good coach because of his strong work ethic.

"I never had a doubt the guy would be a success in coaching," Fultz said. "He was a worker." Fultz said as a player, Brown could "flat-out play guard."

As a senior, Brown scored 761 points while averaging a school-record 24.5 points per game.

Fultz said Brown's death was difficult on the community and himself. "It's really beginning to take a toll on me having so many former players and former students die," he said. "It really hurts me."

Brown is survived by his wife, Sharon, daughters Kim, Karla, and Kandi, and son Kyle.

CALLS GO ON FOR GIBSON, RELIFORD
May 2008

• • •

Losing Greg Gibson as an umpire-mate has been a difficult thing for Charlie Reliford.

Gibson and Reliford have been umpiring major league games together for the past eight years. They know each other like brothers.

Gibson's umpiring mannerisms are exactly like those of Reliford. He's like a clone. If you're watching a game, you have to look closely to tell the difference in how they work a game.

About the only way I could tell was the uniform number. Gibson is fifty-three and Reliford is eighteen.

Even the way they call strikes sounds similar. They were as comfortable with each other as an old pair of slippers.

"We were so connected on the field," Reliford said. "We always worked opposite each other's corners (first and third or second and home). We could look at each other and know what the other one was thinking."

Major League Baseball wanted to mix up some of its umpires so the younger stars, like Gibson, could work with other crew chiefs to gain experience and see how somebody else handles situations.

"Greg's not even a young umpire, he's one of our big hitters," Reliford said. "Guys have different personalities. Crew chiefs give guys different roles. The league will use him to bolster a crew. They plug him in as a heavy hitter. He's a strong, strong umpire."

Gibson has joined Tim McClelland's crew. Reliford said McClelland "is constantly one of our No. 1 rated guys. He's moved over there to see how Tim does things. Greg will be a crew chief some day. This is clearly best for his (Gibson's) career."

Reliford said he was able to get one more year out of Gibson than he expected. But when the bosses came to him in the offseason, he knew it was inevitable that he was going to lose Gibson off his crew.

"I said: 'Can I make a deal? If you take Gibby, you've got to give me Sam (Holbrook),'" Reliford said.

So Holbrook, a Morehead native who lives in Lexington, joined Reliford's crew, which also includes Larry Vanover, another Kentuckian.

"Sam is a terrific umpire, a terrific person," Reliford said. "Three-fourths of the crew is still Kentucky guys. We put UK stickers in everybody's locker. Our fourth umpire is a guy from Connecticut (Dan Iassogna). He's always wearing UConn hats. Sam has an assignment to pick up four UK hats the next time he's home."

Reliford, an Ashland native who is called "Mr. Ashland" by his umpiring peers, said he's already run into at least ten people from Ashland "and it's just the second week of May."

Arliss Beach, Greg Gibson, and Charlie Reliford sign autographs in 2008. KEVIN GOLDY/ THE INDEPENDENT

Reliford said he talked Padre infielder Chris Burke, who is from Louisville, into a little hazing with Iassogna.

"I said 'Talk to Danny between innings and ask him how did you get on the all-Kentucky crew?'" Reliford said. "Chris did it."

Reliford is constantly propping up his hometown and home state. He said having Holbrook on the crew hasn't hurt his cause.

Reliford's ailing back hasn't caused him any problems, he said. "So far I've had a great year healthwise," he said.

The new MLB rulebook also came out and Reliford's name is on the inside cover. He's only the second umpire in MLB history to be a member of the rules committee.

"I'm going to take it to Bobby Lynch (at the Frameup Gallery in

Ashland) and have them take the cover off and blow up that page a little bit where you can actually see the name," Reliford said. "I take a lot of pride in the work that I've put into the rules. It means a lot to me that it's in there."

BOYD TALK OF TOWN
March 1999

• • •

At mid-February, Boyd County was the talk of the 16th Region. But for all the wrong reasons.

Area high school basketball fans, even some of the Lions' very own, had written off the winningest team of the '90s as a candidate for another regional title. This became the year to get Boyd County.

Teams who often dreaded a game with the Lions were suddenly looking forward to playing them. Three 16th Region teams swept the regular-season two-game series with Boyd County—something that hadn't happened in the Roger Zornes' era—and the regular season yielded a rather pedestrian 12 - 15 record.

The prospects of having a winning record hinged on winning the regional championship, and neither seemed probable this time last week.

Boyd County's tradition, so rich in the '90s, was taking a big hit.

"People were saying, 'You can't win it every year' or 'This is going to be a long year.' I was worried, but after I saw how they were coming together, I felt so good about them," said Roger Zornes. "This is what it's all about."

If that baseline-to-baseline smile means anything, Zornes is still feeling real good about the Lions.

That's because January's Team Turmoil is March's Maddening Darling, heading to Rupp Arena this week for the State Tournament.

Again.

It's the Lions' second consecutive trip to the Sweet Sixteen, fifth trip of the '90s and Zornes' seventh regional title overall, only further adding to his own coaching legend.

Boyd County beat Ashland 54 - 52 Saturday night in the regional championship game on Tyler Zornes' three-pointer at the buzzer. It was a game that, frankly, neither team deserved to lose.

"This was like Duke-Kentucky all over again to me," Ashland athletic director Mark Swift in reference to the fabulous 1992 East Regional final.

And the last twelve dramatic seconds did play out that way.

Zornes' big three-pointer came only seconds after Scott Johnson put the Tomcats ahead with a clutch three-pointer of his own with five seconds remaining.

But on this night, it seemed the team that took the last shot was going to win.

"I thought he'd beaten us," said Boyd County senior Bryan Hall of Johnson's shot. "It was the biggest shot I'd seen in my life...until Tyler's shot."

Zornes answered in incredible fashion, running off a screen to catch a pass at mid-court, then dribbling to the top of the key and launching a perfect jumper right at the buzzer that sent a dagger through Ashland's heart.

Johnson and Brad Salyer were defending, but to no avail. Zornes' shot barely even moved the net.

And the Lions, with their less than glossy 17 - 15 record, were making reservations for the Sweet Sixteen.

"I've been waiting for somebody to ask me the question," Roger Zornes said, prodding interviewers who weren't sure what he meant. "How does it feel to take the worst record to the State Tournament? It feels good, real good."

Every regional champion is special, but this one will hold great memories for Zornes in many, many ways.

The main one being, of course, that his son Tyler is the star for the Lions and hit one of the Shot of Shots in 16th Region Tournament history.

Zornes has been accused of letting his son be a "One-Man Show," but Tyler proved in the regional final that he is one of the best clutch players in region history.

The Lions trailed 45 - 41 when Zornes went to work, hitting shots from inside and outside. He scored Boyd County's last thirteen points in an amazing display of offensive ability.

Simply put, he was "The Man."

"I'm so proud of him," said his father. "The things he's had to go through this year, some of the cruel things that adults have said to him...I can't tell you how proud I am of him. This is such a great night."

Tyler, who was rightly awarded the tournament's Most Valuable Player Award, played like a champion the entire regional tournament. He stepped up when the Lions needed somebody to step up big.

Boyd County won the regional tournament not by being a "One-Man Show" or even a "Two-Man Show."

It was Jake Nein who set the screen that freed Zornes, giving him a chance to create a last-second dream come true.

Roger Zornes coached Boyd County to seven regional championships. Probably none was more fulfilling than in 1999 when son Tyler beat Ashland on a last-second shot. JOHN FLAVELL/THE INDEPENDENT

It was Adam Young who consistently hit big shot after big shot when nobody else thought he could.

And on championship night, it was Hall who played one of his best games of the season.

For Hall, winning the regional title made up for anything that might have happened during the rest of the season. And anything short of winning the title wouldn't be enough for him.

"I told Jake on the way up on the bus that if we didn't win tonight, it was like the four years had been a failure," Hall said. "This year's been tough because our own fans were even turning on us.

"Sometimes it was even tough to go to school because people would say things to us. But when they're out of school on Friday (because of the State Tournament), they can have us to thank for it."

Bob Sparks, who has been the right-hand man on Roger Zornes' bench since 1983, marveled at how the Lions came together.

"You asked me last year if that was Roger's best coaching job and I said yes," Sparks said. "Well, that's exactly what he did again, his best coaching job."

Sparks said the turmoil during the regular season, when three players quit the team after a loss to Greenup County, seemed to ignite the others to work harder.

"The kids that left us were good kids and they still even come to our games," Sparks said. "They left because they wanted to leave. There weren't any hard feelings or anything."

Brian Biggs may have summed up the Lions' feeling best.

"It's storybook, I'll tell you that much," he said. "When people were counting us out, it made us work that much harder. There's such a tradition here at the County and we had to live up to it."

And now there's another story to tell about Boyd County's ever-growing basketball tradition, one that seems to blossom more every year.

Juan Thomas (84) reacts afer scoring a touchdown during the 27 - 15 playoff win over Clay County in 1990. KEVIN GOLDY/THE INDEPENDENT

BABY THEY WERE BORN TO RUN
December 1990
• • •

If ever there were a team born to run, it had to be Ashland's 1990 Class AAA champions.

The team on the run blasted their way to 5,000 yards rushing with three 1,000-yard runners in a backfield that would have made Vince Lombardi proud.

Their numbers are staggering. Just look:

- 5,196 yards rushing as a team;
- Juan Thomas, 1,651 yards rushing and twenty-three touchdowns;
- Chris Hutt, 1,436 yards rushing and twenty-two touchdowns;
- Charlie Johnson, 1,248 yards rushing and nine touchdowns.

The Tomcats may never have a backfield, or an offensive line, more suited for a wishbone attack than this one.

And the beauty of Ashland's wishbone attack was never more obvious than in Saturday's 35 - 13 victory over Lincoln County for the Class AAA crown at Cardinal Stadium.

With Lincoln County keeping close tabs on "Mr. Football" candidate Juan Thomas, and taking away the option whenever it could, the Tomcats turned to other options.

There was Chris Hutt going sixty-seven yards on a simple dive play. Or Charlie Johnson pounding, plodding and powering his way up the middle. Stopping Ashland's wishbone was a near impossible task for the Patriots—and every other team on the schedule.

"They were keying on me big time," said Thomas of Lincoln County. "They were stacking to my side. The obvious thing to do is go away from me and give it to Charlie, Hutt, or David (Brown). Just use me as decoy."

The fact that Thomas wasn't the star in the championship game mattered little to him. What did matter a lot was just winning.

But the best part of Ashland's wishbone is its versatility. The Tomcats were a juggernaut offensively.

"It was the only decision to make," said Ashland Coach Vic Marsh of inserting the wishbone in preseason. "We've never looked back. But I have to give credit where credit is due. (Ashland assistant) Dave Arthur was the one pushing hard for it. He saw what Charlie could do (at fullback)."

The wishbone was born of necessity really. Ashland had a shortage of running backs and an overload of good linemen.

So 245-pound Charlie Johnson, who may have been an All-State offensive lineman, became a fullback—the key element to any wishbone offense.

"It's really a very simple offense to teach if you've got the quarterback to run it," Marsh said. "It's not complicated at all. We picked it up like a right-sized shoe."

Charlie Johnson (45) was known to drag tacklers during his days with the Tomcats. Johnson was the fullback on the 1990 state champions at Ashland. KEVIN GOLDY/THE INDEPENDENT

Nobody had a chance to be critical of Marsh's decision. Right away, when the Tomcats pounded out 363 yards rushing in the season opener against Raceland, it was obvious Marsh had made the correct call. And the wishbone just kept getting better and better.

And while in a two-back offense Thomas appeared headed for a record-breaking season and possible Mr. Football award, the team came first. Thomas understood and so did everybody else.

Thomas still nearly got the Ashland rushing record, finishing 103 yards short of cousin Gary Thomas' super '75 season. But the Tomcats—and Thomas—got something even better: a state championship.

"If you stop us, you have to stop the wishbone," Marsh said.

If didn't come without some work, Hutt said. "We've worked on it all year and just kept working. If something isn't broken, you don't fix it."

Ashland offensive coordinator Lee Evans had the pleasure of calling the plays this season.

"With the backfield we have, you can give the ball to any of the three and expect to get three yards," he said.

Arthur, who is the defensive coordinator, said he did push for the wishbone after taking on Johnson and Thomas in practice. "I told Coach Marsh that there wasn't a high school defensive end anywhere that could take on those two guys," he said. "It was that first practice. That's when we knew it was going to be something special."

Probably the coach that stood the most to lose was Steve Salyers, the offensive line coach. He sacrificed Johnson to the backfield.

"I thought the wishbone was a good idea but I hated losing a two-year starter on the line," Salyers said. "But we had people like Jason Suman and Tyler Huffman to put in there and everything worked out great. We had an abundance of good linemen."

And they had a quarterback that could run the option without fear. Brown, a 6-foot-2 senior, made the wishbone go with his daring pitches.

"Give our line credit," Brown said. "They've opened up holes all year. We've been playing together for quite some time and talked about winning a state championship. This is what it's all about."

Brown didn't want to be a quarterback when he was younger. He preferred tight end, where big brother Dan played. "I guess I wanted to follow in his footsteps," David Brown said.

The state championship victory marks this team forever. They join the '67 Tomcats, and many others, in the winner's circle. And winning is worth remembering for the fans, for the players, and for the coaches.

This backfield will be the standard for years to come in Ashland. And, as the years go by, so will the legend of the 1990 Tomcats.

The team born to run is now part of a proud Tomcat tradition.

Hail to the champions.

LADY COMETS
GET WIN OF LIFETIME
March 2001

• • •

Years from now, when some of these players from the 2000 West Carter girls state championship team are bouncing grandchildren instead of basketballs, the memories of these last three precious days will flood back.

They will remember this week as the time of their lives, a time when playing basketball was the most important thing they ever did, a time when they achieve one of life's ultimate goals.

They will tell that grandson about the Lady Comets' miraculous 38 - 1 season, about the exasperating championship game win over Shelby County, about the fireworks before the introduction, about the celebration that turned a small town upside down.

That grandson will nod his head as he sees the twinkle that remains in Grandma's eyes. She will remember it like it was yesterday. Great memories. Golden memories. Delicious memories.

He, too, will know how special this basketball team was to a school, to a community and even to an entire part of northeastern Kentucky.

He can hear that in his grandmother's voice, as it cracks with emotion, remembering how a group of teenagers—some barely old enough to drive, some still with a two-year wait before getting their license—came together in a crescendo of hoops and hurrahs.

West Carter is special today and special tomorrow. They are legends in the making.

The day of March 25, 2005, is now a day that will live in West Carter sports history forever because it's the day the girls state basketball championship came to Olive Hill. This one is for Jack Fultz, who took those great Olive Hill boys' teams to the State Tournament some forty years ago. This one is for the past Lady Comet basketball teams that went home from the State Tournament disappointed. This one, friends, is for a lifetime.

We never appreciate the moment like we should. We make too much of the wins and too much of the losses. This is a moment in their lives that should be swished around and around. It should be savored for now, saved for later and celebrated forever.

State championships are like that.

West Carter's run to a near-perfect season was accentuated with a near-perfect Saturday. There was a beauty of a 73 - 55 victory over Manual in the semifinals and the true grit displayed in the 58 - 50 championship game triumph over Shelby County.

West Carter's special season will sit alongside the one of the last state basketball champions in the 16th Region—the 1961 Ashland Tomcats. That team's legend has grown over the years and deservedly so. It's still being called the greatest high school boys champion of all time.

The Lady Comets carry some of that kind of magic, too. Like the Tomcats of lore, West Carter obliterated opponent after opponent. Inside the 16th Region, there seemed to be no match for them.

There was only one blemish on the season, a regular-season loss to Hart County. That defeat was avenged in the quarterfinals of the State Tournament. The '61 Tomcat suffered only one defeat as well.

Wizard-like passing and team play was the stamp of the '61 Tomcats and it could be the stamp of the '00 Lady Comets, too. West Carter's girls of 2000 are, without question, one of the greatest teams in the modern era.

The reason the Lady Comets were so successful, so fun to watch and such a worthy state champion was their team play. Unselfishness was their trademark from November to March. They truly cared for each other and they put winning above individual achievement.

Kandi Brown is the Larry Conley of her day. She can pass, she can shoot, she can rebound. Kandi Brown, the consummate team player, made things happen in a wonderful way.

There is so much to like about this team it's a shame they don't have more games to play. Watching them work was like watching Picasso paint a picture.

Hop Brown's status as one of the coaching legends is also now secure. He deserved this state championship, too. He embraced each victory at the State Tournament because he didn't know what tomorrow would hold.

When daughter Kandi sank two free throws to make it 58 - 50 with 8.2 seconds remaining, her dad called timeout and give her a bear-hug of a lifetime. And the celebration had started.

It hasn't ended yet and probably won't for decades to come.

Way to go West Carter. You're a great champion.

Mark Surgalski celebrates Ashland's 16th Region championship in 2001.
JOHN FLAVELL/THE INDEPENDENT

SURGALSKI'S BIG MOMENT
March 2001
• • •

With Ashland's Sweet Sixteen victory over Hazard secured, Mark Surgalski went to the bench and gave Arliss Beach a high-five.

With his left hand.

It was that kind of day for Surgalski, who carried the gigantic burden of his team, his school and maybe even his community on his shoulders Thursday afternoon in Rupp Arena.

Less than forty-eight hours after smashing his right hand in a car door—that's his story and he's sticking to it—Surgalski and his heavily bandaged right hand did some heavy damage to Hazard.

Surgalski scored nineteen, sparking a 47 - 35 victory over the Bulldogs in the opening round of the State Tournament in Rupp Arena.

"The whole bus ride up here I was kind of worrying about it," Surgalski said of the broken hand. "When it happened, I felt like I was letting a lot of people down. I didn't sleep the night I hurt it, and it wasn't just the pain."

It was that inside mental anguish, the kind that starts in the pit of your stomach and makes you pull the covers over your head and hope nobody misses you.

But when you're 6-foot-8 and the star of the basketball team going to the Sweet Sixteen, it's hard to hide.

Surgalski needed this kind of gritty performance so he wouldn't be a footnote in Tomcat history. If Surgalski hadn't been able to play, or couldn't be effective because of the injury, then this game may have been his legacy, as unfair as that seems to be.

For that reason, he was a very motivated young man. He tipped at balls with the swollen hand, dove on the floor for loose balls, blocked shots, and even made eleven of fourteen free throws.

Surgalski was, in a word, superb.

"That play when he ran the length of the floor and dove head-long said it all for me," said Ashland coach Mike Flynn.

Surgalski took a page from Larry Bird's playbook.

"Coach Flynn said that when the Celtics knew Larry Bird was hurting the most, he would dive on the floor for a loose ball," Surgalski said. "I want to show my teammates I was ready."

The Tomcats wouldn't have advanced without Surgalski's overall play. And certainly, he played with a lot of pain. On Tuesday night, the hand had swollen to nearly twice its size. Ice, ice, and more ice got it to where he could clinch his fist Wednesday night.

Then, with even more help from Ashland trainer A.J. Stadlemeyer, Surgalski went over for pregame warm-ups Thursday afternoon.

"He saved me," Surgalski said of Stadlemeyer. "He's absolutely done everything he can to get me ready."

Beach, the active point guard who played equally well in the Sweet Sixteen opener, said when the players learned of Surgalski's injury, they were livid.

"Everybody was like, he let us down," Beach said. "We didn't think he was going to play. Then it was like 'OK, he's hurt.' We're going to play with him or without him. We can still play good."

Surgalski played thirty minutes and twelve seconds against the Bulldogs. In some instances, it was obvious a healthy right hand would have made a difference, especially when it came to rebounding.

Surgalski took a lob pass from Beach early in the game. He went up for a dunk, but couldn't grip the ball, so he kind of guided it in the basket. "I went up to dunk it and it slipped out of my hands," he said.

"Any other time, that would have been a dunk," Beach said. "Once we started playing, I didn't even think about him being injured. I tried to feed him the ball.

"When he turned and shot that little hook shot, I knew he was fine."

Surgalski completed a three-play play to finish a 13 - 0 run late in the third quarter that put the Tomcats ahead 32 - 21. Hazard never fully recovered and Ashland was moving on to the quarterfinals.

Surgalski smiled and wore a look of relief when it was finally over.

"After today, it should relieve the pressure off me," he said. "I know how important this is. There's nothing saying for sure we'll be back down here next year. I think we have a good chance, but there's nothing for certain. The last time they'd been before this year was '96. That's five years. I'll be out of college in five years."

Flynn said Surgalski's latest injury is simply a microcosm of the center's season.

"He's had a lot of practice fighting through sickness and injuries," Flynn said. "Sometimes when you have an injury, you tend to concentrate a little bit more. He had a nice soft touch (on his free throws)."

The touch wasn't so soft Tuesday night when, in an awkward moment, Surgalski said he slammed the door on his hand in front of his house. Such awkwardness is not completely uncommon for

Surgalski, who twisted an ankle before the 16th Region Tournament last week stepping off a curb at a pizza place in Morehead.

Even before school started Wednesday morning, the rumors were flying about how Surgalski injured his hand.

"I've heard I've punched people, punched walls, and punched tires," he said. "I was walking around here last night and people—total strangers—were asking me about it and how it happened."

But Surgalski maintained that the injury was self-inflicted, with the help of his car door. He dismissed all the rumors, all the talk, as just that.

"People talk," he said.

Today, though, they are not talking about the particulars of how Surgalski hurt his hand but how courageously he responded to one of those life challenges.

Surgalski nested into a place in Tomcat history Thursday night, but for all the right reasons.

TOMCAT BASEBALL TRADITION ON DISPLAY
April 2009
• • •

From 1965-69, Ashland was Baseball Title Town. The Tomcats won high school state titles in 1966, 1967, and 1968. Those championships were sandwiched around 1 - 0 losses in the 1965 semifinals and 1969 finals.

It was dominance like you've never seen before or will likely see again.

Pleasure Ridge Park repeated Ashland's three-peat feat from 1994 - 96, but it would be hard to match the Tomcats overall during that golden era. They were 107 - 11 during that five-year span.

This spring marks the fortieth anniversary of the end of the amazing run and Ashland plans to commemorate the occasion in its last home game of the season on May 15.

It's a recognition that's long overdue

"It's time we did something," said Ashland coach Jeff Wilcox.

Billy and Bob Lynch were the dominant pitchers of the day but the Tomcats were more than just them.

"I really want these guys to get their due," said Bobby Lynch, who is helping to organize the reunion. "A lot of them played great baseball. It wasn't just me."

In baseball, it's never a one- or two-man show. Sure, you have the stars, but everybody has to be good. Ashland was good. No, make that great. There were no weak links. These were baseball players who cut their teeth in a fairly new Little League, then moved over to Central Park to play Babe Ruth and where they eventually became high school giants.

Bobby Lynch was a link to the three consecutive state titles. He was undefeated in state tournament play in his career and one of about a dozen Tomcats who earned All-State Tournament recognition.

But even that honor hasn't been duly noted on Ashland's All-State record board in the James A. Anderson Gymnasium. That needs to be rectified as well.

"I've got a list of the All-State players from '65 - 69 and there may be more," Lynch said.

It has been Lynch's quest for several years to get those players' names on the All-State board. This looks like the perfect opportunity to fix that situation as well.

In the 1965 semifinals, Ashland came in with a 19 - 0 record and lost a 1 - 0 decision to Bowling Green. Bill Lynch was pitching and he tried to pick off a runner at first base. "He had the guy dead," Bob said. But the ball zipped past the first baseman and into a long foul territory. The baserunner came all the way around to score the game's only run.

In the 1969 finals, it was an errant throw by pitcher Tim Huff that led to a 1 - 0 loss to Owensboro. The Red Devils had a runner on first and were sacrificing. Huff fielded the bunt and threw toward second but the ball sailed into center field, then took a bad hop and the runner came around to score the game's only run.

"I've talked to Tim about it," Bob said. "He said 'You have to move on, but I think about it every day.' He said the umpire told him after the game he kept wondering why nobody came over to him. He said the guy clearly missed third base."

The winning pitcher in the game, Bernie Strom, went on to Alabama where Bob Lynch was playing basketball.

The '69 Tomcats even had to get past McKell and fireballing Don Gullett. They did it with a 1 - 0 victory in Morehead in the 16th Region semifinals, with Huff outdueling Gullett in one of the great pitching matchups in area history.

Ashland defeated Shelby County and the late Mike Casey, 2 - 1, in the 1966 finals. The Tomcats downed Fort Knox 7 - 4 in the '67 finals and then downed Louisville Southern 1 - 0 in the '68 finals to complete the first three-peat in state history.

Lynch said he's suggested in previous years about trying to honor this group of Tomcats but it has been met with lukewarm response.

"Nobody really seemed to be that interested in it," he said. "I talked to Jeff (Wilcox) at the state tournament and he wanted to do something. It's kind of short notice but, at the same time, it's been forty-some years. We're not going to have much longer.

"I talked about having this before Steve Hemlepp got sick (he died in June 2004)," Lynch said. "I actually talked about it four or five years prior to that."

Ashland likes to honor its tradition, especially in basketball and football. It's time for baseball to be added to the salute.

Athletic director Mark Swift is also behind the project to honor the Tomcat baseball teams and individuals. As a former player, he knows the names of these Tomcat greats.

Lynch, who will be the Elks Sports Day honoree this summer, is happy that Ashland is behind doing something for this golden era of Tomcat baseball.

There will be a reception for players, coaches and managers from those teams at the May 15 game. Several other projects to honor the 1965 - 69 Tomcats are in the planning stages, including a possible display of the state championship trophies or possibly hanging championship banners that could fly over the Ashland press box on the Blazer campus.

Whatever is done, it's a good thing. It's time to recognize one of the area's most dominant eras, regardless of sport.

HAVING A BALL IN '43
February 2009
• • •

Once again, here's news from the Small World Department.

A man in Tacoma, Washington, recently visited a flea market in that area and purchased an old football containing signatures and a score from a game played on October 9, 1943—in Huntington.

It was an Ashland Tomcat football game against the Huntington Central Pony Express and the score was 7 - 2 in favor of the Tomcats. Later, of course, Huntington Central became Huntington High School and the game for the Little Red Wagon waged on.

It was the first time in eight years the Tomcats had beaten Central at Fairfield Stadium.

The gentleman, Wilson O'Neal, knew nothing about the Tomcats and their proud tradition. But he was curious about the football and its signatures. He wondered who may still be living and if any were still living in the Ashland area.

The man went to the Internet—where else do we get our information these days?—and found a link to Madge Haney's Web page about the class of 1957. It contained a link to the Boyd County Public Library, and another link to Ashland's 1944 yearbook.

He found in the '44 yearbook, from the library's genealogy room, the names of some players whose signatures were on the ball.

He contacted Madge, who put him in touch with Ashland Superintendent Steve Gilmore. O'Neal has agreed to sell the football to the school so it can be placed in a prominent place. The cost was only $35, including postage.

He listed some last names in an e-mail to Madge, including Ellis, which she said is probably H.L. Ellis, who was her principal at Ashland High School. There's also a Coburn listed, and it's assumed to be Bob Coburn, who still lives here.

Some of the other names were: Charles Barber, Johnny Bill McWhorter, Gerald Jarvis, Doug Robinson, Hugh Callihan, Earl Heffner, Bobby Webb, James Clark, Leonard Manley, Philip Layne, Bob Fidler, Jack DuPree, Bob Kash, and Dick Falk.

Ashland's 1943 team was a very good one, finishing 9 - 2 - 1 with the losses coming to Charleston High, 34 - 19, and Fort Thomas Highlands, 19 - 0, in the last game. The coach of the Tomcats that season was Floyd Roberts.

Ashland was coming off a 10 - 0 state championship season the previous year when it outscored opponents 341 - 30.

Hopefully, as word gets out about the football's arrival back in Ashland, we can figure out how in the world it ended up in Tacoma.

Stay tuned.

TRACKING THE 1943 FOOTBALL
February 2009

• • •

The story about the 1943 autographed football from an Ashland-Huntington Central game that was found in a flea market in Tacoma, Washington, has received a few e-mail responses, although the mystery of how it landed that far away remains.

A little background for those not familiar with the story. Wilson O'Neal, who lives in Tacoma, purchased the football at a flea market and was curious about its history. He found a link to Madge Haney's Web page about the 1957 AHS Class and information rolled from there.

O'Neal got in touch with Haney, who put him in contact with Ashland superintendent Steve Gilmore. O'Neal is sending the football to Ashland so it can be properly placed in a trophy case. O'Neal and Gilmore agreed on $45 for the price of the football and shipping.

The ball was from a 1943 game between the Tomcats and Huntington Central that Ashland won 7 - 2. Huntington Central later became Huntington High. It was the first time in eight years the Tomcats had beaten Central at Fairfield Stadium.

Some of the other names on the football were: Charles Barber, Johnny Bill McWhorter, Gerald Jarvis, Doug Robinson, Hugh Callihan, Earl Heffner, Bobby Webb, James Clark, Leonard Manley, Philip Layne, Bob Fidler, Jack DuPree, Bob Kash, and Dick Falk.

Ashland's 1943 team was a very good one, finishing 9 - 2 - 1 with the losses coming to Charleston High, 34-19, and Fort Thomas Highlands, 19 - 0, in the last game. The coach was Floyd Roberts.

Ashland was coming off a 10 - 0 state championship season the previous year when it outscored opponents 341 - 30.

Gerald Roberts e-mailed me after the story was in the paper last Thursday. He said the Ellis autograph was probably Lawrence Ellis, who was a manager on the '43 team. Originally, it was thought it might be H.L. Ellis, who was a math teacher at AHS that year.

He did confirm that Bob Coburn, who still lives here, played football his senior year (1944). Roberts remembered when he was a sophomore in high school in the 1954 - 55 school year and Coburn was his history teacher.

"I always thought that he was younger than close to thirty at the time because I always had the impression, perhaps from Bob, that the 1954 - 55 school year was the first he had taught," Roberts wrote.

Chet Strother, a graduate of the Ashland High School 1950 class, remembered watching the '43 Tomcats.

"Those Tomcats were all my heroes," he wrote. "I watched their practice sessions in Central Park and watched them as they walked back to the gym. They stopped at Freddy Doer's house for a sip of water from the outside spigot that tasted so good when I retraced their steps a few years later. An empty milk bottle was kept beside the spigot, just for Tomcats! And best of all, a friend showed me how to find Putnam Stadium, so I could see some of their games in person, mostly played on Saturday afternoons."

It's amazing how a football from sixty-six years ago could evoke so many good memories. How the ball arrived in Tacoma—some 3,000 miles from Ashland—is a mystery that probably won't ever be solved. But at least the old football has reminded us about a special era in area sports.

MYSTERY OF
1943 FOOTBALL SOLVED
February 2009

· · ·

The mystery of how a 1943 Ashland High School autographed football wound up in Tacoma, Washington, may have been solved.

The football was likely the property of Gerald Jarvis, the big Tomcat end who caught the game-winning touchdown pass in Ashland's 7 - 2 victory over Huntington Central at Fairfield Stadium in late October of 1943.

Don Virgin, who was a lineman for the Tomcats that season and now lives in Richmond, said Jarvis, who is deceased, was a lawyer who lived in the Northwest for much of his life.

That would be perfect logic as to how the football wound up in a flea market there.

"Gerald would do things like that more than anybody ever knew," Virgin said. "The ball should never have gone to an individual. It should be in a trophy case somewhere. I think he (Jarvis) lived in Washington (state), turned out to be a lawyer."

Ashland's victory over the Pony Express was the first victory in

Huntington since the 1935 season, although the Tomcats whipped Huntington 21 - 6 in Putnam Stadium in the undefeated 1942 season.

The Tomcats trailed 2 - 0 when they put together what turned out to be the game-winning drive late in the first half.

Running the single-wing, Ashland had driven to the three-yard line after J.C. Kennard completed a twenty-eight-yard pass to Charlie Lemaster. After a one-yard gain, Lemaster was tackled for a near five-yard loss and then Kennard threw an incomplete pass. But on fourth down, his pass to Jarvis was gathered in for the game's only touchdown. Bob Fidler added the extra point for the 7 - 2 lead, which turned out to be the final score.

Ashland's Leonard Manley intercepted a pass in the end zone near the end of the half, barely dragging defenders with him to the one-yard line to avoid another safety.

The first safety—and Huntington's only points—came in the first quarter when it blocked one of Kennard's punts. The ball rolled backward into the Ashland end zone, where Kennard covered it up.

Ashland went on to a 9 - 2 - 1 season, the tie coming against Manuel and the losses coming to Charleston High School and Fort Thomas Highlands in what was essentially the state championship game.

Highlands defeated the Tomcats 19 - 0 at UK's Stoll Field.

The previous season Ashland was 10 - 0 and the mythical state champions.

That '43 season also produced one of the greatest individual performances in Tomcat history when Kennard led Ashland past Ironton 33 - 0. The Tomcat triple-threat ran it thirty-four of the first thirty-five running plays and scored four touchdowns in an incredible performance.

ADI Sports Editor John McGill wrote this about Kennard after the game: "It was Kennard, a human dynamo with legs of steel and the endurance of a Flying Fortress, who twisted the Tiger's tail the hardest. Playing the best game of his starry career and turning in one of the outstanding performances of all time in this section, Kennard carried the ball thirty-four times on Ashland's first thirty-five running plays. Battering savagely through the Ironton line, he plowed forward with such momentum it took two and three Tigers to haul him to earth."

Ashland had to play Ironton on the road in those days because blacks weren't allowed to play against whites in the state of Kentucky. But a throng of 6,000 fans showed up at Beechwood Stadium.

Rev. Charles Stewart remembers those early 1940s teams well. He was in his first year as a student manager in the 1943 season.

"I had such a great time," he said. "All those boys on there were terrific people. I loved them and I tried to do a good job for them."

Stewart said the players from the '43 team "taught me a lot about life."

Stewart's responsibilities included cleaning the cleats and uniforms, along with giving players rubdowns before games.

"I asked them to buy me a washing machine but they never did," Stewart said. "Doing my job as manager, I didn't get all my grades. I had to stay another year to pass (graduate)."

The football will soon be the property of the Ashland school system. Superintendent Steve Gilmore worked out a deal with Wilson O'Neal of Tacoma, Wash. It was O'Neal who purchased the football in the flea market there.

The football has the score of the game and several autographs of players from the team.

There are several theories on how the ball may have traveled some 3,000 miles, including one from J.D. Atkinson, a 1944 Ashland High

School graduate. He suggested that someone who had joined the service had taken the ball with them.

"When he had to ship out to wherever he went, probably to the Japanese Theater, he couldn't take it with him so he probably pawned it," Atkinson said. "Everybody at that age in 1943 was drafted (or joined) after graduating high school."

But Virgin's theory that the ball belonged to Jarvis makes the most sense since he did score the only touchdown in that game and was prone to do such things, according to Virgin.

Many players from that team, including Bob Coburn and Earle Heffner, still live in Ashland. Their autographs were among those that were legible, according to the man who bought the football.

"When you get that ball, my name ought to be on that ball, too," Virgin said. "Let me know, would you?"

The football will hopefully arrive home sometime next week.

MAN WHO FOUND '43 FOOTBALL RECALLS JOURNEY
March 2009

• • •

Wilson O'Neal, the man who picked up the 1943 Ashland Tomcat football at an antique show in Tacoma, Washington, a few weeks ago, has enjoyed the journey as much as anyone.

O'Neal, who collects military jackets and vintage golf equipment as a hobby, came upon the football while perusing other items.

"I see this football sitting there and kind of glanced at it," he said. "A guy walked over who had it for sale and started talking to me about it."

The seller didn't know the football's origin, or really much about it at all. But O'Neal saw the mystery associated with the football, purchased it for $30 and then began his journey to find its true home.

"I knew it was at least sixty years old," O'Neal said. "I first ran (Googled) the score Tomcats 7, Pony Express 2 and came up with Ashland High School. I saw Bob Morris' name on the ball and found out he was head coach in '45. Then I knew I'd nailed it."

From there he kept surfing and he landed on Madge Haney's

Web site about the Ashland High School class of 1957. She also had yearbook links through the Boyd County Public Library. O'Neal looked through the 1944 yearbook online and scrolled through eighty-six pages before getting to the football section.

"Then, there it was, the score, group pictures, pictures of players, everything," he said. "Doing the research and then finding the story is the fun part behind it. Obviously, there's a story behind it."

The biggest question was how the football ended up in the Northwest. But a player from the '43 team shared with me that the man who caught the only touchdown in that game, Gerald Jarvis, had moved to the Northwest and become a lawyer. He died in 1998.

"I've been keeping up with the stories in the paper online," O'Neal said. "It's a great story. It created a stir."

O'Neal, fifty-five, said the football "deserves to be back home," so he sold it to Ashland schools through superintendent Steve Gilmore for $45 ($30 for the football and $15 for shipping). He shipped the ball to Ashland on Saturday.

When O'Neal first saw the ball, he could read several of the names and noticed two-digit numbers under the signatures. At first, he thought it was the uniform number. But when all of the numbers were 42, 43, and 44 he figured out it must be graduation years.

The ball's seller said he'd gone online to find out information, but came away empty.

O'Neal's search was obviously more fruitful.

"Some names you couldn't read at all," he said. "Some of them, like Bob Morris, were perfectly clear. I'd heard you might be able to read it better under a black light. I tried that, but it didn't improve it much. There might be some other way to read the names."

O'Neal, who works for a sporting goods company, had the ball slowly inflated. He said it kept the air for awhile before losing it again.

"It still has some shape," he said. "For a ball sixty-five years old, the valve is not going to be the same. I know of some places that restore old balls. One method is they use this fiber fill. It keeps its shape completely like its blown up."

O'Neal said he's glad the football is going home where it belongs. He's also expressed an interest in talking to some of the players on the team.

O'Neal said the football would never have found its way home without today's modern technology.

"Without the Internet, how would I have ever found out about a town of 20,000 where a game was played sixty-five years ago?" O'Neal said.

Doc Rice was a star on Ashland's 1942 state champions. MARK MAYNARD

KENNARD ENJOYING MEMORIES
March 2009

• • •

J.C. Kennard has followed the trail of the 1943 Ashland Tomcat football with keen interest.

No wonder.

Kennard was the star of those '43 Tomcats, a no-nonsense running back typical of that era. He was the workhorse, taking most every snap and either running (mostly) or passing out of the single-wing formation.

These were his Tomcats.

The team's quarterback was Frog Swift, but in the single-wing formation, that wasn't the glamour position it is today. It meant lead blocking back or, back in Tomcat maroon-and-white in '43, it meant one of those responsible for clearing the way for the hard-charging Kennard.

"The quarterbacks then were pretty much running guards, so to speak," Kennard said.

Kennard was also a key player in 1942 when the Tomcats were the mythical state champions with an unbeaten 10 - 0 ledger. That season, the snaps went to Kennard or fullback Doc Rice, who Kennard said was as good as they come.

"He took most of the snaps at fullback," Kennard said. "Oh, man, he was just tops. That's all there is to it."

Rice is mostly underrated, almost forgotten, in Tomcat history, Kennard said. But there weren't many better than him during that time. "I'd love for the Elks to take a look at him" for Sports Day consideration, he said.

Kennard said the '43 Tomcat team was championship-worthy, too. But in the mythical championship game that year against Fort Thomas Highlands at Stoll Field in Lexington, Ashland lost 19 - 0.

Kennard knows partly why the outcome didn't go in the Tomcats' favor. He said the entire Fort Thomas team came to watch Ashland's 22 - 7 victory over Portsmouth—and apparently learned a lot about what the Tomcats liked to do.

"They got to scout us and knew exactly what we were doing," he said. "I never did get to the line of scrimmage."

Kennard remembered something else about the game. "The Army was using Stoll Field for indoctrinating drills. There was chicken dung all over that field. It was a mess. I never played in anything like that."

Kennard learned about Fort Thomas' "scouting trip" from Bluebird player Roger Ross, who attended the University of Virginia when Kennard played football there. That was one of three schools where Kennard played, the others being Duke and Kentucky when the great Bear Bryant coached.

Kennard likes the attention the football from the Huntington High-Ashland game in 1943—that was found in Tacoma, Washington, at an antique auction—has given that era of Tomcat football.

He's followed it with great interest through stories that have appeared online on the newspaper's Web site. Kennard lives in Columbus, Ohio.

One of those stories involved Kennard himself when he ran

thirty-four of thirty-five running plays against rugged Ironton in a surprising 33 - 0 victory. His yardage total wasn't included in the game account, but Kennard estimated it had to be "somewhere in the neighborhood of 250 yards anyhow."

He played three quarters before coach Preacher Roberts took him out of the game. That's because the Tomcats had a game the next day against Catlettsburg in a 39 - 0 victory.

"I played about two quarters in that one," Kennard said. "I think I scored two or three times. They would have kicked out the school superintendent, fired the coach, the principal, and everybody else if you tried to do that (play two games in two days) today. But it was a different time."

It was Kennard who threw the game-winning touchdown pass to Gerald Jarvis in the Tomcats' 7 - 2 victory over Huntington High at Fairfield Stadium. Jarvis, who died in 1998, is believed to have been the one who somehow had the game ball. He became a lawyer in the state of Washington and lived in the northwest most of his life.

Kennard said it didn't surprise him that it was probably Jarvis who had somehow managed to get the game ball.

"He was a case, let me tell you," Kennard said chuckling. "I'm glad he caught that ball. That was a really big win for us living down there in the valley."

Earle Heffner, who lives in Ashland still, was a tackle on the '43 Tomcats. He said Jarvis told him the touchdown catch shouldn't have counted. "He told me personally 'We're lucky we won that game because I was out of bounds when I caught that pass.' That's what Gerald told me and he didn't keep it a secret."

But Heffner said Jarvis was "awful happy we won that game. He was slick, I'll tell you."

Heffner said Kennard threw the touchdown pass while running to his left. He flipped it across his body to the back of the end zone where Jarvis had broken open. "Gerald was out there by himself," he said.

Heffner, a '44 AHS graduate, still has a sharp mind for remembering detail. "The older you get, nobody can prove you wrong," he said with a chuckle.

Kennard remembered playing Saturday afternoon games in Putnam Stadium and some night games at Armco.

"One of our games the lights went out and we had to play again," he said. "It was against Ceredo-Kenova. We were winning before the lights went out." The 1941 Ashland-Ceredo game ended in a 14 - 14 tie, although Kennard didn't remember if that was the game or how it all turned out.

"Don't hold me to all of that," he said. "This is all from the memory of an eighty-three-year-old guy."

And also one very good football player who, because of a football found some 3,000 miles from home, is reliving some of his fondest memories.

COACH'S OLD SCHOOL
FOOTBALL TRIUMPHS
December 2005
• • •

Russell coach Ivan McGlone is pure old school football.

Score one for his generation.

Old-school Russell defeated high-tech Owensboro Catholic 27 - 14 in the Class AA state championship game on Saturday in Papa John's Cardinal Stadium. McGlone, the godfather and maybe the grandfather of Red Devil football, has another state championship trophy to put in the case.

It's been twenty-seven years since the last one, in 1978, but there's not much that's different about McGlone or his philosophy. He's run the Wing-T offense since he started coaching here in 1976 and rock-solid defense has been another staple.

Want a blueprint for a championship program? Just look down Red Devil Lane.

McGlone, whose football roots run deep in West Virginia, may be the classiest coach in Kentucky. He's won 252 games as Russell's head coach, which is more than half in the program's storied history. There are nine players on the Red Devils' roster whose fathers played for the sixty-seven-year-old McGlone.

And think about this: Any players involved with Russell football who are forty-five years or younger know nothing but Ivan McGlone football—and they wouldn't have it any other way.

"He's the god of Russell football," said senior blocking machine Drew Mell.

That sums it up well. Russell football is Ivan McGlone.

McGlone is much more uncomfortable in front of a podium surrounded by reporters than he is prowling the sidelines. He's not in this for personal glory or accomplishments. Ivan almost acts embarrassed when asked questions about how many things he's done at Russell.

The guy just likes to coach football. If the stands had been empty on Saturday afternoon, Ivan wouldn't have minded one bit.

"We got down here and everybody was all excited," he said. "It's just like a plain 'ol football game."

Leave it to Ivan McGlone to simplify what others make complicated.

The victory was one that Russell's program has been waiting on since last celebrating a championship in 1978. The Red Devils have built one of the best programs in the state but programs are measured with state titles. Now, Russell has a pair of them and one it can cherish for a long time to come. The '78 team now has a friend.

This championship will elevate Russell football not only in northeastern Kentucky but in the eyes of the state. It's also a big one for McGlone, who had to be wondering if another championship shot would come for him.

"This win's huge for him," said longtime assistant and offensive

Ivan McGlone holds up the 2005 state championship trophy. KEVIN GOLDY/THE INDEPENDENT

coordinator Mike Jones. "He's the patriarch for the football program. He never puts demands on anyone."

Also, don't believe for a second that Ivan McGlone is the head coach in name only. Whatever is done with Russell football goes through McGlone.

"I tell everybody there's one boss around here and it's that man right there," Jones said, pointing to McGlone. "We've run the Wing-T

261

a long time and I understand what we're trying to do. He goes 90 to 95 percent with what I send down. But sometimes he'll take the game over, and that's his prerogative."

Watching Ivan McGlone work on the sidelines is a study in concentration. He'll pace and look down at the ground, far away from the rest of the coaching staff. He'll cross his arms and look out onto the field. The distress signal at Russell? That's when McGlone raises his arms up (like a touchdown signal) and then follows by putting his hands behind his head.

We've all seen the signals, and the wheels working. The distress sign never came out on Saturday. It wasn't necessary.

Old school football was doing a fine job of knocking off new school football.

Owensboro Catholic came into the championship game for the second year in a row behind passing guru Tony Franklin's high-octane offense. The Aces were hardly slowed by anybody all season, except for a loss to Owensboro (also nicknamed Red Devils) when they committed nine turnovers and fell only 19 - 7.

Russell doesn't boggle the mind with an imaginative offense. The Wing-T's roots are basically simple, unlike the spread offense that seem to be overtaking college and high school playbooks. But the Red Devils do it so well, and that's what makes their offense go, go, go.

No matter what the offense, be it the Wing-T or the spread, it is all a matter of execution. If there was one supreme offense wouldn't everybody be using it?

The difference on Saturday? Russell out-executed Owensboro Catholic on every turn.

Call it McGlone-Ball, because that's what has happened most Fridays in the fall for the past thirty years at Russell High School. By now, we should be getting used to this scene.

Russell quarterback Tommy Brown celebrates the Class AA football title with his king crown in 2005. KEVIN GOLDY/THE INDEPENDENT

"Everything about this game was for him," said Jacob Sizemore, a two-way junior starter. "They've got guys from UK (Franklin was a former Hal Mumme assistant) calling plays for them over there. Coach McGlone and coach (Garry) Morris both outcoached them."

McGlone is also smart enough to utilize one of Kentucky's best coaching staffs. Morris's defensive game plan was brilliant and Jones and Tracy Edwards' offensive calls were pure old-school, just like their head coach.

While many speculated that McGlone would retire if the Red Devils won the state championship—sending him out on top, so to speak—that thought never crossed his mind. He said winning or losing in a state final wouldn't determine when he quits coaching. That's a family matter.

"I told somebody if I won the state championship, I'd come back because I'd like to gloat about it for a year," he said with a grin.

Ivan McGlone enjoyed this victory ride like he enjoys all of his victories, with wife Gloria cheering in the stands.

While the players were celebrating on the field following the victory, McGlone went over to the stands to help his sweetheart down onto the field. The look on their faces was pure love, respect and admiration. It would have the exact same look if the Red Devils had lost the game. Their story is a true love story if there ever was one.

Now Coach McGlone, go ahead and gloat. You deserve it.

ELLIOTT WILL BE
FONDLY REMEMBERED
March 2009

• • •

Elliott County's amazing basketball run came short of the intended goal of cutting down the nets in Rupp Arena on Saturday night.

But years from now, the 16th Region—and especially those who live in Sandy Hook—will still be talking about the pride and hope they gave this little town.

The names of Ferguson, Faulkner, and Knipp will always be dear to those who followed the team's rise to become one of the state's best basketball teams in 2009.

It didn't have a Hoosiers-like ending, but the memories provided will be everlasting.

What made Elliott County's run so special is that it was accomplished the old-fashioned way, with hard work, homegrown talent, and a team of players who had a passion for the game that's not seen much these days. There were no hired guns on the roster, no agendas for individual players who wanted to be the star. They played for Elliott County because that's where they lived, where they grew up, where they learned to play together.

Rick Mays led Elliott County to three consecutive 16th Region titles from 2007 to 2009.
JOHN FLAVELL/THE INDEPENDENT

Since these players were in seventh grade, they banded together on AAU teams in the summer, working on skills and learning each other's every move while playing more than 1,000 games together. That's why Elliott County's basketball team was so fluid. Watching them play was like watching someone pour water out of a pitcher and into a glass. There were no ripples, just pure flow.

In the end, reaching the state semifinals, while quite an accomplishment, was short of the goal that the players set for themselves before the season. That goal was to win a state championship. And while the disappointment and hurt is still fresh, it will soon go away.

By reaching the semifinals, Elliott County put itself in select 16th Region company, becoming only the fifth team in the last forty years to go that far, joining 1969 Ashland, 1974 Greenup County, 1977 Ashland, and 1996 Ashland (a state finalist).

While the opportunity to become the first state champion from the 16th Region since the 1961 Tomcats existed for Elliott County, it wasn't to be. That team, still one of the grandest champions in state history, will be celebrating a fiftieth anniversary in a couple of years.

But for the folks in Sandy Hook, the thrills and chills that this Elliott County team provided them over the last four years, including three consecutive regional championships, will be something that's hard to duplicate but forever remembered. The national media converged on the little town to found out what the buzz was all about. There were stories in USA Today and ESPN.com, not to mention how the Lions captured the imagination and attention of the entire state.

Elliott County is on the map again, thanks to this basketball team that represented the 16th Region so well last week.

Basketball is better in Kentucky because Elliott County passed through it the last three years. It showed once again that it's not always the size of the school or community, but the size of the heart.

Probably somewhere today in Sandy Hook, somebody is pretending to be Jonathan Ferguson, shooting a shot while fading backward out of bounds (Who made more of those than Ferguson? He dared to make shots that most others wouldn't have even thought about shooting).

Or maybe they'll be Ethan Faulkner, coolly cutting down the lane and then, without looking, flipping a pass to a teammate for an open three-pointer (His basketball IQ is off the charts).

Maybe they'll want to be Timmy Knipp, a shot blocker supreme and a big man with more range than most guards (His upside is tremendous, with two years still to go in high school).

They might want to be Evan Faulkner, the defensive specialist who, like his brother, carried amazing basketball knowledge (Who wouldn't want this guy on their team?).

And don't forget about wanting to be Chris Knipp, the unsung guard who hit his share of big baskets (He was a role-player supreme).

The 16th Region is not likely to see a team like this again for a long, long time.

TIPTON GETS THRILL FROM EAGLES' RUN
March 2009
• • •

When Morehead State captured the Ohio Valley Conference tournament championship last Saturday, the flashbacks were inevitable for Jeff Tipton.

Twenty-five years ago, Tipton was a 6-foot-11 senior on MSU's last team that earned a bid to the NCAA tournament.

"I had a lot of great memories come back, I sure did," Tipton said. "Especially when they showed coach (Wayne) Martin in the crowd. I'd already had a lot of conversation with some old players. It was like a twenty-five-year reunion."

The forty-six-year-old Tipton was watching the game on television from his home in Lexington—and he was admittedly a little nervous during the Eagles' double-overtime 67 - 65 victory over Austin Peay in Nashville.

"When they said it had been twenty-five years (since the last OVC tournament title and NCAA bid), it kind of blew me away," Tipton said. "I'm feeling old all of a sudden."

Tipton went to Morehead State after an All-State career at Ashland that culminated in him helping the Tomcats reach the State Tournament in 1980—Ashland's fifth consecutive trip to the Sweet Sixteen.

Tipton's greatest high school game was his last one when Covington Holmes defeated the Tomcats in double overtime during the state quarterfinals in Freedom Hall.

Tipton scored forty-one in that epic loss to Dicky Beal—led Holmes, a team that had hammered the Tomcats during the regular season.

"I love the State Tournament," Tipton said. "I go every year. I always look at the program to see how many have got (passed) me (in highest games). I'm on the back page now.

"I love it. There's nothing better than watching kids in Kentucky play basketball."

Tipton said he learned from the regular-season game with Holmes that he needed to get the Bulldogs' frontline in foul trouble for the Tomcats to have a chance.

"I did that (in the state tournament game)," he said. "That was my personal goal. That was, without a doubt, my best game ever."

But that was in high school. Tipton went on to sign with Morehead State—a critical and pivotal commitment in Martin's building project. Tipton went on to become an All-OVC performer as a senior and scored more than 1,000 in his MSU career.

The Eagles went to consecutive NCAA tournaments in 1983 and 1984 with Tipton as the starting center both seasons. State Rep. Rocky Adkins was a senior guard on the '83 team as well when Morehead State played Syracuse in the NCAA tournament.

"We kind of snuck up on them the first year," Tipton said. "The second year, we got beat by Middle (Tennessee) and then didn't lose again (in the OVC).

"I'll never forget walking into McDonald's out there at Morehead after we won it. They were like clapping and everything, like you'd done something great. There was my picture and Earl's (Harrison) in the trays. It was the greatest time of our life.

"I'd love to be around it, love to be part of it, and smell that locker room. I miss that old mildewy smell."

Tipton said he's impressed with MSU coach Donnie Tyndall, who in three years has taken the Eagles from last in the OVC to tournament champions.

"In my opinion, he's a young Wayne Martin," Tipton said. "He's done a helluva job."

As the game was winding down, Tipton said he was rooting hard for the Eagles. "I was nervous," he said. "I'm not going to lie."

Tipton remembers winning the OVC title in '84 when it was played in Ellis T. Johnson Arena. The Eagles defeated Murray State 80 - 64 in the semifinal and then Youngstown State 47 - 44 in a deliberate championship game.

Tipton had eighteen points and six rebounds in the semifinal win and ten points in the championship game. He has stayed close to team members, including point guard Jeff Fultz, a former roommate.

Morehead State had to win a play-in game against North Carolina A&T to make the NCAA field. The Eagles did that with a 70 - 69 victory over the Aggies when Guy Minnifield hit a short jumper with four seconds remaining.

In was in that game in Dayton, Ohio, that the referees used television instant replays to correct a call for the first time.

NC A&T and Morehead were tied at sixty-eight when the Eagles committed a foul. But A&T sent a different player to the foul line than was fouled. MSU's bench noticed the switch and called foul. The referees weren't sure so they went to the ESPN replays where the announcers were Larry Conley and Tom Hammond.

After watching replays it was determined that the player fouled was James Horace—a 51 percent free throw shooter—and he made one of two to put the Aggies ahead 69 - 68. Minnifield then came down and nailed the jumper that sent Morehead to its first NCAA tournament victory since 1961.

That put MSU in the forty-eight-team field where it was matched against Louisville in Milwaukee. The Cardinals defeated the Eagles 72 - 59, a much closer game than the regular season when Louisville routed Morehead 85 - 50. Fairview great Jeff Hall was a member of the Cardinals.

Also at that venue, Villanova defeated Marshall 84 - 72 in an opening-round game.

Tipton said Martin put Morehead on the map by following a plan. "I have more respect for him than anybody I ever met," he said. "He took a few of us boys from Kentucky and brought in some other athletes and we flourished."

Tipton is enjoying life in Lexington where he works as the finance director for an automobile dealership. He received a scare last October when he had an aneurysm removed. "They cracked me open," he said. "I'm OK, I can take the hours but I'm more tired. They said it would be a year before I'd start feeling good again."

Tipton, who is married to the former Christina Pruitt of Russell, is also having a blast with his eight-year-old son Jeffrey. "I can't get enough of my son," he said. "I think the light is coming on."

Tipton is also proud to be a Morehead alum. He will be in Atlanta next week for work, but hopes to keep an eye on the Eagles whenever they play in the NCAA tournament. "I'm going to be crazy," he said. "I may have to excuse myself for a two-hour lunch."

ELLIOTT HAS COME A LOOOONG WAY

March 2009

• • •

Rowan County and Elliott County will meet tonight for the girls' 16th Region championship at Ellis T. Johnson Arena.

It's a scenario that, twenty-five years ago, no one would have dared dream possible.

On November 27, 1984, in the first game of the Eastern Kentucky Conference Tournament, Rowan County romped Elliott County 123 - 6 in a game that eventually led the Lady Lions to drop basketball.

Elliott County had only five players—a junior, a sophomore, a freshman, and two middle schoolers—on its roster. The coach at the time, Steve Lupkin, was given the job and told to do the best he could.

"The only thing I remember about him is he kept snakes," said Elliott County boys coach Rick Mays. "He really didn't know that much about basketball."

Robin Whitt Adkins, a teacher at Lakeside Elementary, was the sophomore point guard on the Elliott County team that was pummeled by 16th Region powerhouse Rowan County in November of 1984.

Elliott County girls coach Mark Cantrell took the Lady Lions to the 16th Region finals in 2009. JOHN FLAVELL/THE INDEPENDENT

"I remember we couldn't get the ball past halfcourt," she said. "We'd get the ball to halfcourt and they'd take it away from us. It was quite embarrassing."

Adkins said Rowan County coach Claudia Hicks ran up the score.

"Coach Hicks, I remember her real well," Adkins said. "I think she wanted to pad their scoring average for the state."

The 123 points is tied for the second-most in modern state history. Elliott County is also on the list for giving up 119 points and 117 points in games.

Rowan County dressed only ten players for the EKC game and Hicks was quoted in the newspaper as saying she played all ten in the first quarter.

"This type of game is not good for girls' basketball," Hicks said in '84. "We had an idea what it might be like when we heard Elliott only had five girls on the team just a couple of weeks ago."

It would be the only game Elliott County played that season and the last game for Adkins. The school didn't have a team during her junior and senior years.

In the fall of 1986, Terry Puckett re-started the program, but it lasted only two years. Elliott County didn't have a team from 1988 - 93 until Sally Greene started one back again. Mignon Flanery, a star player on that team, was one reason the program got another chance, Adkins said. "She was a really good player." Adkins began coaching an elementary school team in 1990, helping feed players to get the program going again.

Elliott County's girls basketball has a checkered and mostly losing past and had never won a district game before this season. The school does have an outstanding cheerleading program. That, Adkins said, is one reason the girls' basketball team hasn't done better.

"Most of our athletes are cheerleaders," she said. "We have very large cheerleading teams."

The Lady Lions snapped an 0-for-26 district record with a win over West Carter and then defeated East Carter on its home floor for the 62nd District title last week.

In three short years, coach Mark Cantrell has turned Elliott County girls' basketball from lovable losers to a legitimate regional contender.

"I'm excited," Adkins said. "I follow them as much as I can (she has two sets of twins, all boys). I'm not the cheerleading type. If I had little girls, they'd be ballplayers."

While Elliott County's boys have received national recognition, the girls' team has gone about the business of winning, too, but without the fanfare.

Both the boys' and girls' teams have Fergusons—Jonathan and Shae are siblings and Kelsey is a cousin—and both teams play a free-wheeling style that's fun to watch but hard to defend.

Cantrell has said he has tried to model the girls' program after the boys' program. He loves to chat it up with Mays, even graciously taking his good-natured jabs about being, uh, vertically challenged.

"I pick at him a lot. He doesn't get mad at me," Mays said. "Anybody that can take me that long has to be a good fella."

Cantrell isn't a teacher at Elliott County. He's a physical therapist who works two- and three-day shifts in Louisville. His drives back and forth to Sandy Hook for practice and games.

"He does a good job," Mays said. "He loves it. He always wants to talk basketball. The other day I said 'Let's talk about something else. Let's talk about fishing.' But that's not him. He's all basketball."

Mays said the girls appreciate Cantrell's passion for the game.

"He's the most passionate I've seen," Mays said. "He keeps his mind on it every second. The kids notice those kind of things."

Elliott County may not complete the dream tonight and win the 16th Region championship. But at least they don't have to worry about losing games by ridiculous scores of 123 - 6 anymore.

And that's a good thing not only for Elliott County but also for girls' basketball in general.

REGION HISTORY WORTH TELLING
March 2009

• • •

Most of you know, diving into area sports history is a passion of mine.

The stories of our sports legends grow with each passing day.

We're watching a bit of history this season with Elliott County's amazing boys basketball team. Years from now, somebody (maybe me?) will be re-telling the story of the Lions' magical run in the 16th Region. If there's an upset this weekend, we'll be writing about that for years to come, too.

So either way, history will be made.

If Elliott County somehow becomes state champions—and that's not something that falls into the category of the Impossible Dream—then there will probably be books written and movies produced about the boys from Sandy Hook. The Lions could become Kentucky's version of "Hoosiers."

But that's getting ahead of ourselves.

For now, step back into the Wayback Machine with me on a fifty-year journey, in ten-year segments, about some other memorable moments in 16th Region history.

1959

It was the Year of the Comets.

Olive Hill High School had one of its best teams ever under legendary coach Jack Fultz.

Bert Greene, whose fifty-year record of being the region's No. 1 scorer was broken only this season, led the Comets to their third regional title in five years.

Olive Hill reached the state semifinals before injuries to both starting guards led to a bitter 67 - 65 defeat to North Marshall that Fultz went to his grave bemoaning. Lexington Dunbar beat the emotionally and physically drained Comets 88 - 45 in the third-place game.

Greene was the star but Larry Ader, Dale Barker, and Larry Williams were other shooting stars for the Comets.

Olive Hill defeated Clark County 60 - 59 in the regional finals and also eliminated one of Vanceburg's best-ever teams 65 - 46 in the opening round.

The Comets saddled Vanceburg, led by Harold Billman, with four of its six losses in a 21 - 6 season. Two of those losses came in the postseason—the district finals and the regional opener (the regional was blind draw then). Vanceburg's coach was Bob Wright who, after that season, became coach of the Ashland Tomcats. In 1961, Wright guided the Tomcats to the 16th Region's last state title with a 36 - 1 season.

Billman, the fourth all-time scorer in Vanceburg/Lewis County history and the half-brother of 16th Region official Joe Billman, scored forty-one against Olive Hill in the opener that season. That was a school record at the time. Gary Kidwell was a sophomore at Vanceburg High

School who was a statistician '59 before being a player himself as a junior and senior.

1969

Ashland won the regional title behind the play of all-tournament selections Ray Kleykamp, Roger Baldridge, Fred Leibee, and Johnny Mullins.

The Tomcats were never pushed in the regional, winning by margins of 26, 20, and 33 (84 - 51 over Menifee County in the finals) in one of the most dominating tournaments in history.

In the State Tournament, it was nail-biter time. The Tomcats edged Harlan 69 - 66 and then downed Shelby County 81 - 80 in the quarterfinals. The run for the title ended with an 82 - 80 loss to Ohio County on a last-second shot in the semifinals.

Louisville Central, a state powerhouse, went on to win the state title in runaway fashion.

It would be the best finish Ashland would make under Harold Cole.

1979

Ashland won the regional championship to end one of the most incredible streaks in area sports history.

This was coach Paul Patterson's last season for the Tomcats and he finished his four-year Ashland career with a perfect record against 16th Region competition.

Ashland defeated Holy Family 65 - 53 in the regional championship game at Summit Junior High School (now Boyd County Middle School).

The Fighting Irish were a wonderful story that year as well with the likes of David Layne, Art McCullough, Mike Stewart, and Danny Phillips.

Kenny Cobb, Greg McCauley, and Doug Smith were among the stars for Ashland, which beat Owensboro 54 - 51 in the first round of the State Tournament and then bowed out in the quarterfinals to Mayfield, 56 - 54.

1989

Rowan County made it a three-peat of regional championships under coach Tim Moore with a win over Boyd County 74 - 59 in the finals.

Kelly Wells completed his high school career with a fourth consecutive appearance on the All-Region team, winning MVP honors. Rowan County broke out to a 20 - 0 lead in the championship game against the Lions, who never recovered.

The Vikings were eliminated in the first round of the State Tournament by Clark County 45 - 43

1999

This one was sweet for Boyd County and bitter for Ashland.

Tyler Zornes' last-second bomb from about thirty-five feet gave Boyd County a 54 - 52 victory over the Tomcats. It came only seconds before Scott Johnson's clutch basket had put Ashland in front 52 - 51.

The Lions ran Zornes from the far sideline around midcourt. He curled around a screen and drilled the long bomb that stuck a dagger into Ashland's heart.

Boyd County coach Roger Zornes revealed to the press after the game that he dreamed his son was going to hit the game-winning shot the previous night.

Sometimes dreams do come true.

Pikeville beat Boyd County 58 - 51 in the first round of the State Tournament. Bryan Hall and Brian Biggs were other members of that Lions' team.

ELLIOTT COUNTY AMONG FINEST
February 2009
• • •

When the curtain drops on Elliott County's amazing basketball season—whether it's against East Carter in the opening game of the 62nd District Tournament on Tuesday or hoisting the state championship trophy in Rupp Arena later next month—it will be a time of tears and flashbacks.

The Lions have supplied the little town of Sandy Hook with hope, and joy, and pride, for the past four years. Calling them special doesn't do it justice. This basketball team, which plays so fluidly and so unselfishly, can already take its place among the greatest in 16th Region history.

Those who remember watching the 1961 state champion Ashland Tomcats compare the teams favorably. Like the '61 Tomcats, one of the most beloved teams in state tournament history, Elliott County plays with a different passion and court awareness than most teams. Their basketball IQs are off the chart and their talents immense.

They can score from anywhere and with anybody. But it's not just an offensive juggernaut. The offense is fueled by the defense, much like it was for Ashland in '61. It's the relentless kind of defense that makes runs of 20 - 2 or 18 - 0 or 28 - 3 rather commonplace.

Elliott County's top three scorers—Jonathan Ferguson and twins Ethan and Evan Faulkner—have combined for more than 7,000 points in their careers. Ferguson is the new scoring king of the 16th Region, with more than 3,000 points.

Their numbers boggle the mind. Besides the scoring, there have been ninety-nine victories in the past four years.

Now they have one more March left to play. Maybe.

Where they eventually rank in 16th Region lore may be determined by this March's last maddening ride. Elliott County is going for a region three-peat, but that's really small potatoes for this team. There's got to be more for them to consider this wild ride a success.

Before the season, they laid out their goal in very specific terms. Anything short of playing on Saturday night in Rupp Arena, on the last day of Kentucky's high school basketball season, would be a disappointment.

That's a tall order for any team, including this one, and especially given the unfriendly State Tournament draw given to the 16th Region last month. Destiny looked Elliott County square in the eye and said "What do you think of that?"

If Elliott County can get to the Sweet Sixteen—and there's not a reason to think they won't, considering they are 16 - 0 against region competition this season—the hurdles are plenty. There's potentially a matchup with Anderson County, which took the Lions to overtime earlier this season.

They could meet up again with Dakotah Euton and Chad Jackson, now wearing the red-and-white of Scott County instead of the blue-and-white of Rose Hill. There may be a rematch with Shelby Valley,

Elliott County coach Rick Mays led the Lions to three consecutive 16th Region titles from 2007 - 09. JOHN FLAVELL/THE INDEPENDENT

the only team in Kentucky to tame the Lions this season. And those obstacles are in place just to make it to Saturday night.

Nothing worth having is ever easy. Elliott County's players know that better than anybody.

Basketball has been their life, their passion, their dream for a lifetime. They've been playing together since elementary school. They've spent summers together on the AAU trail, along with their parents who no doubt have a vested emotional interest in all of this as well.

This team wasn't built with a transfer here or there. That's what makes them so unique, so revered, so special. They've become the pride and joy of a community and are legends in the making. Years from now, they'll be remembered for what they accomplished.

And for veteran coach Rick Mays, it's been the Dream Team that comes along once in a lifetime. He's experienced four years of bliss. He knows what's at stake as another March beckons—the last March Madness for one of the greatest 16th Region basketball teams ever.

ROSE HILL TO HONOR
PAST BASKETBALL COACH
February 2009

• • •

Rose Hill Christian School will be recognizing Joe Dillow, the first boys' basketball coach after the school joined the Kentucky High School Athletic Association in 1989, at a ceremony tonight before the Royals play the Tomcats at Charles Stewart Gymnasium.

Dillow took over the Rose Hill program before it had a basketball facility on campus. The Royals practiced in the church gym and played games at Alumni Gym or the Ashland Armory.

One of Dillow's best players was Tommy Holbrook, who held the school's all-time scoring title until a player named O.J. Mayo showed up.

Holbrook, who is expected to be at the ceremony tonight, is the head coach for the Lawrence County girls' basketball team.

Rose Hill has had a long line of coaches but few did more than Dillow and, by that, I mean literally. He not only coached seventh grade through varsity, but he also loaded the concession stands for games, cleaned up the gyms afterward, and drove the bus on road trips. He was a one-man coaching band.

"It was fun," said Dillow. "I had great kids who were there for the right reason—to get a Christian education.

"They weren't there just for basketball."

Holbrook was Rose Hill's first 1,000-point scorer. He was a player that could have started for anybody in the 16th Region, Dillow said.

"His senior year, if he'd gone to Boyd County, they'd have gone to state," Dillow said. "He almost averaged a triple-double for us as a senior."

Dillow's first team at Rose Hill didn't have any seniors and Holbrook was among a group of sophomores who gained valuable playing time. The Royals went only 1 - 24 with a toughened-up schedule—including games with Ashland, Russell and Ironton—but Dillow saw some good signs.

"The first thing I told them when I got there was we were going to win," he said. "We had a lot of disadvantages back then. We practiced on a concrete floor with wooden backboards and then played games on wooden floors with glass backboards. It was difficult."

But true to Dillow's thinking, the Royals had seasons of 15 - 14 and 13 - 12 in his next two seasons. In 1991, Rose Hill looked poised to make it to the regional tournament for the first time but lost to Lawrence County—a team the Royals had beaten twice in the regular season—in the 64th District Tournament opener in Louisa. Ashland and Boyd County had drawn each other in the district first round that season.

"Tommy was sick with a temperature of about 103," Dillow said. "They ended up beating us by seven."

Rose Hill's first win over a public school came against Elliott County in Dillow's second season. "I remember J.R. Pack hitting them from way out," Dillow said. The Royals also defeated West Carter and Bath County that season.

But one of his most memorable games came when future UK player Chris Harrison scored 50 against the Royals while playing for Tollesboro.

"I thought he was Rex Chapman," Dillow said. "The guy could jump and score."

Rose Hill's team also included Brad Greene, Gary Crites, and Michael James, all who were in Holbrook's class. Greene is now the principal at Crabbe Elementary where Dillow teaches.

Dillow also rattled off the names of David Harris, Pat Daniels, Nathan Webb, Dewayne Mills, John Adams (who transferred to Ashland), and Charlie Pack (who transferred to Raceland) from those early Rose Hill teams.

In Dillow's first two seasons, he was actually the interim coach for David Seals, who was the acting head coach and athletic director. But everybody knew it was Dillow who was doing the coaching and, since Rose Hill wasn't much of a threat to the area powers in those days, there wasn't much said about it. Scott Walters and Dave Vanover were also assistant coaches.

"Those are fond memories," Dillow said. "There wasn't much pay for it but the memories are great."

Jerry Klaiber, the athletic director at Rose Hill, was on Russell's football coaching staff when Dillow went to school there in the early 1970s. Dillow was a first-team All-Stater who played center and noseguard and went on to earn a full scholarship at Morehead State University.

He was a captain at MSU his junior and senior years. Dillow was second in tackles in the Ohio Valley Conference as a junior, making all-OVC honors that year. His senior year, he was told to "take the pitch man" and saw his tackles decrease. "I just did what I was told," said Dillow, a defensive end.

Dillow also was fifth in the state in the shot put as a senior at Russell and played basketball for coach Marvin Meredith. After his college playing days, he became one of the most feared softball players in the area.

"In the twenty-six years I was at Russell, he was in the top three as far as best athletes—maybe No. 1," Klaiber said. "That's pretty good for a lineman. He's a marvelous person to be around."

It was during Dillow's senior year in 1970 when Russell beat Ashland 6 - 0 in Putnam Stadium—the first time the Red Devils won a football game against the Tomcats. The week before that game, Russell defeated McKell 17 - 0 for the first time since 1959. The Red Devils finished 8 - 2 - 1 under Lafe Walters that season.

Klaiber and Dillow later coached together at Russell and also officiated basketball together for a time.

"Joe Dillow is someone who made the most out of athletics," Klaiber said. "Religion is a big part of his life, too. He talked at a Super Bowl party that Steve Day's church had and Steve said he did a fantastic job."

HOWELL'S BIG NIGHT RECALLED
February 2009
. . .

Few players have ever had a better Senior Night than Ryan Howell did for Russell back in February 1993.

Howell went on a shooting spree that night against West Carter, scoring 53 to become Russell's all-time single game leader—a record that still stands today.

Howell, who is thirty-three and lives in Frankfort, will be back in Russell's gymnasium—now known as Marvin Meredith Gymnasium—to be honored for the achievement at halftime of tonight's Elliott County-Russell game.

Howell's fifty-three-point explosion came on some dynamite shooting. He was sixteen of twenty-four from the field and thirteen of seventeen from the foul line. Not known for long-range shooting, Howell connected on eight of eleven attempts from three-point range.

"I kind of got hot early and went with it," Howell said.

It was definitely one of those nights.

Led by Howell's gaudy total, the Red Devils raced past West Carter 105 - 70.

Ryan Howell fires a jumper against Ashland.

Howell's performance eclipsed Don Ratliff's school record of fifty-two against Catlettsburg back in 1961. Ratliff's record held for thirty-two years before some uncanny shooting from Howell knocked it down.

"Up to that point I'd never scored thirty points in a game," Howell said. "I was kind of joking with some of the guys that I was going to make sure I had over thirty that night. I told them it was time to get my name in the program." Howell nearly took care of that in the first half with twenty-eight, matching West Carter's total as the Red Devils took a 54 - 28 advantage.

The game was never in doubt but climbing to fifty-three points wasn't going to be easy—except that Howell wasn't missing and the crowd was buzzing and motivating.

He drilled five consecutive three-pointers in a four-minute span during the second quarter.

"It was one of those nights," said Ron Reed, who was Russell's boys coach at the time. "He was literally in a zone."

West Carter was helpless against Howell's onslaught.

Grady Lowe, West Carter's coach at the time, saw an early sign it was Howell's night.

"One of Howell's shots in the first quarter hit out off the rim, but somehow went back in," Lowe said back in '93. "I knew right then, look out."

The Russell crowd knew history was happening and got behind Howell with chants of "Ryno! Ryno!" as he closed in on the record. He tied it with 2:55 remaining and broke the mark on a free throw with 2:10 left.

Howell left the game to a standing ovation with fifty-one seconds remaining.

"At halftime I came out and a good friend of mine was yelling from the stands already," Howell said. "We also had another guy on our team, Pat Young, a starter, who had a career night, too. We scored 105 points and everybody got involved."

Howell said he knew about the school record because Russell listed everybody who had ever scored thirty or more points in a game in the program. He also is humbled by his part in Russell basketball history.

"I know there have been a lot of great players," said Howell, who said he sticks mostly with golf these days. "Other nights, if somebody else focused on it, they could have broken it. I always felt team accomplishments were more important than personal accomplishments."

Russell improved to 16 - 6 at the time and the Red Devils would go on to reach the 16th Region finals against Ashland, losing an overtime game at Summit Junior High School gymnasium that the Russell faithful say should never have happened.

A layup by Chris Hughes at the end of regulation that would have won the game was ruled to have come after the buzzer. Russell players, coaches, and fans will never believe it was the right call.

Russell made it into the regional tournament that season with a 45 - 44 victory over Greenup County in the opening game of the 63rd District Tournament at Raceland. The Red Devils also surprised Boyd County in the first round of the regional and then Rowan County in the semifinals.

So for many reasons, it was a season to remember, including Howell's game in February that will go down as one of the best individual performances in region history.

SPORTS HISTORIAN UNLOCKS ANDERSON
March 2009

• • •

Most everyone associated with sports in Ashland knows of James A. Anderson.

He coached the Tomcats basketball and football teams in the 1920s and '30s, including leading the basketball team to an unprecedented national championship in 1928.

The Tomcat gymnasium is named after Anderson, at the prompting of Ashland superfan David Payne.

It's no wonder Payne wanted Anderson's name on the building. Anderson led Tomcat basketball to a 187 - 59 record in nine seasons as head coach.

He also coached some football for the Tomcats back in the day, going 41 - 12 - 6 from 1922 - 27 before concentrating his efforts only on basketball.

But Randy Ross, an Arkansas sports historian who was researching the 100-year history of El Dorado High School Wildcat football, knew nothing of Anderson until he ran across his name as part of that school's legacy.

The 1928 national champion Tomcats were coached by James A. Anderson.

Anderson's roots were in Arkansas—he was born in Fort Smith, Arkansas, in 1888—and he worked as a principal and coach at El Dorado from 1915 - 17 until entering the Army for World War I.

Anderson graduated from Hendrix College in Conway, Arkansas, in 1915. It was a private methodist school. His father, James Sr., was a methodist pastor in Arkansas.

He coached the Hendrix Academy Bullpups—the college mascot was the Bulldogs and the academy was the Bullpups—for two years before settling in at Ashland.

Ross found plenty of information on Anderson in about a week, he said.

Through the Boyd County Public Library, which provided phone numbers, he even talked to Anderson's daughter, Carolyn Beimdiek, who is in St. Louis and a son, James Anderson III, who lives in Georgia.

"I am still amazed that in a little over a week not only did I find out who James Anderson was but I talked to his children," Ross said.

Ross also uncovered old photographs of Anderson with the Tomcat teams, including one with the five starters from the 1928 team where Ellis Johnson—Adolph Rupp's first All-American—is holding the ball.

One of the photos that Ross found from Anderson's college days had him with the nickname of "Goober." The note with the photo said "'Goober' was by far the smallest man on the team, but he never failed to deliver the goods. In fact he played star football all season. He has a quick eye, good head-work, and dodges like lightning. He outclassed his opponents in returning punts."

Another mini-profile said "Goober did not exactly take to his studies like a duck to water, but instead became interested in more worthy things—athletics." Anderson played baseball, football, and was a track sprinter at Hendrix College.

It also said he was the only pigeon-toed member of the class and liked to sing.

Ross found a clipping where Sgt. Anderson came home to see his parents in 1918 during World War I. He later was promoted to the rank of captain.

An article in the *Log Cabin Democrat* talked about how the Ashland 1928 team, along with Carr Creek, were part of a big feature in the Louisville *Courier-Journal* on April 16, 1928.

The newspaper invited Ashland and Carr Creek to Louisville to honor the teams for their showing in the national tournament in Chicago. It showed pictures of the coaches of the teams taking an airplane ride and also one of them seated in a box at the opening St. Paul-Louisville baseball game of the American Association.

The champions were guests of several civic clubs in Louisville, were introduced from the stage of a Louisville theatre and also introduced over radio station WHAS.

Anderson, in a radio interview, said "it was the beating beneath each white shirt of his Tomcat team and the echo of thousands of Kentuckians pleading for Ashland to fight for 'Ole Kentucky' and the southland that brought his team to the highest laurels in the United States."

After his coaching career ended, Anderson enjoyed life in Ashland as a principal at Coles Junior High, Putnam Junior High, and Ashland High School, along with operating a public golf course, before entering the insurance business.

The trophy-chair that went to the winners of the Kiwanis Bowl—the annual football game between Ashland's two junior highs—was also named after Anderson.

Anderson is a member of the National Basketball Hall of Fame and was the first Ashland Elks Sports Day recipient. He died on February 19, 1980.

"When I started out, all I knew was his name," Ross said.

Ross, a retired counselor at El Dorado High School, has been working on the history project for twenty years, he said. The school won 580 games in 100 seasons, including five state titles with the last one coming in 1958.

But Ross never figured that El Dorado and Ashland, Kentucky, would have such a link to the past.

Swing of a Lifetime
April 2009
• • •

Kevin Bair sometimes wonders what would have happened if that hanging curveball had fooled him.

But it didn't. Bair got all of it, and then some. The towering home run with two outs in the bottom of the seventh inning capped a miraculous four-run rally that made a state champion out of East Carter.

Twenty-five years later, they still talk about the home run in Grayson.

"There's a lot worse things to be remembered for," said J.P. Kouns, the Raiders' coach that season.

They probably remember in Cynthiana, too, the hometown of Harrison County, the stunned victim in the 10 - 9 state championship game loss to the Raiders in 1984 at Johnson Central High School.

With one mighty swing, Bair made history

While it hasn't exactly defined his life, it does give him a bit of celebrity status, especially in Carter County.

Bair will always be the player who hit the home run that won the state championship for the Raiders in '84.

"I think about it, I'm not going to say I don't," he said. "It comes back when I drive by the field. My son (Kyle) plays basketball for East Carter. I've been to Paintsville several times and always point out that Johnson Central field, which they've changed. He's not near as interested as I am but I make sure he knows about it. He doesn't want to talk about it as long as I do."

It's more than that magical home run that Kevin Bair remembers. The Raiders were a team built on good hitting, great fielding, and crafty pitching.

They were improbable champions, having entered the 15th Region Tournament as a district runner-up to Rowan County. East Carter outscored three foes, 22 - 1, in the regional tournament.

But the Raiders got on a roll, winning seven consecutive postseason games to claim the only team state championship in school history.

"It's definitely a blur," Bair said. "I remember bits and pieces of it. If I see a photo, I can remember that."

East Carter trailed Harrison County 6 - 0 in the fifth inning, but rallied for four runs to get back in the game. Then Harrison County scored three in the sixth to make it 9 - 4. Again, the Raiders rallied, this time for two runs, to make it 9 - 6.

But could they keep coming back?

"I know we thought we had a chance," Bair said. "We had the top of the lineup (coming) up."

Bair was the No. 6 hitter in the lineup, the designated hitter with a looping left-handed swing.

With one out, Cass Hall reached on an error and then Jamie

Swanagan walked. A popup to second base brought the Raiders down to their last out.

Steve Lambert laced a two-run double to right center field that barely eluded the diving centerfielder to make it 9 - 8.

Then it was Bair's turn to bat.

With the count 1 - 1, pitcher Billy Fisher tried to get ahead with a curveball. Bair didn't blink. He made him pay and the rest, as they say, is history.

"I can still see the pitch and remember hitting it," he said. "Hanging curveball. I knew when I hit it that it was gone."

Bair was a junior on the senior-dominated team that included Art Daugherty, the best three-sport athlete in East Carter history. Daughtery was the shortstop and Hall the second baseman, a keystone combination that led to many double plays.

The pitchers were the durable Swanagan, who won three games in eight days over the regional and sectional tournament, freshman Craig Collier, and senior Joey Thomas. At least, that's the only pitchers they needed in the postseason.

The rules were different in those days and it's a good thing for the Raiders, who finished the season 29 - 8.

"It was one of those special teams," Kouns said.

Those Raiders grew up together, played on the same Little League, Junior League, and Senior League teams. They played other sports, too. Daughtery was the quarterback and Bair the center on one of East Carter's best football teams in 1983.

Others on the team were basketball players. It was just a good collection of athletes who came together.

"Those guys were close-knit because they played together for years," Kouns said.

Kouns considers himself lucky to have won a state championship. He's in the Kentucky Baseball Coaches Hall of Fame but the state title is the major achievement.

"It's a once-in-a-lifetime deal when you can win that thing," he said.

SCAFF'S TIES TO PAGE STRONG
May 2009
• • •

Sam Scaff was sitting at the barber shop waiting for a haircut when he read the news about the passing of former heavyweight boxing champion Greg Page.

"I hadn't read the paper the day before," he said. "It hit me like a ton of bricks."

Scaff and Page have some history, both as competitors and friends.

When Scaff was growing up as a boxer in northeastern Kentucky, Page was being called the next Muhammad Ali in Louisville.

The two young fighters met in the state Golden Gloves championship in Louisville in 1978. Page won that fight and went on to win the National Golden Gloves championship, springboarding him to a highly anticipated professional career.

Scaff, who also turned pro in 1983, would meet up with Page later, too. This time he was on the same boxing card in Las Vegas, a Don King Show. "Everybody on the card was in the top ten except me," he said. "I was the only white guy in the whole show. Here's a kid from Flatwoods out in Las Vegas on this boxing card."

His next meeting with Page came as a corner man during his heavyweight championship bout with Gerrie Coetzee in South Africa in 1984. That's where Page was crowned as WBA heavyweight champion.

One of the national magazines had a photo of Page being lifted in the air by the 6-foot-7 Scaff, who was wearing a red jacket with Page written on it, in the middle of the ring.

"He was one of the most precious people to me as far as my whole career," Scaff said. "He treated me like family when we were in South Africa.

"Even when we fought as amateurs, before and after the fight we were friends. He was the closest thing to Muhammad Ali that will ever be."

Scaff said Page chose him to be a corner man and sparring partner because he had a similar style to Coetzee. "I sparred with him for six weeks," he said. "He requested me. That's how far back we went. He said the reason I sent for you was you reminded me of him."

The hard work paid off. Page had the title that at least used to be one of the most precious titles in all of sports.

Page's reign as champion only lasted five months before he lost to Tony Tubbs on points in a WBA title bout.

He boxed until 1993, took two years off and began fighting in 1996. It was a fight in 2001 that was his last. He suffered severe brain damage and was never the same. Page died at fifty.

His last fight was for only $1,500 and it took place at the Peels Palace in Erlanger, near Cincinnati, against Dale Crowe, an up-and-coming boxer who was twenty-four. Page went down after ten rounds and never got up. He was left with debilitating injuries.

Because of what happened to Page, who won a $1.2 million settlement in 2007 with Kentucky boxing officials over the lack of medical personnel at the 2001 fight, the state is now a safer place to box. That will be part of Page's legacy.

Scaff's pro career ended in 1991 after he lost the West Virginia state heavyweight belt. On the ride home, Scaff's daughter, Ashley, asked her father to quit fighting.

"When she said that, tears came to my eyes," he said. "I got beat by somebody who shouldn't have beaten me. I held that title for six years."

Scaff finished his pro career with a 32-12 record. He fought against four former world champions and countless boxers who ranked in the top ten. His most famous loss may have been one to a young Mike Tyson.

"I was on NBC, Sportsworld, ESPN, HBO, USA, and fought in Rupp Arena," Scaff said.

But he wouldn't recommend the pro route for the young boxers in the area. Scaff said he's glad that boxing seems to be taking on new life locally.

"Fighting in the (National Guard) armory was like fighting in Madison Square Garden," he said. "Doc Walsh was my amateur coach. He was one of the greatest men who ever walked the earth. He started me out as a twelve-year-old with the Westwood Boys Club.

"Amateur boxing teaches discipline. As far as these kids wanting to turn professional, no, don't do it. I would never tell an amateur boxer to turn professional. I know all the problems catching up to me."

Scaff was a standout athlete at Russell where he played a little bit of everything. During his sophomore year in 1972, coach Marvin Meredith told him he would let him out of practice early so he could go to boxing.

Scaff declined the offer and the Red Devils won the 16th Region title. He played basketball his junior and senior seasons. He also played football his senior year.

But as far as training went, nothing matched boxing.

"Boxing is the most demanding training sport there is as far as I'm concerned," he said. "When I won the West Virginia (heavyweight) title, I went twelve three-minute rounds. That's absolutely a lifetime."

Scaff said the news of Page's untimely death was difficult for him to take.

"We went back pretty far," he said.

1960s Was an Amazing Ashland Sports Era

April 2009

• • •

This year marks the fortieth anniversary of the end of an amazing streak when Ashland won three consecutive high school baseball state titles and came within a pair of 1 - 0 losses of winning five in a row.

Like anything else, there's always more to the story.

More to this story actually came before when the players that became Tomcats from 1965 to 1969 were growing up in Ashland.

They were the beneficiaries of organized baseball being in its stride.

The fathers of Little League baseball in Ashland, which eventually prompted other area towns into having similar programs, had a hand in making the Tomcats of 1966 - 68 state champions.

From 1961 to 1964, Ashland National Little League won a state title ('61) and finished runnerup ('62) and Ashland American Little League ('63) also won a state title—and came within one victory of making it to the Little League World Series.

Ashland's Babe Ruth League won the state championship in 1963 and lost in the state semifinals in 1964.

The players from those teams would be the key components of that Tomcat juggernaut from 1965 - 69.

Looking back on it, the 1960s as a decade is arguably the best days in Ashland sports history.

The Tomcat basketball team went to the state tournament the first three years of the decade, was state champion in '61, runnerup in '62 and a semifinalist in '69. Ashland won the '67 state football championship and the three state baseball titles.

They also shined in track and field, both boys and girls, with multiple individual championships.

While not yet sanctioned by the Kentucky High School Athletic Association, the Kittens had girls' basketball teams that rarely, if ever, lost.

Jack Ditty and Jim Fannin were two of the best tennis players in the state.

Those indeed were the days to be a Tomcat.

John Thomas, who played on Ashland's 1965 and '66 baseball teams, is a principal at a high school in Florida today.

"You think about things when you get older," Thomas said. "You never leave Ashland. I tell everybody that's where I'm from even though I've been here since 1976."

Thomas keeps up with his hometown through *The Independent* and has had his memory stirred since reading about Ashland recognizing the golden era of Tomcat baseball on May 15.

Thomas was in the 1966 graduating class where he played catcher for the undefeated state champion Tomcats.

The cornerstone of that team was fireballing lefty Billy Lynch, who Thomas called "a phenom."

"I played with him all the way through," Thomas said. "I was his catcher and it about killed me. The first game I caught him, my left hand swelled up around the thumb area. I said 'This is not going to work.' They got me a glove and special padding."

Thomas was a hard-throwing Little League pitcher who once plunked good buddy Tom Burnette three times in a single game. To this day, Thomas swears it was accidental.

"I could throw it like a bullet in Little League but I never knew where it was going," he said. "We were playing over around McGurk Street, that's where we grew up, and I told him 'You mess with me, I'm going to hit you.' I was with the Giants and he was with the Reds. It was never on purpose, although he swore up and down it was. If I was aiming at him, I'd have never hit him."

Unlike Thomas and his Little League days, the amazing thing about Lynch was the pinpoint control. "He could put it anywhere," he said. "He was easily throwing in the nineties in high school. It was kind of comical. He had a breaking curveball that would buckle you. I know because I was a left-handed batter."

Thomas said Lynch's father, Jack, taught both Billy and Bobby Lynch how to pitch and how to pitch well.

"Billy is the best I've ever seen and I've seen some good ones down here in Florida," he said. "Nobody was better than Billy."

Of course, he wasn't alone. John Sieweke was a star pitcher in '66 as well, along with Bobby Lynch.

"We knew we were good," Thomas said. "We'd had such good teams in Little League and Babe Ruth. That '66 team, going 25 - 0, is probably the best all-around team. It was a good group."

Ashland was 44 - 1 in 1965 and '66 combined. Of course, state titles followed in '67 and '68 before a 1 - 0 loss to Owensboro in '69 ended one of the best runs in state history.

Of the players on the roster from 1966 to 1969, a dozen received college scholarships (for baseball or other sports) and one was drafted:

- Billy Lynch (1966), drafted by the Indians.
- Billy Workman (1966), signed at UK and played four years.
- Benny Spears (1966), signed to play basketball at UK.
- John Thomas (1966), signed at UK, transferred to Georgetown to play football and baseball for four years.
- Don Lentz (1967), signed at UK and played four years.
- Wayne Workman (1967), signed at UK and played four years.
- Toby Tolbert (1967), signed track scholarship at Eastern Kentucky University.
- Ellis Childers (1967), signed basketball scholarship at Union College and played four years.
- Bobby Lynch (1968), signed basketball scholarship at Alabama and played basketball for four years and baseball one year.
- Tim Huff (1969), signed baseball scholarship to Cocoa Beach (Florida) Junior College.
- David Staton (1969), signed baseball scholarship to Eastern Kentucky University.
- Bobby Ison (1969), signed baseball scholarship to Morehead State.
- Bo Carter (1969), signed baseball scholarship to Millsaps College.

That list gives you an idea of what a special group of athletes it was that came through Ashland from 1966 - 69.

It would certainly have to be considered a Golden Era for the Tomcats.

Huff Had Right Stuff
May 2009

• • •

The pitching heroics of Billy and Bobby Lynch with the 1960s Ashland Tomcats are well-chronicled.

And, certainly, without the Lynches the Tomcats would have never won three consecutive state championships from 1966 - 68. Billy was the ace in '66 and Bobby in '67 and '68.

But a left-hander named Tim Huff had the stuff of champions, too.

It was Huff who outdueled McKell's Don Gullett in the 1969 regional tournament in Morehead, winning a 1 - 0 battle as major league scouts crowded the stands to watch the McKell fireballer throw.

What they saw that day was a gritty performance from Huff, whose win in that game put the Tomcats in the region championship later that afternoon where they swamped John's Creek.

"It's funny, probably only ten people watched the game but to hear it today, thousands saw it," he said. "A lot of people think it was in the park, but it was at Morehead. And a lot of people think it was the finals, but it was the semifinals."

And a lot of people think it was Bobby Lynch who outpitched

Gullett. But it was Huff. Lynch had already graduated and was playing basketball for Alabama.

Huff remembers the preview before the state tournament started.

"I think the world of Bobby Lynch, but I remember the article in the (Lexington) paper and the headline was 'Can Lynchless Tomcats win it again?' That fired us up. We were all like, 'yeah, we can do it,'" he said.

Ashland made it to the finals for the fourth consecutive season but lost a 1 - 0 decision to Owensboro. The game's only run came when Huff threw a ball into centerfield trying to pick off a runner.

"I relive that every moment of my life," Huff said. "I didn't get over it; I learned to live with it. I have to live with that error the rest of my life."

While that may be a memory for Huff, those who followed Tomcat baseball in those days remember how competitive a pitcher he was and how wicked his curveball broke.

"I had the ballplayers behind me," Huff said. "If I just threw it over the plate, the defense was there."

Ashland's teams were so good they even overshadowed Gullett, whose McKell teams never beat the Tomcats in that era.

"People always said if he was on our team how much (more) publicity he would have got," Huff said. "They had some good ballplayers besides him, too. Russell was our big rival. They were good. We had some good battles with them. We'd all hang out together after the games."

Huff was in the starting rotation for three years, two of those being championship teams. Back then, freshmen seldom if ever made the varsity teams.

"Johnny Mullins played as a freshman, but in my graduating class, none of us played (as freshmen)," Huff said.

Even today when Huff drives past Central Park the memories of days gone by are fresh.

"You can't help but go back," he said. "It's not just the boys you played with but the families, too. We made a lot of good relationships.

"We just loved to play the game."

Coach Herb Conley gives direction to Rob Ratliff. THE
INDEPENDENT

MEMORIES OF JAWS: ASHLAND'S 1975 TEAM
August 2005

• • •

Thirty years ago, one of Ashland's most memorable football teams embarked on a season that's still discussed today.

The 1975 JAWS team, which devoured fourteen consecutive opponents before falling to St. Xavier 20 - 0 in the Class 4A overall championship game in Louisville, is beloved in Tomcat history.

"I don't have favorite teams or favorite players," said Herb Conley, who was the Tomcats' head coach from 1968 - 76. "But that team, more than any other, is one I hear the most about. Not only here but guys I run into throughout the state. They say 'Oh, we remember that '75 team. They called them JAWS.'"

Maybe the nickname was part of what made the team so memorable.

Looking back now, Conley admits putting a nickname on a team or defense can be a gamble.

Back in '75, Conley had taken his family to Myrtle Beach for some fun in the sun. His sons would venture out further into the ocean than either Herb or Janice, his wife, liked.

"I saw the movie (JAWS) was on and I took them to that movie," he said. "After they watched that, I didn't have to worry about them. They wouldn't even put a foot in the ocean."

Conley said it was in the middle of two-a-days that summer that he relayed the story to his coaching staff.

"We'd let the kids get in the swimming pool (at the high school) and swim to cool off," he said. "We were all in there, getting cooled down, and I told them that story."

Bill Tom Ross, one of Conley's assistant coaches, came up with the idea of nicknaming the defense JAWS.

Conley wasn't completely sold on the idea.

"Bill Tom said 'Let's tell them now.' But wanted to wait. I said we'd tell them at practice tomorrow that there was a possibility we'd name our defensive unit JAWS. I told them I'm not going to name a team something so vicious and then go out and play like a bunch of sissies."

Conley waited until after Ashland's first game—a 47 - 14 victory over Johnson Central—to officially give the team the nickname that would become its calling card.

"You have to be careful about those kind of things," he said. "You name a defense something like that and they give up forty points and everybody would laugh you out of town."

Once the nickname was installed, Ross went to work. He went to the band director so they could learn the JAWS theme; talked to the cheerleaders and basically made sure everybody knew.

"Those kind of things can backfire on you," Conley said. "Luckily for us, it didn't. Everybody picked up on it, even outside of Ashland. The Lexington paper called us JAWS, the Huntington paper, all the television stations. It was something else."

Part of the 1975 team's mystique is its nickname.

"When people talk about that team, they call it the JAWS team," Conley said. "I don't remember a team as beloved by the student body and community as that one."

The one trait that the 1975 team had that was similar to Conley's better teams was the co-

Dougie Paige is flanked by Tomcat head coach Herb Conley (right) and assistant coach Bill Tom Ross (left).

hesiveness of the unit. He said it was the same for the 1967 state champions (where he was an assistant coach) and the 1971 and 1972 teams.

"All four of those teams loved to play and hit," Conley said.

Even though the 1975 team isn't "officially" a state champion, at least according to Kentucky High School Athletic Association records, most of Ashland considers it a state championship team.

The landscape was different in Kentucky high school football thirty years ago. The Class 4A teams in Jefferson County basically had their own playoff to determine a Louisville "champion." Meanwhile, the rest of the state's 4A teams played for the "at-large" championship.

The JAWS team started its playoff trek with a 36 - 6 victory over Dixie Heights, then defeated Lexington Lafayette 21 - 6 to set up a battle with Paducah Tilghman for the at-large championship.

The Tomcats were down 7 - 6 with only 1:30 remaining when Gary Thomas, then a junior, went eighty-five yards for the game-

Some members of the 1975 Ashland JAWS team line up during the 25-year anniversary at Putnam Stadium.

winning touchdown. Thomas, whose son Matt is a sophomore on this year's Ashland team, ran for 1,754 yards and twenty touchdowns that season.

Conley knew going into the overall 4A championship game with St. Xavier that it would take an amazing effort. He also sensed a team that was tiring after six months in pads.

"I thought we had a chance," he said. "The only thing I was worried about was the last two ballgames we'd played, against Lafayette and Paducah, we weren't as sharp as we'd been all year. I thought we were getting tired."

St. Xavier, a team with more than 100 players, was waiting for the Tomcats in Louisville. When St. X came out before the game, there were enough players to encircle the entire field.

"They kept fresh people in the whole game," Conley said. "Our kids were pounding but our kids were tired. We couldn't stay with them."

Ashland opened the championship game with a march inside St.

Xavier's ten but an offside penalty stalled the drive and then a short field goal attempt was missed.

"People told me after the game that we moved the ball better on St. X than anybody did all year," he said. "A lot of people thought us not scoring was a big factor in us not winning."

Ashland trailed only 6 - 0 at the half but St. Xavier's numbers eventually wore down the Tomcats.

After the game, Conley said it was quiet in the dressing room except for some sobbing.

"I think it really hurt them bad," he said. "I've never forgot going inside the dressing room after the ballgame. Everybody was empty inside. It was devastating to see them. We all went down thinking we were better and could beat them."

Even though Ashland fell to St. Xavier, the team's legend has grown throughout the past thirty years. The players from the squad have remained close, too.

"That team did have a lot of togetherness, a lot of mental toughness," Conley said. "Those guys still today talk Tomcat football. They love it."

The quarterback, Chuck Anderson, was also a middle linebacker and one of the hardest-hitting players in Tomcat history. He's now a general in the United States Army.

Anderson's bone-jarring block on an unsuspecting Bryan Station player in the second week of the season led to a punt return for a touchdown by Rick Sang and an eventual 22 - 12 victory over the top-ranked Defenders, serving notice that JAWS was here to stay.

The Tomcats also did something that's become highly unusual, defeating Ironton, with Ohio State signee Kenny Fritz, 14 - 0 in Putnam Stadium. Ashland captured the Tri-State Athletic Conference thanks to

Herb Conley at the Ashland JAWS 25-year reunion in 2000.

a 12 - 6 overtime victory over Huntington High in old Fairfield Stadium.

The backfield had speed galore with Thomas, Jeff Slone, and Greg Jackson. The receivers were Sang and little Dougie Paige, two of the best downfield blockers around. The power of Jay Shippey at fullback won't be forgotten nor will the names of linemen Terry Bell, Yancey Ramey, Casey Jones, Raymond Hicks, Terry Lewis, and David Early.

It was also a special time for a Tomcat coach who just appreciates being part of the tradition.

"I'm proud I had the opportunity to coach there, play there, and live in this community," he said.

For 15-Year-Old, Mayo Leaves Huge Legacy
April 2003

• • •

O.J. Mayo has left the building—and the 16th Region.

There's probably some dancing in the streets around the area about Mayo's departure from Rose Hill Christian School.

But Mayo has left his stamp on the region after only two short years. He brought more national attention to our area than any player in history. Two years ago, ESPN cameras followed his every move for about half the season. He has been on CNN and appeared in national publications like *Sports Illustrated* and *USA Today*.

His departure shouldn't be that much of a surprise. How many have predicted that he wouldn't be long for Rose Hill? It happened to be a steppingstone for a fifteen-year-old who will be leaving as an area legend. Mayo's brightest days are surely ahead.

Twenty years from now, they will recall the O.J. Mayo years at Rose Hill.

He was the reason the Royals had such an enormous fan following the past two years. They came in flocks to watch him play.

There are many "O.J. moments" from the last two years. The last one came in the State Tournament's opening round when he split two defenders and raced in for a one-handed dunk to end the half against South Laurel.

Locally, his biggest moment was the three-pointer he hit at the buzzer to beat Ashland in his first varsity season, when he was a seventh-grader. That game, as much as any, fueled an Ashland-Rose Hill rivalry that burned hot the past two years. The Royals and Tomcats split six games during the Mayo Years.

While Mayo's leaving obviously damages Rose Hill's basketball team, it also takes some excitement and notoriety from the rest of the area—and the state hoops scene for that matter. We may never see another player with as much potential, as much star power, even in an area where high school basketball is darn good.

Mayo will take his skills to Cincinnati where he's expected to reunite with Bill Walker, an athletic 6-foot-5 forward who played at Rose Hill for almost half of last season. Walker's mother withdrew him from the school on the day the team was leaving for the All "A" Classic State Tournament because Rose Hill refused to move him from ninth grade to eighth grade. Walker is currently enrolled as an eighth-grader at North College Hill Middle School.

The Walker-Mayo tandem will make any high school team anywhere a state contender. It will be interesting to follow their progress through the years.

Mayo and his father, Kenny Ziegler, publicly said he would be coming back to Rose Hill next season. Apparently, circumstances changed or maybe they just didn't want to show their hand when asked about O.J.'s future at the State Tournament last month.

Ziegler was critical of Rose Hill's handling of Mayo and even said the school wasn't full committed to basketball.

Rose Hill's O.J. Mayo soars to the basket in the 16th Region Tournament in Morehead against Raceland in 2003. JOHN FLAVELL/THE INDEPENDENT

If anything, Rose Hill has been too committed to basketball. A lot of what Rose Hill did in basketball was with Mayo's future in mind.

Coach Jeff Hall made a schedule based on the assumption that Mayo was returning. It included a trip to the King of the Bluegrass in Louisville where the O.J.-led Royals were a big hit last season.

So now what happens at Rose Hill?

The Royals obviously won't be the team they've been the past two seasons. Not only has Mayo withdrawn, but promising eighth-graders Michael Taylor and Jamaal Williams also left the school and enrolled at Cammack Junior High in Huntington this week. How many more will follow Mayo out the door?

The Royals' emergence from doormat to region champion was a transformation that happened almost too quickly. There was no time to build a foundation. It came overnight and it could fall overnight.

321

Rose Hill won't close down its basketball program because Mayo is leaving town but it will be scaled back from what it has been the past two seasons. Of course, there was always some baggage that came with having such a high-profile player. At times it became almost a circus-like atmosphere at the Royals' games. Truth be told, some of that won't be missed.

Many of the players on Rose Hill's roster the past three years, including Mayo, didn't even live on this side of the river—a fact that didn't sit well with detractors. Because the players weren't really from this area, and didn't come up through Rose Hill's program, they also didn't have knowledge of the region as a whole or much school loyalty.

Until school starts in August, it's really hard to predict what will happen with Rose Hill basketball next season. There could be more shuffling to come, both in and out.

But the O.J. Mayo Era at Rose Hill, short and sweet as it was, is over.

WEBB'S DAD OVERWHELMED
April 2003

• • •

Philip Webb arrived at the Shea Stadium parking lot three hours and forty minutes before game time. They hadn't even let security into the park yet.

Philip, the father of Arizona Diamondback rookie Brandon Webb, wanted to savor every second of his son's first major-league start.

Philip paced the pavement hours before the game, rolling over the many scenarios in his head.

"You know, if he gives them five innings, just five innings, that'll be good enough," he reasoned.

The rookie from Ashland did better than Dad expected—and better than the Diamondbacks' organization expected—in winning his first major-league start with seven innings of scoreless, three-hit pitching. He also struck out ten.

It was the kind of performance a father doesn't even dare to dream.

"I can't believe it," he said, numb from the experience. "It's amazing."

Webb was amazing in the place where the Amazin' Mets play baseball. A wicked sinkerball held the Mets hostage in their own ballpark.

While Brandon was working his magic from the mound, his father was sitting in the stands, nervously tapping his leg and listening to the game on Mets' radio. The broadcasters were heaping praise on his son.

"This twenty-three-year-old right-hander from Ashland, Kentucky has absolutely got a sinkerball to die for," said one of the announcers.

"Batter after batter, pitch after pitch, they're pounding the ball into the ground," said the other.

There was a buzz in Shea Stadium about the rookie from Ashland.

Even Philip Webb, who is the picture of calm and cool, was starting to get a little excited.

"YES!" he yelled after Mike Piazza grounded into a double play in the fourth inning—the only inning that his son was really in any trouble at all. "That's poise, that's all there is to it."

In the seventh inning, Webb struck out Mo Vaughn for the second time to run his total to nine for the game. He then had a 2 - 2 count on Raul Gonzalez.

"I know I'm getting greedy, but I'd like to have ten (strikeouts)," his father said.

Floyd Paris, the pastor of Unity Baptist Church who made the trip to New York with Webb, took off his baseball cap and said: "I'll pray about it."

But it was the Mets who never had a prayer against Webb. On the next pitch, Gonzalez went down swinging and No. 10 was in the books.

Dad has his reason to be proud of a son who he has helped reach the major leagues. He would never take any credit for what has transpired with Brandon but anyone who knows this family, knows the truth. Brandon Webb wouldn't be anywhere near a major-league field today if not for his father.

When the game was over, Brandon walked off the field and through the tunnel to the Diamondbacks' clubhouse. There waiting for him was his father.

They exchanged handshakes and hugs, just like it was a Little League game instead of the biggest game of their lives.

Webb's Parents Watch Scoreless Streak
August 2007

• • •

The parents of Arizona Diamondback pitching sensation Brandon Webb don't like to miss a pitch their son throws.

Especially when he's throwing zeros in record fashion.

Webb, who has thrown forty-two consecutive scoreless innings, resumes his chase for Orel Hershiser's record of fifty-nine scoreless innings tonight in Phoenix when the Diamondbacks play the Milwaukee Brewers at Chase Field.

Phil and Dreama Webb are crossing their fingers, not just for their son but also for electricity.

Separated by 1,700 miles—the distance between Ashland and Phoenix—Phil and Dreama Webb rely on television and satellite dishes to follow their son's every pitch. And with a scoreless streak on the line, every pitch counts—literally.

But last Friday, one day after the storm that pounded the Boyd County-Greenup County area and knocked out electricity to nearly 6,000, the Webbs found themselves in the dark—still.

In the dark meant no television to watch Brandon, who took his thirty-three-inning scoreless streak into Atlanta to face one of the National League's best-hitting teams. Just going to a friend's house wouldn't do it because the game wasn't on cable television—TBS showed only one game of the three-game series between the Braves and Diamondbacks last weekend.

So Phil and Dreama, along with Brandon's uncle and aunt (Larry and Beverly Carr, who live in Ashland and were also without power), crowded around a seventeen-inch computer screen at Brandon's home in Boyd County. Their noses pressed against the screen, they watched another masterpiece—Brandon's third consecutive shutout, running his streak to an amazing forty-two scoreless innings—through the Carr's membership on MLB.TV.

Phil and Dreama have the MLB Extra Innings package. His father not only nervously watches every game on a sixty-inch big screen but also burns a DVD for Brandon.

"To think that it's been forty-two innings is kind of mind-boggling," Phil said on Monday.

Webb's confidence level has never been higher, his father said. Brandon has drawn compliments from some of baseball's best players.

At the All-Star Game in San Francisco, home run king Barry Bonds struck up a conversation with Webb, according to Phil.

"Barry came over and said 'Hey Webby, I think you're dodging me.' Brandon said 'I think the last time we played, and I pitched, you didn't play. I think you're dodging me.' Then Barry told him 'Webby, I want to tell you something. No matter what anybody ever tells you, you're a great pitcher,'" Phil said.

Then in Atlanta on Sunday, pitcher John Smoltz spoke to Webb before the game, Phil said. "He said 'Listen Webby. I've been doing this a long time and what you're doing is absolutely incredible.'"

Words like that from Bonds and Smoltz have done nothing but further stoke the confidence of last year's National League Cy Young Award winner. Webb goes into tonight's game with a 13 - 8 record and 2.63 ERA. He's also second in the NL, with 160 strikeouts. The forty-two-inning scoreless streak has put Webb's face back in the national spotlight.

But the unassuming Webb has stayed true to himself.

A story on the Diamondbacks' Web site described this moment. In the ninth inning of the game with the Braves, Webb was on deck when some Braves' fans in the front row began talking to him. "Aren't you getting tired yet?" Webb told them he was feeling good and they told him they thought he was pitching well, to which he said, "Thank you very much."

All that happened in front of D-Backs CEO Jeff Moorad and team president Derrick Hall.

"Are you kidding me?" Hall was quoted as saying on the Web site. "That tells you right there what kind of person Brandon Webb is."

Webb is the first pitcher since Roger Clemens in 1998 to throw three consecutive shutouts. Phil Webb said the three complete games in a row impressed him the most.

Of course, Webb and his parents know the streak won't last forever. But being on the same list as Hershiser, Don Drysdale, Bob Gibson, Walter Johnson, and Carl Hubbell is pretty humbling stuff.

"It's kind of surreal," his father said. "To see his name up there with Bob Gibson. I remember going to Riverfront Stadium to watch Gibson and (Don) Gullett pitch. Never in my wildest imagination could I have dreamed something like this would happen."

Webb's streak almost ended in the ninth inning of Friday's game with the Braves when Willie Harris drove a grooved fastball to deep right center. His father said Brandon told him he thought the streak was over.

"He said 'Well, I threw that and I knew he hit it good. I turned around and thought, 'Well, that was a good streak I had.' Then I saw C.Y. (Chris Young) under it out there," Phil said. "Whether it's a no-hitter or a perfect game like (Randy) Johnson threw, you need some luck. You need some luck just to win games."

Tonight against the Brewers, Webb will certainly have to pitch carefully to Prince Fielder—the NL leader with thirty-nine home runs. Fielder went 5-for-7 against Webb last season, including a home run.

Phil said the scoreless streak has provided even more unforgettable moments for Brandon's family and friends in what is becoming a storybook career. At Ashland Sporting Goods, owner David Payne has put up Webb's baseball vitals—record, ERA and scoreless streak—on a sign outside the store.

"You know how much God's blessed him," Phil said of his son. "We're just waiting on Wednesday."

And hoping the power stays on.

Reliford to Receive Sports Day Honor

June 2008

• • •

There's no doubt how Charlie Reliford feels about his hometown.

His umpire peers in major league baseball call him "Mr. Ashland" for his frequent references of which he seems to have no shortage.

"I wear them out with it," Reliford said. "I don't know if this is a good one or a bad one but we were in the locker room the other day and there was something showing on TV about Charles Manson. I say 'Hey, did you know Manson's parents are from Ashland?' Two of the guys about fell out of their chairs. They were like 'Oh, come on.' I said, 'It's true. I don't make this stuff up.'"

During a recent Fox national Saturday telecast, Reliford was wearing a microphone while umpiring second base.

"It was a series with the Diamondbacks (and Giants) a couple of weeks ago," Reliford said. "I was miked and I knew I was miked. I kept talking to Arizona's second baseman every half inning, telling him about all the people from Ashland. 'Did you know O.J. Mayo played basketball at a small school in Ashland? Brandon (Webb) is from

Ashland, Don Gullett, used to pitch for the Reds and Yankees, he was from that area, too...There was a Legion team in Portsmouth—I figure every other big city in a forty-mile radius (of Ashland) counts—that had Al Oliver and Larry Hisle on it.' Every half inning, I kept them coming."

Then, after the game, Reliford asked Fox producer Glenn Diamond how much was used in the telecast. "He said 'We didn't use a thing.' I was like, 'Oh, man.'"

Reliford, one of Ashland's favorite sons and a highly regarded nineteen-year veteran MLB umpire, will be the honoree for the 34th annual Elks Sports Day next month. Tickets are $30 for the reception and banquet at the Elks Lodge on July 18 - 19. Longtime Ashland Tomcat radio voice Dicky Martin will be the speaker.

For Reliford, the Sports Day honor is a humbling one.

"I've called two World Series, which is the top of the mountain in the baseball world," Reliford said. "But this and the Distinguished Tomcat Award (which he won in 2000) are above that."

Reliford's professional career as an umpire has kept him from attending Elks Sports Day activities in the past. He had to obtain special permission from MLB for the time off to receive the honor.

"Baseball is very finicky about letting us off for an event," Reliford said. "It's supposed to be a family event. When I talked to them about this they said 'That's not a family event.' I told them I didn't ask off for my ten-year, fifteen-year or twenty-year reunions. I'm not one of those guys who asks off a lot, but a lot of people who will be sitting in that room are my family or are like my family. I approached my boss and told him this may or may not sound like a big deal to you, but it's a big deal to me. They agreed to let me come."

Reliford said having his photograph on the Elks Wall of Fame with the past honorees is unimaginable.

Charlie Reliford has been a major league umpire since 1991. He's also been touting Ashland as one of the world's greatest places ever since. STEPHANIE CLARK

"I look up there and look at the wall itself and can't believe I'll be up there," he said. "Bo McMillen gave me my first job at the Y, which led me into umpiring softball and baseball and that eventually guided me to where I am today. People like Herb Conley and so many others up there who have been so important in this community."

Reliford graduated No. 1 in the Harry Wendlestedt Umpire School in 1982 and became the school's chief instructor in 1987. Twenty-two of the sixty-eight current major league baseball umpire staff trained under him. "As I get a little bit older, those are numbers I'm really proud of," he said.

Reliford, regarded as one of the top rules umpires in baseball, has had a highly decorated career that includes assignments in the 2000 and 2004 World Series, the 1996 and 2007 All-Star Game, three Division Championship Series and three League Championship Series.

He and his wife, Laurie, have a daughter, Logan, and reside in Bradenton, Florida.

Reliford is a 1974 graduate of Paul G. Blazer High School, a former YMCA director, and a proud Ashland native. Before every game he umpires, Reliford said he prays "to please not do anything that would embarrass the folks back home."

Mission accomplished.

HOST OFFERED THE MOST
August 2009

• • •

Of all the interviews that were done for the "Ashland's Field of Dreams" documentary—and there was about seventy-five in all—one stood out above the rest.

Jim Host was simply mesmerizing.

Host, the communications mogul who started Host Communications in Lexington, was so eloquent, so comfortable, with the tape rolling on a summer morning in Morehead City Park back in June. That's no surprise, given his public persona and time behind a microphone.

There wasn't any prodding with Host. He was an interviewer's dream, at least when it came time to talking about one of his favorite subjects—Central Park and baseball in Ashland.

"He wasn't just the best one, he's head and shoulders above any other," said Dave Carter, who produced the documentary. "I asked him two questions the whole time and he gives me a half hour."

That's not to say some of the others weren't compelling and emotional interviews because they were. Some of their words will send chills down your spine the size of a baseball.

But Host delivered the most.

Host has deep roots to Central Park and baseball in Ashland. He credits the men who taught him the game for giving him the opportunities toward making him the person he is today.

And he's forever grateful, not only to those men but to the game itself, and to Ashland's back yard—Central Park.

Host didn't come to Ashland until he was in the eighth grade and spent only five years here before going on to the University of Kentucky as one of the first scholarship baseball players in school history.

But all these years later, Host still considers Ashland home and Central Park the best place he ever knew.

"I really think kids today miss a great deal without having what I had—being able to play whenever I wanted to play," he said. "Kids today are forced to play. I only wanted to play baseball. I learned everything about the game."

It was when Host was in ninth grade that he first played organized baseball in Ashland. It grew from there.

"My sophomore year in high school, they organized a team in the summer," Host said. "We had some great summer teams. All I wanted to do was play baseball and pitch."

Marvin Hall watched Host pitch and found someone who was willing to listen. He molded Host into a pitcher that would not only be good enough to pitch in college but also in professional baseball before a shoulder injury cut short his career.

"Marvin Hall taught me to pitch," Host said. "He worked hundreds of hours with me. What he did for me can never be repaid. He taught me how to throw a curveball the right way. It was all volunteers (coaching). No words can express my feelings for him."

Jim Host credits his upbringing in Ashland, including baseball in Central Park, for his lifetime of success. MARK MAYNARD

Like hundreds of others in Ashland, Host also expressed how he owed a debt of gratitude to Bo McMillen and Ernie Chattin, the YMCA mentors who paved the way for so many. They hired Host to work at the YMCA for sixty cents an hour, forty hours a week, so he could have money to purchase books.

Host was in Ashland during the early 1950s when the Tomcats ruled in basketball. The 1953 and 1954 teams were two of the best in history. Host was a manager on the basketball team for fiery George Conley, who knew how to use fear as a learning tool. Host loved basketball and "could shoot really well" but baseball was his passion. Conley knew that too but invited Host to be a manager for the basketball team.

It was a life-changing move because the lessons he learned from George Conley were invaluable. They were lessons about toughness and never backing down. He learned respect and how to do what you were told in no uncertain terms. "I learned words I never knew existed," Host said.

Cecil Bush and Emmor Evans were two others he mentioned who were instrumental in Host's development as a baseball player. His big break came when he was playing for a semi-pro team and outdueled lefty Steve Hamilton 2 - 0 in Paintsville. That opened so many doors, including one to become the first full baseball scholarship to UK. He didn't know it until years later, but it was Ernie Chattin who had made sure Lancaster was there to watch him pitch.

"Ernie Chattin had called him and said 'You've got to see this kid pitch.' I never knew that's why Harry was there (until later in life)," Host said.

Wayne Blackburn, a scout for the Tigers, was there too and offered Host $25,000 to sign in 1955.

"My dad said to me 'You're going to be the first one (in the family to graduate from college),'" Host said. "You're going to college."

He already had a scholarship offer from Eastern Kentucky, a half each from baseball coach Turkey Hughes to pitch for the Colonels and basketball coach Paul McBrayer to be a manager. But now UK was offering a full ride, something they'd never done before in baseball.

"I'd cut off my left arm to go to UK," Host said. "I told Turkey Hughes what had happened and he understood."

He went from UK, where he would graduate, and then tried pro ball in the Chicago White Sox organization before a shoulder injury stopped his career in its tracks. It was over, just like that.

As Host reminisced, his thoughts kept drifting back to Central Park, back to a time and place that will remain special to him forever. "The heritage of Central Park and the heritage of baseball in Central Park is something else," he said.

Host never did it for the glory, but for the love of the game. He once pitched a no-hitter and his parents didn't know about it until they read about it in the newspaper. "It was no big thing," Host said. "I never thought I was better than anybody else."

Anybody who ever played in Central Park will feel the tug on their heartstrings when watching the documentary that has its world premier on Friday at the Paramount Arts Center.

The film is about the boys who played there in the 1950s, the fathers who brought organized baseball to this town and how the baseball landscape in Ashland was forever changed for the better because of it.

And it shows how Central Park has been a large part of the equation for the youth in Ashland from then to now.

"You're talking about something that's very emotional to me,"

Host said, his voice cracking, while talking about CP-1. "Something in me always remains here."

DADDY GETS TO CADDY
August 2009
• • •

Who's your caddy?

How about Loren Ledford?

The Ashland doctor will be carrying the bag for fellow Kentuckian Kenny Perry today in a pro-am event at the Barclays in Jersey City, New Jersey.

Ledford earned that right through an auction on eBay a couple of weeks ago that goes to support a charity—"Caddies for a Cure"—that fights leukemia.

"I was thumbing around on eBay a couple of weeks ago and typed in Kenny Perry," Ledford said. "There was an offer to caddy for him. I didn't think it was real. I put in a bid and the next thing I know, Bernard Langer's caddy was calling me and telling me I'd won and would be the caddy for Kenny Perry in the pro-am."

Ledford was elated. He's always been a fan of Perry, who was born in Elizabethtown and lives in Franklin.

"I've followed Perry throughout his whole career," Ledford said. "He's been a favorite player of mine, basically because he's from my home state."

Perry, who turned forty-nine on August 10, is having the best season of his career. He's won twice and been in the top 10 seven times in twenty tournaments. Perry is fourth in the FedEx Cup point standings and finished second in the Masters, losing a two-stroke lead with two holes to play.

"It was exhilarating and then disappointing," Ledford said.

So will he bring up the Masters today?

"Absolutely not," Ledford said. "I think we'll talk Ryder Cup or maybe Kentucky basketball and leave it at that."

Smart caddy.

Ledford will look the part. He's already been sent a shirt and hat and the other entire "caddy garb."

He was also given a mini-tutorial about the do's and don'ts in the caddy world.

"It's mostly etiquette," he said. "You're not allowed to wear golf shoes. It has to be flat-soled tennis shoes. It was things like being respectful of the other golfers in the group. Like don't run in front of them because you got excited when your player hits a good shot. It's pretty much common sense and courteous type of things."

That the Ashland caddy can handle.

He's also supposed to get a last-second crash course from Perry's caddy.

"It'll kind of be fun and educational," Ledford said. "Hopefully he'll have a good sense of humor and we'll have a fun day."

Langer's caddy told him he could offer Perry as much advice as he wanted. Just don't expect Kenny to take it.

Perry will be having fun but he'll also be preparing for the first of four tournaments that will determine the FedEx Cup champion. The top 125 golfers were invited to a four-tournament playoff and a certain number of golfers will be cut each week.

Ledford's group will also include three businessmen or sports personalities. "It could be Eli Manning or (pro) hockey players or Donald Trump. Who knows?" he said.

No matter. Ledford will have his own gallery cheering for him. His wife Amy and their two children, Preston and Bethany, will be following the caddy's every move today.

The Ledfords are staying for Thursday's opening round before coming back to Ashland. "Amy and the kids have to get back for school and I have to do some work, too" he said.

After all, a donation to caddy for one of the best players on the PGA Tour can't be cheap. Loren didn't reveal exactly how much he paid. "It was a nice donation that will help the little children with leukemia."

And help this daddy become caddy for a day.

MORE RICH HISTORY FROM ARMCO FIELD
July 2009
• • •

For the past few weeks, I've written about the old Armco Field and some of the amazing events that took place there.

The other day, Jim Graham gave me a Tomcat program from a 1932 Ashland High School game that was perhaps the greatest ever played there when Erie East, Pennsylvania, defeated Ashland 19 - 13 to snap a seven-year winning streak that dated back to 1925.

It was the Tomcats' fourth game of the 1932 campaign and everybody knew that Erie East posed the biggest threat to the streak in years. They had snapped a Steubenville, Ohio, win streak in 1931 and a week before coming to Ashland snapped Campbell Memorial's twelve-game winning streak.

Ashland had graduated four linemen, two who were named All-Southern by a Florida newspaper, and two from the backfield off a 10 - 0 1931 team.

But winning was what the Tomcats did better than anybody else.

Brady Black, the sports editor of the *Ashland Daily Independent*, had never seen the Tomcats lose in his six years of covering them. Yet, on the day before the Saturday afternoon game, Black wrote in his column—called "Freelance Sports"—that Erie would defeat Ashland by a score of 19 - 12.

Even the Swami can respect that prediction.

But nobody could have imagined how it would play out on the crisp fall afternoon.

Both teams were evenly matched, as expected, and had slugged their way to a 6 - 6 tie at halftime.

Erie had pinned Ashland deep in its own territory and Bert Johnson had to punt out of his end zone in the third quarter. George Blossey, who Black described as one of the best backs the Tomcats had ever faced, stunned the large crowd with an electrifying forty-one-yard return for a touch-down that put Erie ahead 13 - 6.

But the Tomcats, who hadn't tasted defeat in seven years, weren't going with a whimper.

Behind their heralded captain, Bert Johnson, the team marched to a first down on the Erie five-yard line, most of that coming on passes from Johnson to John "Red" Craig. The next three plays resulted in six yards of losses and it was fourth down from the eleven. The home crowd, which Black numbered to be around 5,000, was on the edge of their collective seat.

Johnson flipped a flat pass to the left that Craig pulled off an Erie player's ear at the five and then danced into the end zone. Frank Gallaher dropkicked the extra point to tie the game at 13 - 13.

Johnson and Craig had fabulous games. It was a twenty-yard pass in the flat to Craig that resulted in the Tomcats' first score to make it 6 - 0 in the opening quarter.

Johnson's kicking, blocking, running, and passing were largely the reason that Ashland was in the game in the first place. Craig was having a break-out game after a slump to start the season.

With three minutes remaining, Erie got the ball and was driving. A pass interference call had given Erie a first down around midfield. Erie moved even closer, driving to the twenty-seven, before Craig intercepted a pass and ran it back to the forty-seven with about forty seconds remaining.

Ashland could have taken a knee and settled for a tie that would have preserved a 60 - 0 - 4 streak, but Johnson went for the win. He turned to a play that had worked time and time again—the left flat pass to Craig—but this time it backfired. Erie's John Gonski read the play and intercepted the pass that was low and short. There was nothing but green in front of him and he raced forty-five yards untouched to the end zone.

When Gonski touched the football to the ground in the end zone, the timer fired the gun ending the game.

It was over—the game and the winning streak—just like that.

As a small contingent of Erie fans celebrated with the team on the field, the Tomcat players were heartbroken. They were spilled all over the field, some bent over and crying, others with their faces buried in the ground. Ashland's fans and "the splendid high school band," as Black wrote, were trying to console them after the first defeat in seven years.

It was an experience that showed how much Ashland cared about its football back in those days.

Black wrote: "The contest was the greatest ever played here. It provided thrills aplenty, a clean, hard football game played by two well-drilled teams."

Back then, newspapers filed play-by-play reports on games. During Erie's drive to its first touchdown, according to Black's statistics, it appeared they were given an extra down.

Fred Burns of WSAZ radio, who announced the game, also remembered thinking the ball should have been turned back over to

Ashland on that drive. The referee, Gayle Mohney, said there must have been a mistake in the play-by-play keeping.

But nobody on Ashland's side ever brought up the mistake, if there was one, after the game. Erie's coaching staff was so impressed with the Tomcats' sportsmanship that they wrote a letter to the Ashland Elks, who had hosted the visiting teams fans before and after the game.

Jim Hyde, the Erie head coach, said Ashland "was one of the best bunch of losers he ever encountered." He meant that in the kindest way. The Tomcats didn't make excuses for the loss, even when the opponent needed five downs to score their only offensive touchdown. They already knew how to win with class and on this day they learned how to lose with class, too.

Ashland used only a dozen players in the game. Neither Johnson nor Craig was able to play the next week, when the Tomcats went back to their winning ways with a 51 - 0 victory over Georgetown.

Johnson took some heat from Ashland fans for throwing the pass that was intercepted on the last play of the game. But Black defended him in his column, talking about how he gambled but went for the win instead of settling for a tie. He said Johnson was the best player on the field.

The 1932 season was the same year that Ashland's players and fans witnessed the horror of the teenager being electrocuted after climbing a power line near the field.

The Tomcats would lose again in 1932—7 - 6 to Huntington High in the next-to-last game of the season. But they had signature wins over Louisville Male (30 - 6) and Martin's Ferry, Ohio (6 - 0) in the last game.

Erie East and Ashland went on to enjoy a great rivalry. The teams played each other every year from 1932 to 1939. The Tomcats held a 4 - 3 - 1 edge in the eight-game series, including a 25 - 7 victory at Armco field in the undefeated 1933 season.

Graham, a Tomcat star in the late 1940s, said his father told him stories about the Erie East-Ashland game of 1932. And he saved the program, which is a bit tattered but has several advertisements in it, including the Ventura Hotel where you could get an excellent room with bath for $1.75.

Given what was at stake and how the game finished, the Erie East-Ashland game of 1932 would have to rate as one of the greatest games in the Armco Field history—even though it was a Tomcat loss.

DIGGING HIS WAY INTO
AREA BASEBALL HISTORY
July 2009

• • •

The more Bill Williams digs, the more information seems to be coming his way about the old Armco Field.

Williams is the seventy-two-year-old Russell resident and Armco retiree who had a photograph of the old ballpark that sat where the AK Steel's Amanda Blast Furnace is today.

Williams was wondering what the name was on the fence of the park. After a story about the park came out in the newspaper, several responded with the answer. The official name of Armco Field, the name most used to refer to the field, is Association Athletic Park.

But that was only the start for Williams, who has continued to ask questions like a veteran reporter.

There aren't too many days that have gone by since the first story appeared in the newspaper that Williams doesn't hear: "I've got something for you."

Jim Frazier, who last year at age eighty-two shot his age on the

Association Athletic Park, more commonly known as Armco Field.

golf course, revealed some old photographs of former Armco baseball teams that intrigued Williams. And Mike Phelps, who lives in Worthington, had photographs his grandfather, Rudy Phelps, had given his father Ray of Joe DiMaggio and Leo Durocher that were taken at the Armco Field when the Yankees and Dodgers played an exhibition game there in 1940. There were some other player photos too, including pitchers Red Ruffing and Goofy Gomez.

"This thing keeps reaching out," Williams said. "I'm amazed. I'm digging into this, making notes. I hope to maybe compile a book of some of the athletic events that have been around here.

"It's an adventure. My phone's rung off the wall."

Williams has been provided with a much clearer photograph of the Armco Field where the Association Athletic Park name is clearly in focus.

On Wednesday, a classmate of Williams gave him a ticket for an exhibition game between the Reds and Tigers from April 10, 1942, that was to be played at Armco Field. The game was scheduled but it was rained out after the area was saturated with 2.51 inches of rain in forty-eight hours.

A game between the Yankees and Dodgers in 1940 is the only major league game ever played in Ashland.

The Detroit players had a ninety-minute workout at the park but didn't take batting practice. The Reds didn't work out but did sign autographs in the lobby of the Henry Clay Hotel. Fans lined up for autographs of their favorite players and were a little disappointed that Paul Derringer wasn't traveling with the team.

The Reds-Tigers game was expected to far outdraw the Yankee-Dodger game that attracted more than 4,000 fans to the park in 1940.

The Reds were only two years removed from the 1940 World Championship team. Elmer Riddle, who was 19 - 4 with a 2.24 ERA in 1941, was supposed to pitch that day for the Reds.

On the day before the exhibition game, a story in the *Ashland Daily Independent* said Reds' left-handed pull hitters Ival Goodman and Lonnie Frey were at the park the previous day and were salivating over the short right-field fence at Armco Field.

Area fans were disappointed that the game didn't work out. But on the ticket was a refund guarantee of four free tickets to a Mountain State League game at Armco Field if the exhibition was cancelled for any reason. The cost of a ticket was $1.50.

While Ashland was anticipating the Reds-Tigers exhibition game, a big-time player from the 1920s and '30s was visiting Ashland earlier that week. Hall of Famer Earle Combs had stopped by to see old friend John Steele, the owner of Steele and Lawrence Drugs.

Combs, a Richmond, Kentucky, native known as "The Kentucky Colonel," played in the same outfield with Babe Ruth for ten years with the Yankees. In 1942, he was a Yankee coach. He had entertained Steele in 1941 in New York when the Yankees played in the World Series.

Williams has enjoyed his part in unveiling some history in the area that had been long forgotten.

He played in the shadows of the old park as a child and understands there aren't many still around who remember much about that era in Ashland history.

"But I'm going to keep digging," he said.

WHAT'S IN A NAME?
PLENTY FOR THIS MAN
July 2009
• • •

Bill Williams grew up in Lower Millseat, in the shadow of what he always called Armco Park, where the Amanda Blast Furnace now sits on the AK Steel grounds.

"I'd like to have a nickel for every time the Armco guards ran us out," he said. "That was quite a thrill to get to play on that."

Williams ran across a photograph of the old park and it has him stumped. It was taken from across U.S. 23, about where the Kentucky Fried Chicken now sits, and the three-word sign on the park wall is partially blocked. The last two words are "Athletic Park" and the last five letters of the first word are "ation." But trees and bushes block out the first part of the word.

"That got my curiosity aroused big time," Williams said. "I grew up in the shadow of that steel mill and all I've ever heard it called is Armco Park."

Baseball and football were played at the old park until around 1941. It's where Armco's professional football team played. The

Ashland Tomcats played there until building Tomcat Stadium—later named Putnam Stadium—in 1937. Semi-pro baseball—the Kentucky Colonels—played there as well at the multi-sport park.

The Dodgers and Yankees played an exhibition there once. Stan Musial played when he was with the Williamsburg Redbirds. Back then, Stan the Man was also an outstanding pitcher.

Williams said his father, William J. Williams, would walk across old U.S. 23 and across the railroad tracks and collect baseballs during batting practice. He would return the balls and get free admission into the game for him and his son.

The photographs of the park came from Bobby and Sandy Moore, who own Country Finds, an antique shop in Flatwoods. "He called me and wanted some information," Williams said. "I told him I had to see those pictures."

Those photographs have stirred memories for Williams, who is doing everything he can to find out if there was another name for his beloved Armco Park.

Williams said his father had told him the story about the boy who was electrocuted while sitting on a high-tension tower watching a football game back in the 1930s but never put any names with it.

It turns out that Williams' aunt, Betty Gunderson, knew the story all too well and actually had clippings of the tragic event that happened on November 5, 1932.

William Dennis and Gerald Gunderson, both sixteen, were watching Ashland High School play Roanoke, Virginia, in a high school football game at the park. They had climbed a nearby tower and Dennis came in contact with a high tension wire carrying 33,000 volts.

More than 1,500 fans witnessed the horrifying incident. Many of the spectators rushed over from the football park after hearing the denotation and watching Dennis fall about sixty-five feet to the ground. Artificial respiration methods were used but Dennis had been instantly killed.

"My dad had told me that story many times," Williams said.

Gerald Gunderson, who had a productive life, was burned badly but he was able to slowly climb down the tower to safety.

In the story that was printed in the newspaper the next day, the field is called the American Rolling Mill football park—another name that Williams hadn't before heard.

"You can look and see that tower behind the chicken place," Williams said.

Williams is seventy-two and retired from working at AK Steel in 1999 after forty-four years of service.

"I followed my dad into the steel mill," he said. "After I graduated from Russell in '55 I knew that's where I was going. Back then, there were a lot of opportunities for us kids with Armco, Ashland Oil, and the railroad. But sports kept me in school."

Williams played football, basketball, and baseball for the Red Devils. He was on Russell's 1954 team that went 9 - 1, losing only to Catlettsburg 13 - 6, while outscoring opponents 295 - 35.

Two of the wins came against Ashland's sophomore team and Ashland's B-team but Russell didn't play the Tomcat varsity.

"Our best teams were in football," Williams said. "Russell has always been a good football school. Back when I played high school baseball, we didn't even have uniforms."

Williams played everything because "I grew up before television."

"We played it if rained," he said. "We'd put sawdust out to play basketball and we burnt tires to have night games."

Williams remembers when the family butchered a hog that one of the prized possessions was the hog bladder. "I played with a lot of bladders," he said.

Williams was an end on that '54 Russell team but he said his athletic claim to fame was facing Ashland and pitcher Jim Host in the regional tournament. Williams never had a chance.

"He had a wicked fastball," Williams said. "He was a big guy anyway. I ran into Jim down at Rupp Arena. I said 'Jim, shake my hand. You proved to me in a heartbeat I'm not a baseball player.'"

But Williams has some memories of Central Park, too, like when a makeshift team from Hale's Supermarket entered Ernie Chattin's midget league and won the title.

"We had a white t-shirt with a stencil on it and a red cap," he said. "We thought we were King Cotton."

Hale's Supermarket had some players they picked up from Catlettsburg, including Curt Cassell, Norm Collinsworth, Tommy Scott, Mickey Hedrick, and Tony Childers.

Later, Williams became friends and co-workers with Ashland's Paul Conley and Buff (Bill) Hopkins, who live in the Russell area. "They'd said 'Bill, who do we play Friday?' They'd be talking about Russell. I'd say 'It does my heart good to hear 'Who do we play?' and you be talking about Russell.'"

Williams likes to say he was a "lot sale" from being a Tomcat himself. His father sold some property on Kansas Street, where he watched Putnam Stadium being built with WPA funds back in the 1930s.

He ended up in Lower Millseat, in the shadow of the old park, which is why he's so determined to find out the name on the photograph.

"I've enjoyed the chase but I'd sure like to know that name," he said.

An Open Letter to All-Star Parents
July 2009
• • •

Dear All-Star parent:

First of all, congratulations on your son or daughter being named to an All-Star summer league baseball or softball team.

It's an important accomplishment in their young athletic lives and hopefully not the last one they'll achieve. Some of you are All-Star veterans whose son or daughter has been playing at this level for three or four years.

Double congratulations to you.

As a former All-Star parent and someone who has covered youth league sports for the past thirty-five years, let me offer some advice to both the newbies and the veterans of what I call the All-Star Experience.

First and foremost, enjoy the experience.

It can be the best time of your life if you'll let it. Your son or daughter will wear the All-Star uniform proudly and do their best to make you proud. My All-Star Experiences were enjoyable and some of my favorite family memories. We had a blast. If I could relive some of those moments, I would.

Let this All-Star Experience be times you'll cherish for a lifetime, too.

Don't be an armchair coach.

It's easy to get caught up in who's starting and who's not and why that has happened. Nothing will ruin the All-Star Experience quicker than a parent who thinks he knows more than the coach. While you may well know more than the coach, he or she is still the coach and is devoting time to lead the team. Don't forget that. Your two cents isn't worth two cents. And if it's your loud mouth that's causing the rift with the team, it will ruin the All-Star Experience for you and your child.

If you want to coach, get involved with the league and start earning your stripes. Most of the time, coaches that win the league are rewarded with All-Star assignments.

All-Star coaches will ask your opinion if they want it. Otherwise, keep it to yourself—and that means at the dinner table, too. Remember, your son or daughter is listening to everything you have to say about the situation.

If you're saying the coach doesn't know what he's doing, guess what that impressionable All-Star is thinking?

Relax, you're going to lose.

No matter how good your team may be, the All-Star Experience is likely going to end with defeat. It's inevitable. Think about it. In youth league history in our area, only one team has ever made it to the World Series of a particular All-Star tournament—Ashland's 1994 thirteen-year-old Babe Ruth All-Stars. And guess what? The first game of their experience started with a defeat and then it ended with a defeat on the biggest stage of all.

Don't let the loss, whenever it happens, spoil the All-Star Experience. And when that loss happens, for goodness sake, don't blame it on the umpires (even if they miss a call). Blaming every loss on umpiring teaches impressionable children a couple of things: 1) We never lose, we only get cheated. 2) It doesn't matter what the authority figure thinks: We're always right, they're always wrong. Is that the message you want to be sending?

Enjoy the moment.

Trust me, this time will pass by too quickly. Don't let it be a time when your son or daughter remembers how ugly you acted because of a silly game. Win or lose, enjoy the All-Star Experience. Savor it inning by inning and pitch by pitch because it'll be gone before you know it.

Good luck to you and your All-Star.

GIVING SANDLOT A CHANCE
July 2009
• • •

Growing up in Ashland during the 1960s and 1970s, being involved in organized youth sports wasn't the only way to participate.

We all had our sandlots, a makeshift field that was good for baseball in the summer and football in the fall.

I took more swings and scored more touchdowns at those places than I did in any organized league.

Our driveways included basketball goals, at least the good ones anyway. Sometimes there'd even be a spotlight attached to the garage. Night games. Ahh...nothing better.

That's where you learned to play. That's where you learned to win and learned to lose.

That's what we did.

If there were only four of us around on a hot summer day, it was off to play Whiffle ball in the Estep's side yard. Double-or-nothing was the game. The place had more quirks than Fenway Park. Ground rules were important, too. If you hit one in the big pine tree and the ball weaved its way through, the opponent could still catch it for an out—if he was patient and quick-footed enough.

We'd not only keep score, we'd keep statistics and standings (Is it any wonder why I became a sportswriter later in life?).

The short bushes that lined the Estep's yard served as the perfect fence for a bunch of young boys. The bushes were short enough that you could reach over and steal a home run as we pretended to be our favorite Cincinnati Red that day.

What do kids do today?

I drove around Ashland the other day looking for outside action. Maybe a Whiffle ball game. Or even a couple of guys throwing baseball.

There was nothing.

It was a picturesque day. Not too hot, not too cold.

I tell you, there was nothing.

The sandlots of my day are gone. Stafford's Field has a couple of houses on it now and has had for several years. But I still look at that corner lot as a life shrine. Few places carry more memories.

In my mind's eye, the big tree along the corner of Gartin and Blackburn Avenue is still standing proud. It was the center field fence for baseball and one of the goal lines for football. If you hit one into the tree, it was a home run. I'm not sure I ever did but it wasn't for lack of trying.

I'm not sure how we didn't knock out every window in the house across the street that happened to be in foul territory behind third base. We also somehow avoided oncoming traffic, as best I can remember anyway.

When it was football season, Saturdays and Sundays were when the games would be played. Sandlot football is tough football. My usual neighborhood gang included kids my brother's age, and he was three years older than me. Those guys took me in and taught me, but expected me to do my part when another neighborhood gang came challenging us. We had our moments.

During the winter, we'd play basketball on the outside courts and driveways from after school until it became too dark to shoot. It was mostly 2-on-2 games. There would be the occasional temper flareup, but mostly it was just good basketball.

My point is, every sport had a season and it didn't have to be an organized season.

The sandlots were our training ground. We didn't blame the refs when we lost because we didn't have any refs to blame. Parents weren't part of the process. We were playing for ourselves, not through our parents. It was something to do and we loved doing it.

We had our youth league coaches and they were good. They were men who taught the game well, men who cared what happened when the game was over.

When the organized sports were finished for the season, it was on to the next sport because, back in the day, each sport actually had a season.

That's not life in today's youth sports world. AAU basketball dominates the landscape. It has pushed baseball practically out of the picture. Soccer, which was never a thought in the 1960s and 70s, takes it share, too.

We are so organized that athletes are made to choose a sport before they turn twelve. Instead of trying them all, they make one their passion for fear of being left behind. Who knows what the future may have held in other sports for them. But because they don't play other sports—organized, sandlot or anything else—we may never know.

When it's all said and done, life is too short. Encourage your young athlete to play them all. Engage him in a 2-on-2 Whiffle ball game in the side yard with some buddies. Make up your own ground rules. Announce the starting lineup.

You might find that little boy in you, too.

CARTER ENJOYING PROJECT
June 2009

• • •

Dave Carter doesn't do things halfway. A little more than a year ago, when he decided to make a documentary on Central Park's baseball impact on Ashland in the 1950s, he did it with an open slate.

Like any good project, "Ashland's Field of Dreams" has evolved into something even bigger than he first imagined. He calls it his most satisfying work and if you consider Carter's body of work, that's quite a statement.

Carter grew up in Flatwoods, but the park was his place, too. His passion for the CP-1 is obvious.

Not only has the documentary become retrospect of the 1950s, which was the original intent, but his broad brush touched players from before and after as well. So many good baseball players—and even more good people—have a personal connection to CP-1. If a place can be considered a friend, the park was it. It was a comfort zone, a place where youth comes alive again. It was the gathering place for neighborhood games.

Any of us who have had any ties to the place can relate to Central

Park's main baseball diamond. You can remember digging in at shortstop, with sand filling your cleats. You remember how it felt to be in right field with the sun setting and causing those blind spots behind the backstop.

And you better have a good catcher on your team because that backstop was extra long. A wild pitch could mean two bases, so that fifty-five-foot curveball had to be blocked.

There were actually two home plates as the field was a 2-in-1 design for softball and baseball. There was the baseball home plate and the softball home plate that was much closer to the backstop.

Softball, fast-pitch softball, was so good here from the 1940s to the 1960s. It was a way of life in the park, too. Slow-pitch softball was big for years, too. But the fast-pitch games drew crowds into the hundreds.

CP-1 was special. It wasn't near the showplace that it is today but more everybody's back yard. CP-1 was where everybody eventually wanted to be playing because that's where the idols played.

They would come out to the park early on a hot summer day, riding bikes from all over town to be the first to get there. The games would last from early in the morning until late at night. Parents didn't worry. It was essentially a free babysitting service. It wasn't until the 1950s that youth baseball truly got organized although from the 1940s and into the 1950s there were fathers who did their best to make sure these young boys knew how to play baseball.

One of those was T.R. Wright, the father of Gary Wright, who is the man who got all the CP-1 buzz rolling with a sizeable donation to upgrade Central Park's field. It was through the impact of men like the late T.R. Wright, one of the early youth baseball organizers, where Ashland's baseball heritage grew.

Wright's name is attached to a sparkling press box that is the centerpiece for the renovation at the park field, Gary Wright's only caveat for handing over $125,000 to make CP-1 a showplace. His generous gesture has spurred so much more goodwill from other CP-1 alum.

There have been so many great baseball players that have played on that field, some from Ashland and many others from the surrounding area. Don Gullett, perhaps the greatest athlete in our area's modern history, played there. Former No. 1 draft choice Drew Hall's fastball zipped and dipped in the park with sturdy catcher Daniel Smith, a future Dodger farmhand, catching him in the late 1970s. WVU record-holder Steve Rolen, a future Giant farmhand, showed off his trade there in the 1980s as one of the best hitters I could remember covering. Future major leaguer Joe Magrane of Morehead had some pitching moments in the park. Larry Conley, Billy and Bobby Lynch, Tim Huff, Jody Hamilton, Jim Host...the list goes on and on. It's like a who's who of area athletes who were part of the CP-1 alum.

I don't know for sure, but it's also likely that future major league All-Stars Al Oliver and Larry Hisle, who both played American Legion baseball for Portsmouth on their way to the major leagues, probably took some swings on the CP-1 diamond. Ken Griffey, Jr. made an appearance for Cincinnati Midland during one of the Fourth of July Tournaments.

Arizona pitcher Brandon Webb, of course, was a park star in the late 1990s. Brandon's father, Phil, an outstanding pitcher in his day with Catlettsburg, rocked the park mound a few times, too.

And who could forget some of the prodigious home runs of Juan Thomas, who blasted nearly 275 on various minor league levels.

Carter has secured interviews with many other CP-1 alum who made it and some whose recollections of the park are just as special to Ashland. They fought their battles in the park, learned how to win and how to lose.

Dave Carter explains the interview process to Bobby Simpson and Reecie Banks at the CP-1 Reunion. Carter made a documentary —"Ashland's Field of Dreams"—that aired in August 2009. MARK MAYNARD

Last summer, the first CP-1 reunion took place on the park field. It was something to witness. So many from out of town came back to Ashland and walked out on that park field that day, reminiscing about their day. It was like they'd taken a long sip from the fountain of youth. I saw the twinkle in their eyes as we interviewed many for the documentary on that sun-splashed Saturday afternoon.

That twinkle, that slice of Americana, is what Carter has captured in this hour-long documentary that will make a world premiere at the Paramount Arts Center on August 28.

You'll see it on their faces and hear it in the voices. It's heartfelt drama as the stories, some of the great stories, are told over and over.

His special effects work intertwined in the documentary will put you back in the 1950s when Ashland—and the world for that matter— was a lot less complicated place than it is today.

DRAFT DAY 25 YEARS AGO
June 2009
• • •

Twenty-five years ago, Ashland's Drew Hall was working out in Central Park while his phone was practically ringing off the hook.

The baseball world was calling.

"The phone was ringing constantly," Hall said. "They kept calling my dad. My dad told me I needed to come home. I remember being completely overwhelmed."

Scott Boras, who was Hall's advisor, told him he needed to get away from all the phone calls, to clear his head, because some big things were about to happen.

It did. Hall was taken with the No. 3 overall selection by the Chicago Cubs, behind only Shawn Abner and Bill Swift.

Hall had positioned himself as one of the top prospects, a left-handed pitcher who had refined his trade under Steve Hamilton at Morehead State University.

Hall was a 1984 Sporting News All-American and arguably the best left-handed pitcher available in the June Amateur Major League Baseball Draft. He was living a dream come true.

Drew Hall was the third overall pick in the 1984 MLB Draft. MARK MAYNARD

However, he also remembers it as being the most confusing and hectic time of his life.

"The NCAA ties your hands so badly on that (negotiating)," he said. "You're not allowed to negotiate. At the time, you can only say yes or no. Luckily, you could have an advisor but, once again, that was bad, too. You needed more than an advisor to negotiate your first contract. You get taken advantage of."

Boras, one of the super agents in baseball today, was good even then, Hall said.

"He was good, but I was not mentally prepared for the onslaught of what it was going to be like," Hall said.

While Hall did get a hefty signing bonus, it's nothing like the demands of the past ten years or so. For instance, top draft choice Stephen Strasburg is asking for $50 million from the Washington Nationals.

"What I got was probably not even close to what a 10th-rounder gets anymore," Hall said. "I just wanted to play."

The stars aligned correctly for Hall, who had a brilliant junior season at Morehead State and then pitched "the game of my life" in the competitive Shenandoah Valley League after the season. He struck out twenty-two of twenty-seven batters, skyrocketing his draft status.

Hall had worked out for the Cincinnati Reds in a tryout at Riverfront Stadium and also pitched in front of Reds superscout Gene Bennett in front of Fairview High School.

"The Reds had the fifth pick that year and I had a pretty good idea they were interested in me," Hall said. "That's when I really started to get excited about everything."

Hall came to Morehead State a raw talent with a lively fastball with control problems. However, Hamilton, a former major leaguer who was also left-handed, taught Hall the slider and how to change speeds on the fastball. Hall went from being a hard-throwing lefthander to a dominant pitcher in a short time.

"I got better and better as far as throwing strikes," Hall said.

"Developing the slider, the pitch I could throw (when) behind in the count, was the big thing."

Hall was the Cubs' first selection in 1984 and the second was a high school player named Greg Maddux.

That same year, Hall made the twenty-five-man traveling squad of the U.S. Olympic Baseball Team in 1984, too. But on the last cut to twenty players, he was cut—along with Norm Charlton and Greg Swindell, the only other lefties on the roster. The U.S. team played with an all right-handed staff.

Hall eventually made it to The Show in 1986 and defeated the New York Mets for his first victory in September of that year. He was only a journeyman in the majors, finishing with a 9 - 12 career record while pitching for the Cubs, Texas Rangers, and Montreal Expos from 1986 to 1990.

But for that one Tuesday in June, Hall was the talk of the baseball world.

How many can say that?

Time has passed and Hall's career has faded, but he's still got baseball in his blood as a pitching coach for Morehead State University.

Hall played in the major leagues and sat side-by-side with Hall of Famer Nolan Ryan and future Hall of Famer Maddux. He pitched with Jamie Moyer, who just last week notched his 250th career victory.

Hall, Moyer, and Rafael Palmiero were part of a trade between the Cubs and Rangers. His best season was in Texas, where he went 3 - 1 with a 3.70 ERA in thirty-eight appearances in 1989.

He was traded to the Expos the following season and worked in forty games before a bout with tendonitis cut short that season and eventually his career.

But twenty-five years later, Hall can still remember the call when he was No. 1 on the Chicago Cubs' speed dial.

Some Lynch "Fact or Fiction"
June 2009
• • •

There used to be a television program on called "Fact or Fiction."

They would show a story, most of the time an outlandish one and, when it was over, the viewer was asked if the story was fact or fiction. It was often a hard call to make and sometimes you were very surprised.

I've many times likened the premise of "Fact or Fiction" to some of our sports heroes. Like the giant fish tale, sometimes the stories get bigger (better?) with time.

That's even truer for local sports legends, whose stories have been told so many times—most of the time not even by them—that they become bigger than life, if sometimes at least stretching the truth.

When interviewing Bobby Lynch, this summer's Elks Sports Day honoree, about a week ago, there were a few things I'd heard that I wanted to get correct with him.

I'll tell the stories, you decide if they are "Fact or Fiction."

1. Bobby Lynch once threw a baseball from home plate onto Carter Avenue at Central Park's main diamond.

"We were playing softball, a few years after I was back from college," Lynch said. "For whatever reason, after one of the games, somebody asked me if I thought I could throw a ball from home plate over the fence. I said 'Yeah, I think I could probably do that.' The first one I threw over the fence, through the trees, and it bounced off the street into the yard (across the street). The second one I threw to Tim Huff, who was standing on the other side of the fence in center field."

FACT.

2. Bobby Lynch outdueled Don Gullett 1 - 0 in the famous regional tournament championship game at Central Park.

"I get credit for that one all the time, but it wasn't me," Lynch said. "I was in Tuscaloosa when that game was played. That was all Timmy (Huff)."

It was Huff who outdueled Gullett in the regional tournament semifinals in Morehead. It came during the 1969 season, a year after Lynch had graduated from Ashland and was going to college at Alabama. He was nowhere near Ashland or Morehead.

FICTION.

3. On a trip to Eau Claire, Wisconsin, to play in a national-level Babe Ruth All-Star tournament, the team bus twice left players behind and had to go back and pick them up.

Back then, there was only one age-level Babe Ruth All-Star team and Lynch had made the 13 - 15 year-old team as a thirteen-year-old. Ashland lost twice and began making the long drive home.

"Coming back, we stopped at a restaurant built over the highway real early, at like six in the morning, for breakfast," Lynch said. "We all piled back in the bus and didn't take a head count. It was like 'Everybody here?' 'Yeah, we're all here. Let's go!'"

Bobby Lynch, left, is one of Ashland's all-time basketball and baseball greats. MARK MAYNARD

But when the bus got a mile down the road, the players noticed Duke Morrison wasn't with them.

"Duke was one of those guys who was shaving when he was ten or eleven," Lynch said. "He had a five o'clock shadow when he pitched in Little League, and he could throw it hard, too. But Duke never grew any after that time."

The bus driver pulled over in the emergency lane and backed the bus down the highway and nearly in the same parking place he had left, Lynch said.

"Duke comes out of the restaurant with his shaving kit," Lynch said.

"He's wiping his face, getting on the bus, and everybody is laughing. He's like 'What's the matter?' Then we told him the story."

At another spot, the team stopped for gas and another of the players, Bobby Stanley, was left behind. "Bobby was a quiet guy and nobody had missed him," Lynch said.

Then all of a sudden, the players look out the window and Stanley was leaning out of a car window waving and screaming, telling the bus to pull over.

"Bobby swears he doesn't remember this, but it happened," Lynch said. "He was so mad. He was a red-headed kid. He just sat down and crossed his arms over."

FACT.

4. When Bobby Lynch played softball in the outfield with his brother Bill, one of the hardest-throwing left-handers in Ashland history, he often had to make the throw in for him.

"Jim Speaks used to play in the outfield with us and Jim couldn't throw it anymore either," Lynch said. "Whenever the ball was hit, if it was hit over their heads, I would run halfway between where they were and the infield. Both of their arms were just done."

FACT.

5. Bobby Lynch also played baseball at Alabama.

As a freshman, he stepped onto the baseball field for one season and finished 3 - 3. He said his first game came against LSU.

"I got started off late," he said. "I was home one day my freshman year because during spring break I was playing baseball. I stayed at Bryant Hall and it was for basketball and football players. I was the only athlete in Bryant Hall (that spring)."

Lynch was also in love with soon-to-be wife Jo Etta, who was attending Anderson College in Indiana.

"I didn't play (baseball) after my freshman season," he said.
FACT.

6. Bobby Lynch started all three (varsity) years at Alabama.

During his senior season, Lynch lost his starting position and never regained it although he was still a co-captain for coach C.M. Newton. The talent level changed while he was at Bama, although he averaged ten points per game both as a sophomore and junior starting guard.

Lynch was at school when Alabama signed its first black scholarship player, Wendall Hudson.

"It just didn't seem like it was that earth-shattering at the time," Lynch said. "We played against black players all the time, so that wasn't a big deal. I don't know if that was part of C.M.'s plan to bring in players familiar with playing with or against them. Wendell Hudson was a fantastic guy."

FICTION.

7. Bobby Lynch had his best college game against Kentucky.

Lynch scored thirty-four points on the Wildcats, who were ranked No. 2 in the country at the time. The Tide lost 86 - 71 but Lynch was on fire, making 14-of-26 shots in Memorial Coliseum.

"Jim Fannin, who is the Sports Day speaker, talks about being in the zone," Lynch said. "I was in the zone. I did not have very many games in the zone but that was one of them. I actually have it on disk. The first half I shot three or four air balls. All my kids looked at it and said 'You must have had a good second half.' Actually, I did."

The thirty-four points was his high-point game at Alabama, although he usually played well against Kentucky. He scored fourteen and sixteen in two other games against the Wildcats.

FACT.

8. Bobby Lynch guarded Pete Maravich not once but twice in his college career.

Lynch was part of the "defense" that held the high-scoring Maravich to an NCAA record sixty-nine points in one meeting, which Alabama won. Earlier in his career, Maravich had fifty-five points against the Crimson Tide's defense, which Lynch was part of as well.

"The amazing part about Maravich was the fact that he never stopped and he always had the ball," Lynch said. "His ballhandling skills were off the charts. His body-type was perfectly suited, long arms, and long legs."

Lynch was stunned when learning about Maravich's death from a heart defect.

Lynch said Maravich's game when he scored sixty-nine came in Alabama before a full house, which was unusual for basketball. "Him coming to town made it like a football ticket—they were hard to come by," he said.

FACT.

Hopefully these "Fact or Fiction" stories give you a better idea of who Bobby Lynch is and what a truly worthy Sports Day honoree he is as well.

FACT.

JOLTIN' JOE AND A DAY TO CHERISH
September 2009
• • •

My phone rang the other day and on the other end of the line wasn't a familiar voice, but it was a familiar name.

Jimmy Rose was calling me. I'd heard about him through my many conversations with Jack Fultz over the years. Rose was Fultz's high school basketball coach at Olive Hill. He was twenty-years old at the time, the youngest man to ever take a team to the State Tournament. He did that with Olive Hill in 1944 and darn near won the thing.

The Comets defeated tournament favorite Brooksville 23 - 20 in the quarterfinals but fell the next day in a heartbreaking semifinal against Harlan and "Wah Wah" Jones. Jack Fultz, I remember, never got over that loss.

Rose's brother is Gayle Rose, who played on Kentucky's 1954 undefeated national championships. "One of the best ballhandlers ever," said big brother Jimmy. Gayle Rose's jersey is hanging in the rafters at Rupp Arena.

Jimmy Rose coached Olive Hill High School to a 49 - 4 record in 1946. It was the most victories in a season ever in Kentucky. "We had dropped football and I had to give the boys something else to do," he said. "We started playing games in October." He was also the first coach to play an all-black team when Olive Hill met Booker T. Washington before the public white schools were even allowed to play the black schools.

But Jimmy Rose wasn't calling to talk about basketball.

He wanted to talk baseball.

More specifically, he wanted to talk baseball in Ashland in 1940.

Jimmy Rose is eighty-five and in failing health. He is housebound in central Kentucky and suffers from dementia and short-term memory loss. "I've forgotten so much of my past," he said. "But I've got a great story for you. For some reason or another, I've never forgotten it."

Over the next forty-five minutes or so, Rose took me on a journey to Ashland in 1940 and one afternoon in April that he will never forget.

You would never have known this was a man who had "forgotten his past." He spoke with such clarity and detail that it was like these events happened yesterday. I was simply mesmerized.

Even though he lived in northeastern Kentucky, in the heart of Reds Country, Jimmy Rose always loved the Yankees.

"I heard Babe Ruth hit a home run when I was six-years old," he said. "From then on, I was hooked. It was dangerous living in Olive Hill because everybody there was for the Reds."

Not Jimmy Rose. He loved the Yankees and especially Joe DiMaggio.

Rose learned that the Yankees and Brooklyn Dodgers were going to stage an exhibition game at Armco Field on their way north for the start of the 1940 season. Rose, who was fifteen at the time, was going to be there, even if he had to walk from Olive Hill.

"I went in the night before and spent the night with friends," he recalled. "My daddy was a doctor and he gave me a prescription pad for autographs.

"I couldn't sleep; I slept very little. At daylight the next morning, I went down to the old railroad depot in Ashland. Walking up and down past the Pullman (sleeper) cars, I was wondering which one Joe DiMaggio was in? He was my hero. The Yankees were my heroes."

Rose watched and waited, anticipating when the Yankees would be coming off the train.

"I saw some man get off the train. I could tell by his size and build, he wasn't a Yankee," Rose said. "That day they were to meet the Brooklyn Dodgers at Armco Field. He said to me, 'Young man, where are we?' I said 'We're in Ashland, Kentucky.' He said 'Oh yes, we have a game here today with the Dodgers.' I asked him 'Are you with the Yankees?' He said 'I'm their equipment manager.'"

Rose's ears perked up. "That got my attention real quick," he said. "I've told this story so many times I've got it memorized. I asked if he knew Joe DiMaggio. The greatest player in the game...what a question!"

But the man just smiled. "He started to get back on the train and he said 'Young man, I need a couple of young men to help me today. Do you know where I could find them?' I said 'You've already got one of them right now.'"

The equipment manager told Rose to recruit a friend and meet him at the Henry Clay Hotel at ten o'clock and he'd give them instructions.

"I called my friend Buster Cartee, who later coached at Olive Hill," Rose said. "I said 'Buster, get your mother to drive you in here quick. We're going to be batboys for the Yankees' and he came."

Rose watched as the Yankees filed into the hotel. He got them to sign autograph after autograph. He got one from Red Ruffing, the top pitcher in the American League, but the one he wanted was DiMaggio.

"The last one to make an appearance—and he didn't come in the same door as the other guys, he came in the side door instead of the front door—was guess who? He was dressed like a Philadelphia lawyer. I got up and started to get his autograph and I couldn't get up my nerve to do it. I stood in awe of him."

Rose and Cartee were given instructions on what to do from the equipment manager. One assignment was to carry the uniforms and gloves to the players' rooms.

"They didn't carry their own uniform," he said. "They were all in suits and ties. They looked like businessmen rather than ballplayers. That was one of their marks, looking like professionals."

They delivered the uniforms to each room and had the thrill of meeting Joe Gordon ("His glove looked like a piece of leather," Rose said) and Red Rolfe. They met George Selkirk, Frank Crosetti, and Charlie "King Kong" Keller.

The Yankees dressed in their rooms and then came to the lobby to board the bus. Rose and Cartee were the last ones on.

"We set on the steps going into the bus and drove from the Henry Clay (Hotel) to Armco (Field)," he said. "I happened to look up and one man had a seat all to himself. That was Joe McCarthy, the great manager of the Yankees. He smiled at us with the sweetest, kindest smile. He gave us the fatherly look."

Once at the park, the players took the field for batting practice. Rose and Cartee were positioned behind the short right field fence to retrieve home run balls.

"They had so many left-handed batters, they wanted us to recover as many of the baseballs as we could and bring them back," Rose said. "They hit balls over there one right after the other."

It was then that Rose caught a glimpse of DiMaggio at the plate.

"When he took batting practice, everything came to a standstill," Rose said. "I remember he hit a line drive that went almost all the way to the center field fence. That ball never got more than ten feet off the ground. It was one of the hardest hit balls I've ever seen."

When the game started, Lefty Gomez sat with Rose outside the dugout. "He had a little change in his pocket and he sent me for peanuts," Rose said. "A little later, he sent me for peanuts again and then again. I came back one time and he said 'What's the score?' He wasn't paying any attention to the ballgame."

After making numerous trips for peanuts, Rose said he was gathering himself when someone came and knelt beside them. "I was busy helping Mr. Gomez and I looked up and it was Joe DiMaggio. I couldn't talk. I couldn't say anything. I said 'Joe, do you think you could hit a ball out of this ballpark?' What a crazy thing to say to him."

Rose can recall some details of the game, including when Yankee outfielder Jake Powell ran into the right field fence and injured himself so badly he had to stay in the hospital here for a week. The Dodgers defeated the Yankees, 7 - 6.

"I'd never known it," Rose said. "I was too busy getting peanuts for Gomez."

The batboys' last job of the day was to go back with the team and collect the players' uniforms and gloves and return them to the equipment manager.

"I still hadn't gotten DiMaggio's autograph," Rose said. "After making that silly statement, I was in such awe, I couldn't go in his room. I passed by it and looked in. He had a strawberry (abrasion) on his hip (from sliding into a base). It was angry looking really. I saw it. When I passed by the door, he recognized me as one of the batboys.

He yelled at me 'Kid, come in here!' Naturally, I ran right up. I didn't get too close, I was in awe of him."

DiMaggio told him to go the equipment room and bring back the medical kit. "He told me with authority," Rose said. "He wanted it right now. He wanted to treat the strawberry on that hip."

Rose carried out DiMaggio's order to the equipment manager, who gave him one of the two medical kits he carried.

"I set the medical kit down at his feet," Rose said. "Then one of the greatest things that ever happened in my life happened. 'He patted me on the shoulder and said 'That's my boy, that's my boy.' And I still couldn't ask him for his autograph. But it's one of the great thrills of my life. I didn't think the world had anything else to offer me."

Of course, it did, through his coaching, which he did at Olive Hill High School, Paris High School, Pfeiffer College in North Carolina, and Asbury College. He later entered the ministry of the United Methodist Church.

But for one day in 1940, he was a batboy for the New York Yankees, right here in Ashland, when he had the thrill of a lifetime.

No KO, but "Rockys" Fall
March 1992
• • •

Rick Pitino would like to think that his Kentucky basketball team had a little "Rocky" in them.

So it probably wasn't by coincidence that Pitino and his coaching staff triumphantly ran up the steps of the Philadelphia Museum of Arts—those same steps "Rocky" made so famous in the movie—during some early-morning jogs Thursday and Friday.

Up against mighty Duke in the NCAA East Region final, they must have been feeling like the underdog "Rocky" felt going against Apollo Creed in that very first Hollywood movie in 1976.

And, like the famed movie boxer, Kentucky kept taking punch after punch against champion Duke Saturday night. It was like a team of "Rockys" going against the Blue Devils in the Spectrum. Duke kept jabbing and Kentucky kept standing.

Jab, jab, jab went Duke. UK went down by eight, down by nine, down by ten. But the Wildcats wouldn't go down completely. Not in regulation anyway. Forty minutes and dead even with No. 1 Duke.

And so it went down to a tantalizing five-minute overtime with the outcome certainly in doubt.

Like the two heavyweights they are, the punches kept coming from Duke and Kentucky. Bam! John Pelphrey bangs a three-pointer. Bam! Bobby Hurley hits a three-pointer. The big shots kept coming from both sides. Stephen Spielberg couldn't have scripted it any better.

And with seven seconds to play in overtime, the Wildcats had the chance of a lifetime and a chance to be in the Final Four. Their dream rested in the balance with one last knockout punch.

Sean Woods, the Wildcat who had played like one of the best point guards in America for the past two weeks, blew past Hurley and took it right at All-American Christian Laettner in the lane. His high-arching impossible shot somehow banked in for a 103 - 102 lead over Duke which, poised as always, called a timeout with 2.1 seconds left in its dream season.

And Laettner had one more dream come true. He took a perfect length-of-the-floor pass from Grant Hill that went between Pelphrey and Deron Feldhaus, and drilled a turnaround seventeen-footer for a heart-stopping 104 - 103 victory.

For a moment, "Rocky" lived again in Philly. And then he died a painful death.

For Kentucky's four overachieving seniors—Woods, Pelphrey, Feldhaus, and Richie Farmer—it was the most bitter of endings to a fabulous season.

Years from now, they will be replaying Laettner's incredible shot over and over in their minds. For the moment, they were stunned, crushed and defeated in one of the worst possible ways. You could feel the emptiness for them and see it in their young eyes. You could almost taste their bitterness. Yes, life will go on for them. But these daunting memories of one of the greatest college basketball games ever played will be with them forever.

They fought with determination and courage—much like "Rocky" did in the movies—for most of their careers. Then, just like that, it was over. Snuffed out. They will never forget this Philadelphia experience and the thrills that come with it. And they will never ever forget the agony of this defeat.

For Duke, it's on to another Final Four. The Blue Devils know they were lucky and knew they were in a fight of survival against these "Rockys" from Kentucky.

And when it was all over, amid the on-the-court celebration, you could have probably heard Duke cry out in union: "There ain't gonna be no rematch!"

INDEX

• • •

ABOUT THE AUTHOR
Mark Maynard
• • •

Mark Maynard has been on the staff of *The Independent* since 1975, first as a sports writer, then sports editor, and now managing editor of the daily newspaper in northeastern Kentucky. He has covered many significant sports events in the area over the past thirty-four years and has won nearly fifty writing awards from the Kentucky Press Association.

Maynard and his wife, Beth, live in Ashland, Kentucky, where they raised two children.

ABOUT THE PUBLISHER
Jesse Stuart Foundation
• • •

The Jesse Stuart Foundation (JSF) is devoted to preserving the human and literary legacy of Jesse Stuart and other Kentucky and Appalachian writers. The Foundation controls the rights to Stuart's published and unpublished literary works. The JSF has reprinted many of Stuart's out-of-print books along with other books that focus on Kentucky and Appalachia, and it has evolved into a significant regional press and bookseller.

The Foundation also promotes a number of cultural and educational programs. We encourage the study of Jesse Stuart's works and related regional materials.

Our primary purpose is to produce books which supplement the educational system at all levels. We have thousands of books in stock and we want to make them accessible to teachers and librarians, as well as general readers. We also promote Stuart's legacy through videotapes, dramas, readings, and other presentations for school and civic groups, and an annual Jesse Stuart Weekend at Greenbo Lake State Resort Park.

We are proud that Jesse Stuart's books are a guideline to the solid values of America's past. Today, we are so caught up in teaching children to read that the process has obscured its higher purpose. Children require more than literacy. They need to learn, from reading, the unalterable principles of right and wrong.

That is why Stuart's books are so important. They allow educators and parents to make reading fun for children while teaching solid values at the same time. In a world that is rapidly losing perspective, the JSF is working to educate tomorrow's adults for responsible citizenship.

TPS 100023